Summary

Contents

CHAPTER 3: SOCIAL AND WELFARE **37**

Introduction

INTRODUCTION

The Northern Ireland Annual Abstract of Statistics is prepared by the Northern Ireland Statistics and Research Agency in collaboration with Northern Ireland Departments, the Northern Ireland Office and other organisations. The name of the department or organisation responsible for providing statistics is given under each table. A list of sources and contact points from which further information may be obtained appears at the end of the Abstract.

DEFINITIONS AND CONVENTIONS USED

Area covered

Unless otherwise stated all statistics relate to Northern Ireland.

Explanatory notes

Each section of the Abstract is followed by explanatory notes which should be read in conjunction with the appropriate tables.

Non-calendar years

Academic year: September 2003 to June 2004 would be shown as 2003/04.

Financial year: 1 April 2003 to 31 March 2004 would be shown as 2003-04.

Migration year: 1 July 2003 to 30 June 2004 would be shown as 2003/4.

Data covering more than one year: 2002, 2003 and 2004 would be shown as 2002-04; 2003 to 2004 would be shown as 2003-04.

A survey conducted over two calendar years, for example 2003 and 2004, would be shown as 2003/4 even though it may not collect data for a complete 12 month period. Surveys which cover financial or academic years would be shown as 2003-04 and 2003/04 respectively.

Rounding of figures

Where figures have been rounded to the nearest final digit, there may be a slight discrepancy between the sum of the constituent items and the total.

Symbols

The following symbols are used throughout the Abstract:

..	not available
.	not applicable
-	negligible (less than half the final digit shown)
0	nil
*	sample size too small for a reliable estimate
p	provisional
r	revised
f	forecast
<	less than
≤	less than or equal to
>	greater than
≥	greater than or equal to
GB	denotes a value which relates to the three countries of Great Britain: England, Scotland and Wales.
UK	denotes a value which relates to the United Kingdom of Great Britain and Northern Ireland.
ROI	denotes a value which relates to the Rebublic of Ireland.

Typeface

Bold text and values denote summary values.

Values in italics denote percentages and rates.

Population

- The estimated population of Northern Ireland at 30 June 2004 was 1,710,300. Over the three decades between 1971 and 2004, the population of Northern Ireland has increased by 11%. This overall increase marks a steady fall in the population throughout the 1970s before a rise into 1979. Without exception, the NI population has continued to rise year on year since that date.

- The 2004 total population was almost 2% higher than it had been five years previously. However, 2004 population estimates for Belfast and Castlereagh Local Government Districts (LGDs) were lower than the 1999 figures, whilst Larne LGD displayed no change. Conversely, the population of Banbridge LGD was almost 10% higher in 2004 than in 1999.

- There were just over 22,300 resident live births in Northern Ireland in 2004. This is a 3% increase on 2003 and represents a 7% decrease on the 1994 figure. Between 1994 and 2004, the NI birth rate per thousand population decreased from 14.7 to 13.0. Thirty years before, the birth rate was much higher at around 18 to 19 births per thousand population.

- Between 1994 and 2004, the proportion of births to mothers under the age of 20 fluctuated between 6% and almost 8%. The proportion peaked in 1999, at 7.8% of all live births, before generally falling through the early part of this decade. Over the same period there has been a rapid increase in the proportion of births to mothers aged 35-39, from 10% in 1994 to almost 17% in 2004.

- In 2004, there were over 14,300 registered deaths in Northern Ireland, or 8.4 per thousand population. The NI death rate per thousand population has been below 10 since 1990.

- In 2004, the Eastern Health Board had the highest death rate per thousand population (9.3); the Western Board had the lowest (7.4). However, standardised death rates, which take account of the age and gender profile of the population, indicate less variation between the four Health Board areas. In 2004, the Western Board had the highest standardised death rate (8.7), with the Northern Board the lowest (8.0).

- For those born in 1890-92, life expectancy was approximately 46 for both males and females. Life expectancy for those born during 2001-2003 is 76 years for males and 80 years for females. Women aged 65 in 2001-2003 could expect to live, on average, another 19 years; males aged 65, another 16 years.

- Between 2003 and 2004 Northern Ireland experienced net inward migration of over 800. This compares to just over 1,000 net outward migration between 1996 and 1997.

Estimated population by gender and age, 2004

1.1

Numbers

Age	Males	Females	**Persons**	Age	Males	Females	**Persons**	Age	Males	Females	**Persons**
0	11,287	10,603	**21,890**	30	11,221	11,739	**22,960**	60	8,900	9,266	**18,166**
1	11,022	10,440	**21,462**	31	11,800	12,165	**23,965**	61	8,585	9,166	**17,751**
2	10,956	10,611	**21,567**	32	12,055	12,348	**24,403**	62	7,813	8,275	**16,088**
3	11,229	10,492	**21,721**	33	12,361	12,959	**25,320**	63	7,086	7,582	**14,668**
4	11,619	10,831	**22,450**	34	12,401	12,812	**25,213**	64	6,976	7,545	**14,521**
0-4	**56,113**	**52,977**	**109,090**	**30-34**	**59,838**	**62,023**	**121,861**	**60-64**	**39,360**	**41,834**	**81,194**
5	11,928	11,403	**23,331**	35	12,490	13,070	**25,560**	65	6,944	7,671	**14,615**
6	12,267	11,518	**23,785**	36	12,710	13,118	**25,828**	66	6,753	7,313	**14,066**
7	12,590	12,012	**24,602**	37	12,767	13,204	**25,971**	67	6,591	7,477	**14,068**
8	12,577	11,637	**24,214**	38	12,898	13,238	**26,136**	68	6,200	7,150	**13,350**
9	12,494	11,758	**24,252**	39	13,037	13,574	**26,611**	69	5,919	6,720	**12,639**
5-9	**61,856**	**58,328**	**120,184**	**35-39**	**63,902**	**66,204**	**130,106**	**65-69**	**32,407**	**36,331**	**68,738**
10	12,473	12,077	**24,550**	40	12,884	13,390	**26,274**	70	5,649	6,697	**12,346**
11	12,673	12,273	**24,946**	41	12,528	12,933	**25,461**	71	5,399	6,652	**12,051**
12	13,262	12,552	**25,814**	42	12,047	12,885	**24,932**	72	5,306	6,451	**11,757**
13	13,439	12,784	**26,223**	43	12,167	12,700	**24,867**	73	4,969	6,534	**11,503**
14	13,354	12,792	**26,146**	44	11,760	12,258	**24,018**	74	4,744	6,323	**11,067**
10-14	**65,201**	**62,478**	**127,679**	**40-44**	**61,386**	**64,166**	**125,552**	**70-74**	**26,067**	**32,657**	**58,724**
15	13,571	12,820	**26,391**	45	11,238	11,793	**23,031**	75	4,422	6,060	**10,482**
16	13,811	13,167	**26,978**	46	11,294	11,856	**23,150**	76	4,040	5,815	**9,855**
17	13,962	13,200	**27,162**	47	10,917	11,323	**22,240**	77	4,035	5,754	**9,789**
18	14,040	13,248	**27,288**	48	10,826	10,833	**21,659**	78	3,661	5,633	**9,294**
19	13,035	12,130	**25,165**	49	10,517	10,198	**20,715**	79	3,394	5,114	**8,508**
15-19	**68,419**	**64,565**	**132,984**	**45-49**	**54,792**	**56,003**	**110,795**	**75-79**	**19,552**	**28,376**	**47,928**
20	12,703	12,017	**24,720**	50	10,357	10,027	**20,384**	80	3,056	4,838	**7,894**
21	12,442	11,764	**24,206**	51	10,057	10,039	**20,096**	81	2,665	4,639	**7,304**
22	11,561	11,501	**23,062**	52	9,708	9,756	**19,464**	82	2,454	4,402	**6,856**
23	11,364	11,060	**22,424**	53	9,735	9,657	**19,392**	83	2,256	4,039	**6,295**
24	11,359	10,826	**22,185**	54	9,591	9,881	**19,472**	84	2,034	3,642	**5,676**
20-24	**59,429**	**57,168**	**116,597**	**50-54**	**49,448**	**49,360**	**98,808**	**80-84**	**12,465**	**21,560**	**34,025**
25	10,637	10,760	**21,397**	55	9,573	9,835	**19,408**	85	1,454	2,865	**4,319**
26	10,377	10,600	**20,977**	56	9,538	10,031	**19,569**	86	1,150	2,413	**3,563**
27	10,458	10,734	**21,192**	57	9,670	10,230	**19,900**	87	890	2,048	**2,938**
28	10,721	10,981	**21,702**	58	9,000	9,249	**18,249**	88	813	1,941	**2,754**
29	10,654	10,995	**21,649**	59	8,765	9,251	**18,016**	89	690	1,777	**2,467**
25-29	**52,847**	**54,070**	**106,917**	**55-59**	**46,546**	**48,596**	**95,142**	**85-89**	**4,997**	**11,044**	**16,041**
								90+	**1,866**	**6,091**	**7,957**

Age group summaries	Males	Females	**Persons**
All Ages	**836,491**	**873,831**	**1,710,322**
All aged under 16	196,741	186,603	**383,344**
All aged under 18	224,514	212,970	**437,484**
All aged 16 & over	639,750	687,228	**1,326,978**
All aged 18 & over	611,977	660,861	**1,272,838**
All aged 16-29	167,124	162,983	**330,107**
All aged 30-44	185,126	192,393	**377,519**

Age group summaries	Males	Females	**Persons**
All aged 45-59 Female/ 45-64 Male	190,146	153,959	**344,105**
All aged 60 Female/ 65 Male & over	97,354	177,893	**275,247**
All aged 16 to 59 Female/64 Male	542,396	509,335	**1,051,731**
All aged 75 & over	38,880	67,071	**105,951**

Source: Northern Ireland Statistics and Research Agency

1.2 Health and Social Services Board (HSSB) and Local Government District mid-year population estimates, 1997 to 2004

Numbers

Area	1997	1998	1999	2000	2001	2002	2003	2004
Northern Ireland	**1,671,300**	**1,677,800**	**1,679,000**	**1,682,900**	**1,689,300**	**1,696,600**	**1,702,600**	**1,710,300**
Eastern HSSB	**672,000**	**671,800**	**669,400**	**668,500**	**666,900**	**665,700**	**663,900**	**664,100**
Ards	70,100	70,900	71,800	72,800	73,400	74,100	74,400	74,600
Belfast	287,700	286,700	283,200	280,900	277,200	274,100	271,600	269,000
Castlereagh	66,200	66,200	66,300	66,400	66,500	66,300	66,100	65,800
Down	62,500	62,500	63,400	63,400	64,100	64,800	65,200	66,800
Lisburn	109,600	109,500	108,900	109,100	109,000	109,400	109,600	110,200
North Down	75,900	75,900	75,800	75,900	76,600	77,000	77,100	77,600
Northern HSSB	**419,400**	**421,600**	**423,200**	**425,500**	**428,200**	**430,400**	**432,800**	**435,900**
Antrim	48,100	48,500	48,700	48,800	48,800	48,900	49,300	49,800
Ballymena	58,300	58,100	58,100	58,300	58,800	59,000	59,500	60,000
Ballymoney	25,500	25,700	26,000	26,400	27,000	27,500	27,800	28,300
Carrickfergus	36,700	37,000	37,100	37,600	37,700	38,100	38,500	38,700
Coleraine	55,100	55,500	55,700	56,000	56,400	56,200	56,000	56,500
Cookstown	32,100	32,200	32,100	32,100	32,700	33,000	33,400	33,700
Larne	30,700	30,700	30,900	31,000	30,800	30,900	30,900	30,900
Magherafelt	38,400	38,800	39,200	39,400	39,900	40,400	40,800	41,300
Moyle	15,500	15,600	15,700	15,800	16,000	16,200	16,300	16,400
Newtownabbey	79,100	79,500	79,700	80,000	80,100	80,200	80,300	80,300
Southern HSSB	**302,600**	**304,300**	**305,400**	**307,300**	**312,200**	**315,600**	**319,000**	**321,400**
Armagh	53,500	53,600	52,600	53,200	54,500	55,000	55,400	54,900
Banbridge	38,700	39,300	39,900	40,600	41,500	42,400	43,100	43,800
Craigavon	78,300	78,900	79,500	80,100	80,900	81,500	82,200	83,200
Dungannon	46,900	47,100	47,300	47,400	47,800	48,200	48,700	49,300
Newry & Mourne	85,200	85,300	86,100	85,900	87,400	88,500	89,600	90,300
Western HSSB	**277,200**	**280,100**	**281,000**	**281,600**	**282,000**	**284,900**	**286,900**	**288,900**
Derry	104,400	105,500	106,200	106,400	105,300	106,200	106,500	106,900
Fermanagh	56,400	56,800	57,000	57,100	57,700	58,100	58,700	59,300
Limavady	31,900	32,500	32,000	32,100	32,600	33,200	33,600	34,000
Omagh	47,400	47,800	47,900	48,000	48,100	48,900	49,600	50,100
Strabane	37,000	37,500	37,800	38,100	38,300	38,400	38,600	38,700

Source: Northern Ireland Statistics and Research Agency

Figure 1.1 Persons per square kilometre by Local Government District, 2004

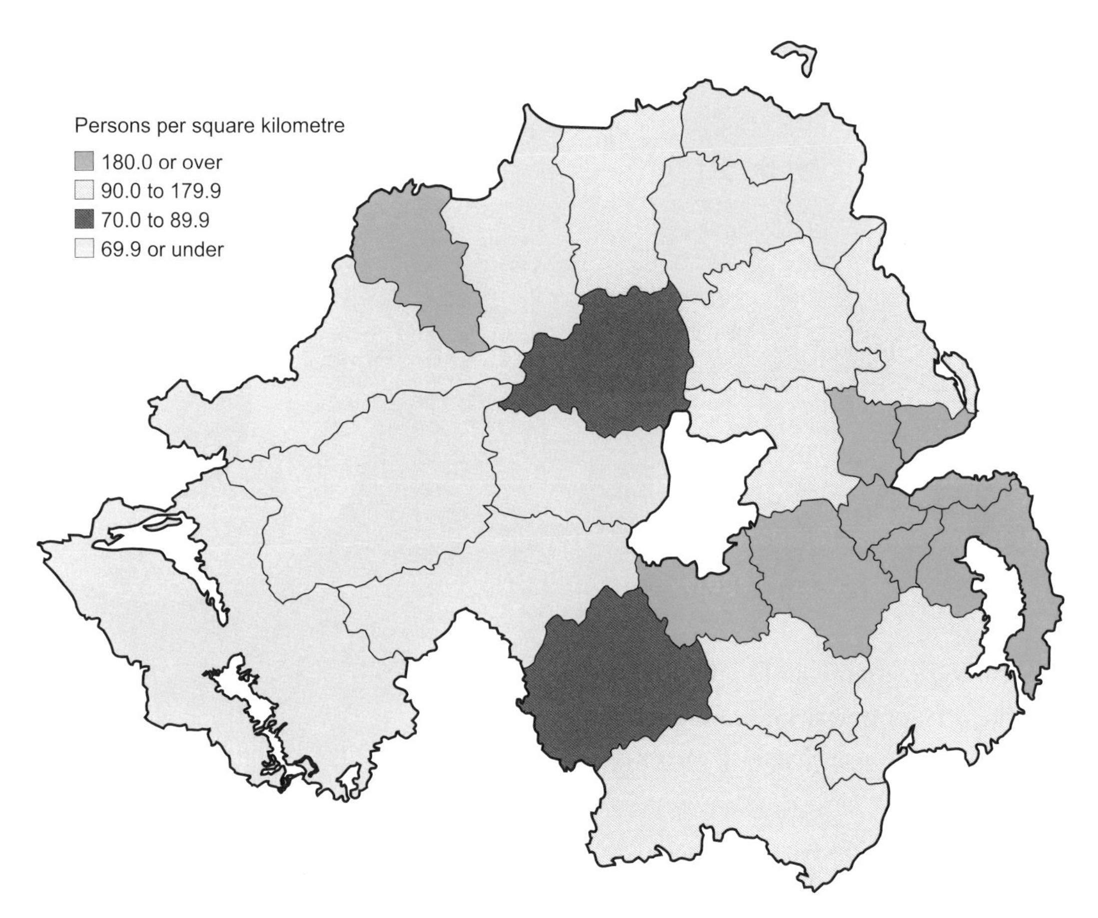

Source: Northern Ireland Statistics and Research Agency

1.3 Population density by Local Government District[1,2], 1981 to 2004

Persons per square kilometre

Local Government District	1981	1986	1991	1996	1999	2000	2001	2002	2003	2004
Northern Ireland	**114**	**116**	**118**	**122**	**124**	**124**	**124**	**125**	**125**	**126**
Antrim	109	110	108	113	115	116	116	116	117	118
Ards	152	166	172	182	189	191	193	195	196	196
Armagh	73	76	78	79	78	79	81	82	83	82
Ballymena	87	90	90	92	92	93	93	94	94	95
Ballymoney	55	58	58	61	63	63	65	66	67	68
Banbridge	67	71	74	85	88	90	92	94	95	97
Belfast	2,886	2,761	2,672	2,632	2,584	2,562	2,528	2,501	2,478	2,454
Carrickfergus	355	367	410	447	459	466	467	471	476	479
Castlereagh	717	712	723	770	780	781	783	780	777	774
Coleraine	97	102	108	113	115	115	116	116	115	116
Cookstown	55	57	61	62	62	63	64	64	65	66
Craigavon	261	262	268	277	282	285	287	290	292	295
Derry	237	250	256	272	279	279	277	279	280	281
Down	83	87	90	96	98	98	99	100	101	103
Dungannon	57	58	59	61	61	61	62	62	63	64
Fermanagh	31	31	32	33	34	34	34	34	35	35
Larne	87	86	88	91	92	92	92	92	92	92
Limavady	47	49	50	53	55	55	56	57	57	58
Lisburn	191	208	226	243	244	244	244	245	245	247
Magherafelt	58	60	65	68	70	70	71	72	72	73
Moyle	29	31	30	31	32	32	32	33	33	33
Newry & Mourne	86	90	93	94	96	96	97	99	100	101
Newtownabbey	481	497	505	523	529	531	532	532	533	533
North Down	827	869	906	936	937	939	947	952	953	960
Omagh	40	40	41	42	42	42	43	43	44	44
Strabane	42	41	42	43	44	44	44	45	45	45

Sources: Northern Ireland Statistics and Research Agency; Ordnance Survey of Northern Ireland

[1] Any major inland water is excluded from the area used in the calculation.

[2] The boundaries of Banbridge and Newry and Mourne Local Government Districts were revised in 1993.

Estimated population by quinary age group, gender and Health and Social Services Board (HSSB), 2004

1.4

Numbers

Area/gender	All ages	0-4	5-9	10-14	15-19	20-24	25-29	30-34	35-39	40-44
Northern Ireland										
Persons	**1,710,320**	**109,090**	**120,180**	**127,680**	**132,980**	**116,600**	**106,920**	**121,860**	**130,110**	**125,550**
Males	**836,490**	**56,110**	**61,860**	**65,200**	**68,420**	**59,430**	**52,850**	**59,840**	**63,900**	**61,390**
Females	**873,830**	**52,980**	**58,330**	**62,480**	**64,570**	**57,170**	**54,070**	**62,020**	**66,200**	**64,170**
Eastern HSSB										
Persons	**664,050**	**39,460**	**43,520**	**47,500**	**51,140**	**47,920**	**41,050**	**45,040**	**49,520**	**48,990**
Males	**319,050**	20,250	22,380	24,180	25,870	24,090	20,260	21,840	23,830	23,290
Females	**345,000**	19,210	21,140	23,320	25,270	23,830	20,790	23,200	25,690	25,710
Northern HSSB										
Persons	**435,930**	**27,600**	**30,400**	**31,770**	**32,400**	**27,350**	**26,190**	**31,760**	**34,000**	**32,260**
Males	**214,270**	14,180	15,630	16,160	16,830	13,980	12,810	15,770	16,810	15,910
Females	**221,660**	13,420	14,770	15,610	15,560	13,370	13,380	16,000	17,190	16,360
Southern HSSB										
Persons	**321,420**	**22,400**	**24,080**	**25,500**	**25,020**	**21,000**	**20,480**	**23,490**	**24,580**	**23,560**
Males	**158,980**	11,530	12,450	13,200	13,040	10,480	10,100	11,530	12,290	11,810
Females	**162,430**	10,870	11,630	12,290	11,980	10,530	10,380	11,960	12,300	11,750
Western HSSB										
Persons	**288,930**	**19,630**	**22,190**	**22,910**	**24,430**	**20,330**	**19,200**	**21,570**	**22,010**	**20,740**
Males	**144,190**	10,160	11,390	11,660	12,670	10,880	9,680	10,700	10,980	10,380
Females	**144,730**	9,470	10,800	11,250	11,760	9,440	9,520	10,870	11,020	10,360

Numbers

Area/gender	45-49	50-54	55-59	60-64	65-69	70-74	75-79	80-84	85+
Northern Ireland									
Persons	**110,800**	**98,810**	**95,140**	**81,190**	**68,740**	**58,720**	**47,930**	**34,030**	**24,000**
Males	**54,790**	**49,450**	**46,550**	**39,360**	**32,410**	**26,070**	**19,550**	**12,470**	**6,860**
Females	**56,000**	**49,360**	**48,600**	**41,830**	**36,330**	**32,660**	**28,380**	**21,560**	**17,140**
Eastern HSSB									
Persons	**43,260**	**38,030**	**37,540**	**32,290**	**27,620**	**24,650**	**20,610**	**15,020**	**10,890**
Males	20,850	18,760	18,170	15,490	12,710	10,640	8,150	5,370	2,920
Females	22,400	19,260	19,370	16,810	14,900	14,010	12,470	9,650	7,970
Northern HSSB									
Persons	**28,590**	**26,010**	**25,060**	**21,990**	**18,290**	**15,300**	**12,180**	**8,740**	**6,050**
Males	14,270	13,140	12,270	10,670	8,670	6,980	5,160	3,300	1,760
Females	14,320	12,870	12,790	11,320	9,630	8,320	7,020	5,440	4,290
Southern HSSB									
Persons	**20,570**	**18,210**	**17,420**	**14,540**	**12,430**	**10,370**	**8,290**	**5,630**	**3,860**
Males	10,460	9,190	8,530	7,140	5,940	4,570	3,400	2,110	1,210
Females	10,110	9,020	8,890	7,400	6,490	5,800	4,890	3,530	2,650
Western HSSB									
Persons	**18,380**	**16,570**	**15,130**	**12,370**	**10,400**	**8,410**	**6,850**	**4,630**	**3,200**
Males	9,220	8,360	7,570	6,070	5,090	3,880	2,850	1,690	980
Females	9,170	8,210	7,560	6,310	5,310	4,530	4,000	2,940	2,230

Source: Northern Ireland Statistics and Research Agency

1.5 Mid-year population estimates by Parliamentary Constituency, 1997 to 2004

Numbers

Area	1997	1998	1999	2000	2001	2002	2003	2004
Northern Ireland	**1,671,300**	**1,677,800**	**1,679,000**	**1,682,900**	**1,689,300**	**1,696,600**	**1,702,600**	**1,710,300**
Belfast East	81,600	81,000	79,800	79,600	79,300	78,600	78,000	77,700
Belfast North	91,100	90,900	89,600	88,000	85,900	84,600	83,400	82,400
Belfast South	94,600	94,800	94,600	94,800	95,000	94,600	94,100	92,800
Belfast West	91,600	91,300	90,400	89,300	87,500	86,900	86,300	85,700
East Antrim	81,500	82,100	82,900	84,000	84,100	84,800	85,200	85,300
East Londonderry	87,000	88,000	87,800	88,100	89,000	89,400	89,600	90,500
Fermanagh & South Tyrone	89,400	89,900	90,200	90,400	91,400	92,100	92,900	93,900
Foyle	104,400	105,500	106,200	106,400	105,300	106,200	106,500	106,900
Lagan Valley	100,800	100,700	100,700	101,500	102,000	102,900	103,500	104,600
Mid Ulster	84,400	85,000	85,400	85,700	86,800	87,700	88,700	89,700
Newry & Armagh	99,900	99,700	99,100	99,300	101,400	102,400	103,400	103,000
North Antrim	99,200	99,400	99,800	100,500	101,800	102,700	103,600	104,700
North Down	84,800	85,000	85,100	85,500	86,300	86,700	86,900	87,400
South Antrim	99,100	99,800	99,900	100,200	100,300	100,700	101,200	101,900
South Down	102,600	102,900	103,800	104,000	105,100	106,100	107,200	109,200
Strangford	95,700	96,300	97,000	97,700	98,400	98,900	99,200	99,600
Upper Bann	99,100	100,100	101,000	102,100	103,300	104,000	105,000	106,200
West Tyrone	84,400	85,300	85,700	86,100	86,400	87,300	88,100	88,700

Source: Northern Ireland Statistics and Research Agency

Population and vital events, 1926 to 2004

1.6

Numbers and rates

	Estimated population			Live births[1]				Deaths				Marriages	
Year	Males	Females	**Persons**	Males	Females	**Persons**	Births per 1,000 persons	Males	Females	**Persons**	Deaths per 1,000 persons	Number	Marriages per 1,000 persons
1926-30	604,000	645,000	**1,249,000**	13,587	12,831	**26,418**	*21.2*	8,888	9,515	**18,403**	*14.7*	7,328	*5.9*
1931-35	617,000	653,000	**1,270,000**	12,926	12,172	**25,098**	*19.8*	8,869	9,157	**18,026**	*14.2*	7,806	*6.1*
1936-40	626,100	660,700	**1,286,800**	13,110	12,423	**25,533**	*19.8*	9,097	9,271	**18,369**	*14.3*	9,073	*7.1*
1941-45	674,000	630,400	**1,304,400**	15,287	14,305	**29,592**	*22.7*	8,778	8,700	**17,478**	*13.4*	10,751	*8.2*
1946-50	695,800	654,600	**1,350,400**	15,336	14,428	**29,764**	*22.0*	8,134	7,905	**16,039**	*11.9*	9,396	*7.0*
1951-55	673,700	708,800	**1,382,500**	14,885	13,913	**28,798**	*20.8*	7,966	7,590	**15,557**	*11.3*	9,359	*6.8*
1956-60	684,700	720,300	**1,405,000**	15,755	14,784	**30,539**	*21.7*	7,872	7,303	**15,175**	*10.8*	9,500	*6.8*
1961-65	705,500	741,700	**1,447,200**	17,171	16,055	**33,226**	*23.0*	8,185	7,443	**15,628**	*10.8*	10,185	*7.0*
1966-70	732,500	769,000	**1,501,500**	16,958	15,908	**32,866**	*21.9*	8,399	7,588	**15,987**	*10.6*	11,357	*7.6*
1971-75	755,200	776,700	**1,532,000**	14,935	13,914	**28,850**	*18.8*	8,954	7,994	**16,948**	*11.1*	11,384	*7.4*
1976-80	754,300	771,900	**1,526,200**	13,807	13,152	**26,959**	*17.7*	8,770	7,980	**16,750**	*11.0*	10,010	*6.6*
1981-85	759,700	792,400	**1,552,100**	13,965	13,229	**27,194**	*17.5*	8,146	7,826	**15,972**	*10.3*	10,049	*6.5*
1986-90	773,800	811,600	**1,585,400**	13,914	13,130	**27,045**	*17.1*	7,879	7,818	**15,696**	*9.9*	10,031	*6.3*
1991-95	795,900	835,900	**1,631,800**	12,704	12,075	**24,779**	*15.2*	7,515	7,713	**15,228**	*9.3*	8,983	*5.5*
1996-00	816,700	857,800	**1,674,500**	11,966	11,356	**23,321**	*13.9*	7,315	7,835	**15,150**	*9.0*	7,881	*4.7*
1971	754,600	785,800	**1,540,400**	16,504	15,261	**31,765**	*20.6*	8,593	7,609	**16,202**	*10.5*	12,152	*7.9*
1972	757,500	781,500	**1,539,000**	15,559	14,435	**29,994**	*19.5*	9,001	8,031	**17,032**	*11.1*	11,905	*7.7*
1973	755,700	774,200	**1,530,000**	15,152	14,048	**29,200**	*19.1*	9,288	8,381	**17,669**	*11.5*	11,212	*7.3*
1974	755,000	771,900	**1,526,900**	13,987	13,173	**27,160**	*17.8*	9,226	8,101	**17,327**	*11.3*	10,783	*7.1*
1975	753,300	770,200	**1,523,500**	13,475	12,655	**26,130**	*17.2*	8,664	7,847	**16,511**	*10.8*	10,867	*7.1*
1976	754,000	769,500	**1,523,500**	13,542	12,819	**26,361**	*17.3*	8,869	8,161	**17,030**	*11.2*	9,914	*6.5*
1977	753,900	769,400	**1,523,300**	13,154	12,283	**25,437**	*16.7*	8,871	8,050	**16,921**	*11.1*	9,696	*6.4*
1978	753,600	769,700	**1,523,200**	13,168	13,071	**26,239**	*17.2*	8,458	7,695	**16,153**	*10.6*	10,304	*6.8*
1979	755,200	773,100	**1,528,300**	14,485	13,693	**28,178**	*18.4*	8,822	7,989	**16,811**	*11.0*	10,214	*6.7*
1980	754,800	778,000	**1,532,800**	14,686	13,896	**28,582**	*18.6*	8,832	8,003	**16,835**	*11.0*	9,923	*6.5*
1981	756,600	786,300	**1,543,000**	13,847	13,319	**27,166**	*17.6*	8,423	7,833	**16,256**	*10.5*	9,636	*6.2*
1982	756,700	787,800	**1,544,500**	13,732	13,140	**26,872**	*17.4*	8,004	7,914	**15,918**	*10.3*	9,913	*6.4*
1983	759,000	791,500	**1,550,600**	13,972	13,054	**27,026**	*17.4*	8,209	7,830	**16,039**	*10.3*	9,990	*6.4*
1984	761,300	796,000	**1,557,300**	14,196	13,281	**27,477**	*17.6*	8,007	7,685	**15,692**	*10.1*	10,361	*6.7*
1985	764,900	800,400	**1,565,400**	14,076	13,351	**27,427**	*17.5*	8,088	7,867	**15,955**	*10.2*	10,343	*6.6*
1986	768,400	805,100	**1,573,500**	14,501	13,474	**27,975**	*17.8*	8,154	7,911	**16,065**	*10.2*	10,225	*6.5*
1987	772,900	809,100	**1,582,000**	14,196	13,457	**27,653**	*17.5*	7,721	7,613	**15,334**	*9.7*	10,363	*6.6*
1988	773,800	811,700	**1,585,400**	14,131	13,383	**27,514**	*17.4*	7,993	7,820	**15,813**	*10.0*	9,960	*6.3*
1989	775,900	814,500	**1,590,400**	13,307	12,524	**25,831**	*16.2*	7,878	7,966	**15,844**	*10.0*	10,019	*6.3*
1990	777,900	817,700	**1,595,600**	13,437	12,814	**26,251**	*16.5*	7,648	7,778	**15,426**	*9.7*	9,588	*6.0*
1991	783,200	824,100	**1,607,300**	13,427	12,601	**26,028**	*16.2*	7,533	7,563	**15,096**	*9.4*	9,221	*5.7*
1992	792,100	831,100	**1,623,300**	12,924	12,430	**25,354**	*15.6*	7,469	7,519	**14,988**	*9.2*	9,392	*5.8*
1993	798,200	837,300	**1,635,600**	12,515	12,207	**24,722**	*15.1*	7,731	7,902	**15,633**	*9.6*	9,045	*5.5*
1994	801,900	841,800	**1,643,700**	12,361	11,737	**24,098**	*14.7*	7,362	7,752	**15,114**	*9.2*	8,683	*5.3*
1995	804,000	845,100	**1,649,100**	12,293	11,400	**23,693**	*14.4*	7,482	7,828	**15,310**	*9.3*	8,576	*5.2*
1996	810,300	851,400	**1,661,800**	12,382	12,000	**24,382**	*14.7*	7,418	7,800	**15,218**	*9.2*	8,297	*5.0*
1997	815,500	855,700	**1,671,300**	12,325	11,762	**24,087**	*14.4*	7,244	7,727	**14,971**	*9.0*	8,071	*4.8*
1998	818,700	859,100	**1,677,800**	12,058	11,610	**23,668**	*14.1*	7,321	7,672	**14,993**	*8.9*	7,826	*4.7*
1999	818,500	860,500	**1,679,000**	11,943	11,014	**22,957**	*13.7*	7,464	8,199	**15,663**	*9.3*	7,628	*4.5*
2000	820,500	862,500	**1,682,900**	11,120	10,392	**21,512**	*12.8*	7,128	7,775	**14,903**	*8.9*	7,584	*4.5*
2001	824,400	864,900	**1,689,300**	11,288	10,674	**21,962**	*13.0*	7,007	7,506	**14,513**	*8.6*	7,281	*4.3*
2002	828,900	867,800	**1,696,600**	10,874	10,511	**21,385**	*12.6*	6,948	7,638	**14,586**	*8.6*	7,599	*4.5*
2003	832,800	869,800	**1,702,600**	11,244	10,404	**21,648**	*12.7*	6,920	7,542	**14,462**	*8.5*	7,757	*4.6*
2004	836,500	873,800	**1,710,300**	11,477	10,841	**22,318**	*13.0*	6,935	7,419	**14,354**	*8.4*	8,328	*4.9*

Source: Northern Ireland Statistics and Research Agency

[1] Live births before 1981 include births to mothers who were not Northern Ireland residents.

1.7 Estimated population, births, deaths and marriages by Health and Social Services Board (HSSB) and Local Government District, 2004

Numbers and rates

Area	Estimated population at 30 June 2004	Resident live births				Deaths				Marriages	
		Males	Females	**Persons**	Births per 1,000 persons	Males	Females	**Persons**	Deaths per 1,000 persons	Number	Marriages per 1,000 persons
Northern Ireland	**1,710,300**	**11,477**	**10,841**	**22,318**	***13.0***	**6,935**	**7,419**	**14,354**	***8.4***	**8,328**	***4.9***
Eastern HSSB	**664,100**	**4,280**	**3,925**	**8,205**	***12.4***	**2,904**	**3,244**	**6,148**	***9.3***	**3,216**	***4.8***
Ards	74,600	461	403	**864**	*11.6*	337	362	**699**	*9.4*	244	*3.3*
Belfast	269,000	1,821	1,602	**3,423**	*12.7*	1,314	1,480	**2,794**	*10.4*	1,517	*5.6*
Castlereagh	65,800	367	346	**713**	*10.8*	271	327	**598**	*9.1*	181	*2.8*
Down	66,800	467	428	**895**	*13.4*	228	267	**495**	*7.4*	313	*4.7*
Lisburn	110,200	754	710	**1,464**	*13.3*	409	404	**813**	*7.4*	456	*4.1*
North Down	77,600	410	436	**846**	*10.9*	345	404	**749**	*9.6*	505	*6.5*
Northern HSSB	**435,900**	**2,892**	**2,805**	**5,697**	***13.1***	**1,757**	**1,783**	**3,540**	***8.1***	**2,060**	***4.7***
Antrim	49,800	404	351	**755**	*15.2*	191	185	**376**	*7.5*	203	*4.1*
Ballymena	60,000	396	388	**784**	*13.1*	235	252	**487**	*8.1*	311	*5.2*
Ballymoney	28,300	195	202	**397**	*14.0*	119	107	**226**	*8.0*	118	*4.2*
Carrickfergus	38,700	204	235	**439**	*11.3*	146	162	**308**	*8.0*	187	*4.8*
Coleraine	56,500	343	329	**672**	*11.9*	257	262	**519**	*9.2*	305	*5.4*
Cookstown	33,700	258	244	**502**	*14.9*	123	117	**240**	*7.1*	193	*5.7*
Larne	30,900	163	153	**316**	*10.2*	172	128	**300**	*9.7*	163	*5.3*
Magherafelt	41,300	302	287	**589**	*14.3*	140	119	**259**	*6.3*	211	*5.1*
Moyle	16,400	101	97	**198**	*12.1*	69	77	**146**	*8.9*	112	*6.8*
Newtownabbey	80,300	526	519	**1,045**	*13.0*	305	374	**679**	*8.5*	257	*3.2*
Southern HSSB	**321,400**	**2,347**	**2,335**	**4,682**	***14.6***	**1,203**	**1,315**	**2,518**	***7.8***	**1,612**	***5.0***
Armagh	54,900	356	372	**728**	*13.3*	201	235	**436**	*7.9*	298	*5.4*
Banbridge	43,800	282	302	**584**	*13.3*	153	171	**324**	*7.4*	156	*3.6*
Craigavon	83,200	577	599	**1,176**	*14.1*	319	331	**650**	*7.8*	348	*4.2*
Dungannon	49,300	400	385	**785**	*15.9*	189	205	**394**	*8.0*	267	*5.4*
Newry & Mourne	90,300	732	677	**1,409**	*15.6*	341	373	**714**	*7.9*	543	*6.0*
Western HSSB	**288,900**	**1,958**	**1,776**	**3,734**	***12.9***	**1,071**	**1,077**	**2,148**	***7.4***	**1,440**	***5.0***
Derry	106,900	746	739	**1,485**	*13.9*	353	394	**747**	*7.0*	506	*4.7*
Fermanagh	59,300	370	322	**692**	*11.7*	296	290	**586**	*9.9*	368	*6.2*
Limavady	34,000	232	194	**426**	*12.5*	111	110	**221**	*6.5*	154	*4.5*
Omagh	50,100	348	298	**646**	*12.9*	172	152	**324**	*6.5*	261	*5.2*
Strabane	38,700	262	223	**485**	*12.5*	139	131	**270**	*7.0*	151	*3.9*

Source: Northern Ireland Statistics and Research Agency

Figure 1.2 Average annual births and deaths, 1926 to 2025

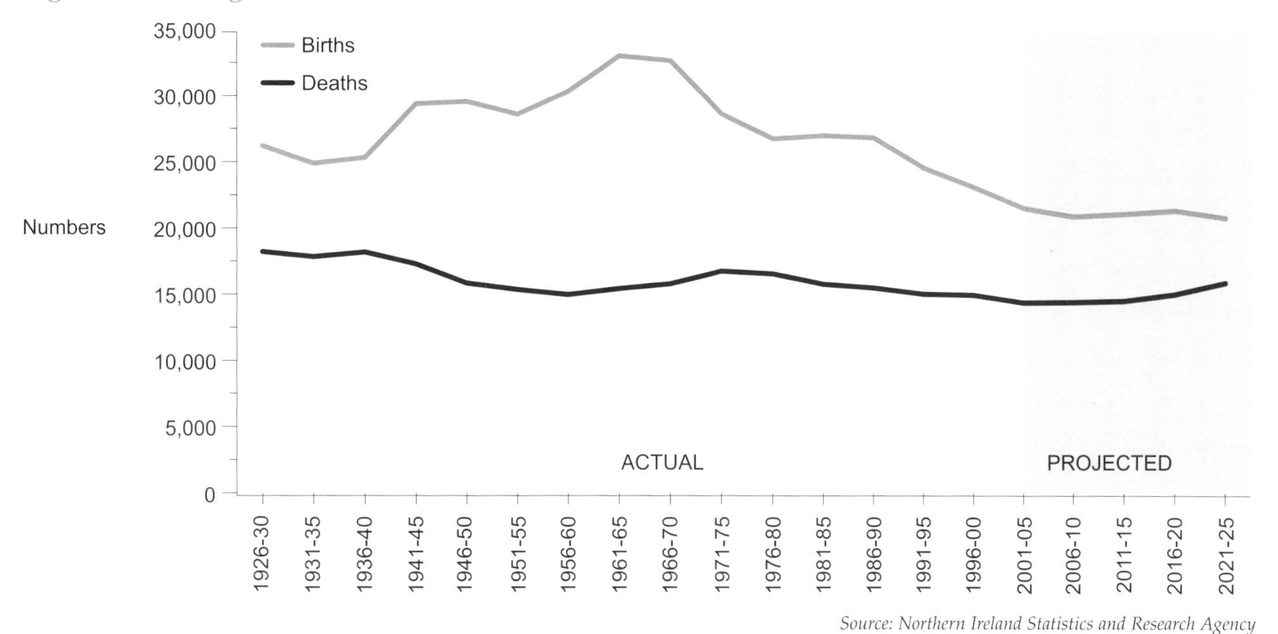

Source: Northern Ireland Statistics and Research Agency

1.8 Live births, birth rates and Total Period Fertility Rates (TPFR) by Health and Social Services Board (HSSB), 2004

Numbers and rates

Area	Live births: Resident in Northern Ireland: Males	Females	**Persons**	Not resident in Northern Ireland	Live births per 1,000 persons	Live births per 1,000 women aged 15-44	TPFR	Males per 1,000 females
Northern Ireland	**11,477**	**10,841**	**22,318**	**575**	***13.0***	***60.6***	***1.87***	***1,059***
Eastern HSSB	4,280	3,925	**8,205**	154	*12.4*	*56.8*	*1.77*	*1,090*
Northern HSSB	2,892	2,805	**5,697**	10	*13.1*	*62.0*	*1.92*	*1,031*
Southern HSSB	2,347	2,335	**4,682**	265	*14.6*	*68.0*	*2.08*	*1,005*
Western HSSB	1,958	1,776	**3,734**	146	*12.9*	*59.3*	*1.82*	*1,102*

Source: Northern Ireland Statistics and Research Agency

1.9 Resident live births by age of mother, 1994 to 2004

Numbers

Age group	1994	1995	1996	1997	1998	1999	2000	2001	2002	2003	2004
Under 20	1,545	1,428	1,582	1,644	1,735	1,791	1,614	1,524	1,502	1,483	1,486
20-24	4,591	4,399	4,332	4,061	3,889	3,874	3,602	3,699	3,619	3,619	3,592
25-29	8,414	8,204	8,243	7,855	7,451	6,866	6,206	6,087	5,779	5,817	5,935
30-34	6,607	6,596	7,075	7,179	7,170	6,953	6,547	6,891	6,691	6,772	6,985
35-39	2,464	2,629	2,706	2,868	2,955	2,957	3,031	3,183	3,203	3,342	3,712
40-44	455	418	425	463	446	497	496	548	565	596	592
45 and over	22	19	19	17	22	19	16	30	26	19	16
All ages	**24,098**	**23,693**	**24,382**	**24,087**	**23,668**	**22,957**	**21,512**	**21,962**	**21,385**	**21,648**	**22,318**

Source: Northern Ireland Statistics and Research Agency

1.10 Deaths, death rates and standardised death rates by Health and Social Services Board (HSSB), 2004

Numbers and rates

Area	Deaths			Not resident in Northern Ireland	Deaths per 1,000 persons	Standardised death rate[1]
	Males	Females	**Persons**			
Northern Ireland	**6,935**	**7,419**	**14,354**	**84**	***8.4***	***8.4***
Eastern HSSB	2,904	3,244	**6,148**	37	*9.3*	*8.4*
Northern HSSB	1,757	1,783	**3,540**	7	*8.1*	*8.0*
Southern HSSB	1,203	1,315	**2,518**	15	*7.8*	*8.6*
Western HSSB	1,071	1,077	**2,148**	25	*7.4*	*8.7*

Source: Northern Ireland Statistics and Research Agency

[1] Adjusted for the age and gender of the population.

Figure 1.3 Life expectancy at birth by gender, 1900 to 2003

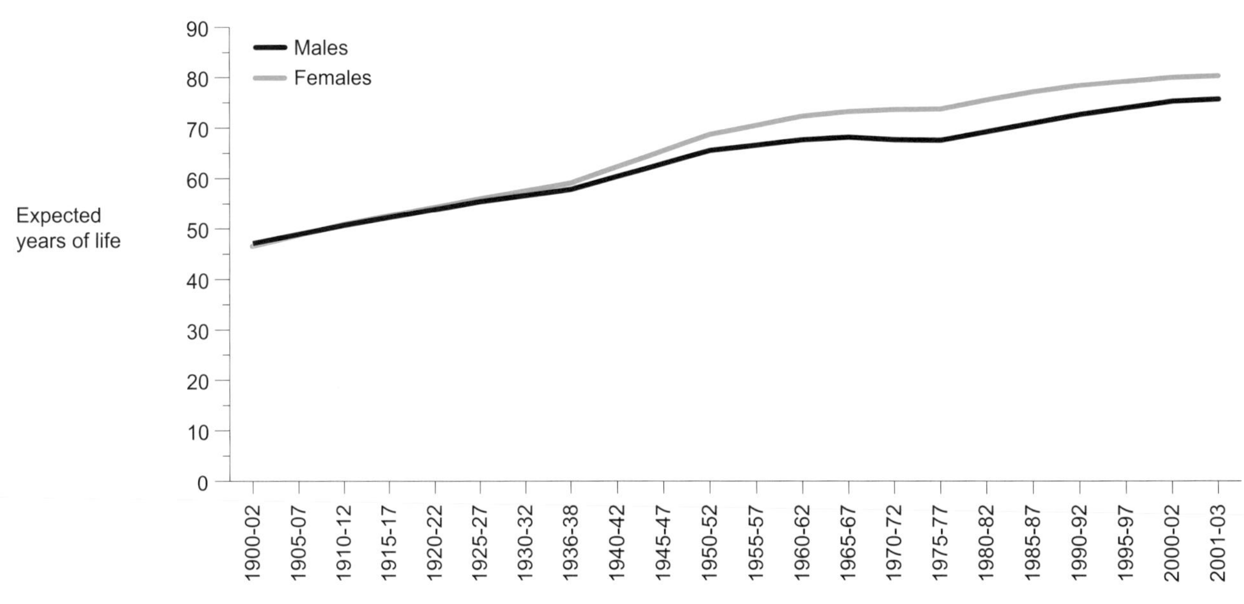

Source: Northern Ireland Statistics and Research Agency

POPULATION

Life expectancy[1] by selected age and gender, 1890 to 2003

1.11

Years

Year	Expectation of life at: Birth		Age 1		Age 65	
	Males	Females	Males	Females	Males	Females
1890-92	46.3	45.7	..	..	10.6	10.6
1900-02	47.1	46.7	..	..	10.5	10.4
1910-12	50.7	51.0	..	..	12.1	12.8
1925-27	55.4	56.1	59.9	59.5	11.9	12.7
1936-38	57.8	59.2	..	..	11.6	12.4
1950-52	65.5	68.8	67.5	70.3	12.1	13.5
1960-62	67.6	72.4	68.7	73.2	12.2	14.4
1965-67	68.1	73.3	68.9	74.1	12.3	15.0
1970-72	67.6	73.7	68.3	74.1	12.0	15.2
1975-77	67.5	73.8	67.9	74.1	11.8	15.3
1980-82	69.2	75.5	69.2	75.4	12.5	16.3
1982-84	70.1	76.3	70.1	76.1	13.0	16.6
1983-85	70.3	76.7	70.2	76.4	12.9	16.7
1984-86	70.6	76.9	70.4	76.6	13.0	16.8
1985-87	70.9	77.1	70.7	76.8	13.2	16.9
1986-88	71.1	77.3	70.9	76.9	13.3	17.2
1987-89	71.5	77.5	71.1	77.1	13.4	17.3
1988-90	71.7	77.6	71.3	77.2	13.5	17.4
1989-91	72.1	78.0	71.7	77.5	13.7	17.5
1990-92	72.6	78.4	72.1	77.9	13.9	17.8
1991-93	72.7	78.6	72.3	78.0	14.0	17.9
1992-94	73.0	78.7	72.5	78.2	14.2	17.9
1993-95	73.1	78.7	72.7	78.1	14.3	17.9
1994-96	73.5	78.9	73.0	78.4	14.4	18.0
1995-97	73.8	79.2	73.3	78.6	14.6	18.1
1996-98	74.2	79.5	73.6	78.9	14.7	18.3
1997-99	74.3	79.5	73.7	79.0	14.9	18.3
1998-00	74.5	79.6	73.9	78.9	15.0	18.4
1999-01	74.8	79.8	74.3	79.2	15.3	18.5
2000-02	75.2	80.1	74.6	79.5	15.7	18.7
2001-03	75.6	80.4	75.0	79.8	15.9	18.9

Source: Northern Ireland Statistics and Research Agency

[1] Expectation of years of life left to persons at birth, aged 1 and 65 who are subject to the current year's mortality probabilities from that age onwards.

1.12 Components of population change by Health and Social Services Board (HSSB) and Local Government District, 2003 to 2004

Numbers and percentages

Area	Estimated population 30 June 2003	Births	Deaths	Natural change	Estimated net civilian migration	Other changes[1]	Estimated population 30 June 2004	Population change	
								Number	%
Northern Ireland	**1,702,628**	**22,018**	**14,585**	**7,433**	**821**	**-560**	**1,710,322**	**7,694**	***0.5***
Eastern HSSB	**663,911**	**8,224**	**6,271**	**1,953**	**-2,314**	**501**	**664,051**	**140**	***0.0***
Ards	74,369	859	708	151	131	-3	74,648	279	*0.4*
Belfast	271,596	3,479	2,834	645	-2,941	-322	268,978	-2,618	*-1.0*
Castlereagh	66,076	706	650	56	-347	10	65,795	-281	*-0.4*
Down	65,195	884	511	373	561	630	66,759	1,564	*2.4*
Lisburn	109,565	1,448	817	631	113	-62	110,247	682	*0.6*
North Down	77,110	848	751	97	169	248	77,624	514	*0.7*
Northern HSSB	**432,834**	**5,499**	**3,575**	**1,924**	**480**	**693**	**435,931**	**3,097**	***0.7***
Antrim	49,260	732	375	357	181	35	49,833	573	*1.2*
Ballymena	59,516	761	522	239	313	-42	60,026	510	*0.9*
Ballymoney	27,809	359	204	155	296	0	28,260	451	*1.6*
Carrickfergus	38,466	453	311	142	157	-50	38,715	249	*0.6*
Coleraine	56,024	629	501	128	-222	600	56,530	506	*0.9*
Cookstown	33,387	471	241	230	43	0	33,660	273	*0.8*
Larne	30,948	314	303	11	-51	0	30,908	-40	*-0.1*
Magherafelt	40,837	572	270	302	157	0	41,296	459	*1.1*
Moyle	16,302	207	153	54	68	0	16,424	122	*0.7*
Newtownabbey	80,285	1,001	695	306	-462	150	80,279	-6	*0.0*
Southern HSSB	**319,026**	**4,552**	**2,521**	**2,031**	**2,166**	**-1,808**	**321,415**	**2,389**	***0.7***
Armagh	55,449	749	409	340	259	-1,172	54,876	-573	*-1.0*
Banbridge	43,083	596	330	266	425	0	43,774	691	*1.6*
Craigavon	82,155	1,097	672	425	572	16	83,168	1,013	*1.2*
Dungannon	48,695	719	414	305	329	-22	49,307	612	*1.3*
Newry & Mourne	89,644	1,391	696	695	581	-630	90,290	646	*0.7*
Western HSSB	**286,857**	**3,743**	**2,218**	**1,525**	**489**	**54**	**288,925**	**2,068**	***0.7***
Derry	106,456	1,486	755	731	-97	-201	106,889	433	*0.4*
Fermanagh	58,705	695	563	132	492	-50	59,279	574	*1.0*
Limavady	33,571	450	218	232	-63	270	34,010	439	*1.3*
Omagh	49,560	636	363	273	214	35	50,082	522	*1.1*
Strabane	38,565	476	319	157	-57	0	38,665	100	*0.3*

Source: Northern Ireland Statistics and Research Agency

[1] Other changes include changes in the number of Her Majesty's Forces stationed in Northern Ireland.

Net migration by gender and age, 1996/7 to 2003/4

Numbers

Gender/age	1996/7	1997/8	1998/9	1999/0	2000/1	2001/2	2002/3	2003/4
Males								
Under 15	307	-172	-72	-133	-196	847	496	102
15 - 44	-1,860	-2,044	-3,575	-2,324	-1,964	-1,372	-1,169	-37
45 - 64	638	637	636	704	694	665	391	349
65 and over	106	204	165	238	161	167	171	169
All ages	**-809**	**-1,375**	**-2,846**	**-1,515**	**-1,305**	**307**	**-111**	**583**
Females								
Under 15	-114	-109	-235	-397	-302	791	406	209
15 - 44	-519	-700	-2,006	-678	-705	-1,718	-1,858	-575
45 - 64	554	305	180	304	449	391	399	328
65 and over	-144	94	92	59	-12	314	168	276
All ages	**-223**	**-410**	**-1,969**	**-712**	**-570**	**-222**	**-885**	**238**
All persons	**-1,032**	**-1,785**	**-4,815**	**-2,227**	**-1,875**	**85**	**-996**	**821**

Source: Northern Ireland Statistics and Research Agency

Figure 1.4 Estimated population, 1926 to 2025 (2003 based projections)

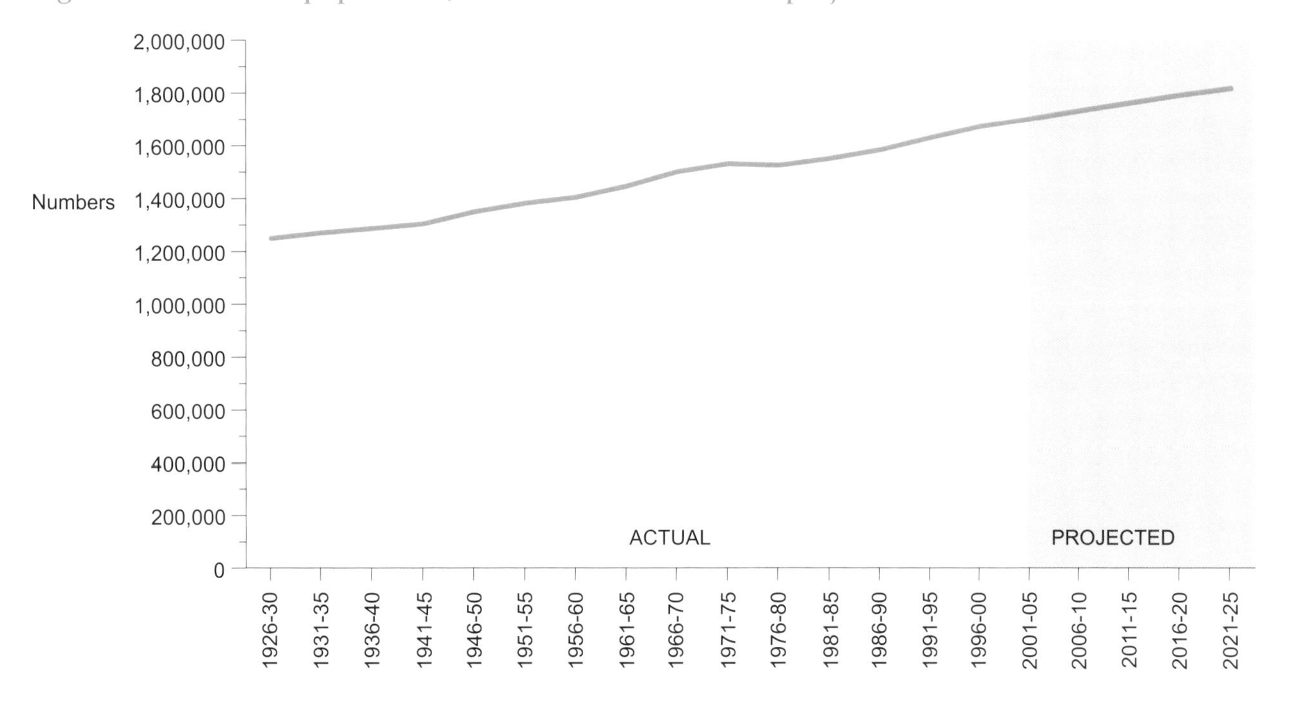

Source: Northern Ireland Statistics and Research Agency

POPULATION

1.14 Projected population (2003 based) by age and gender, 2003 to 2043

Thousands

Age/gender	Estimated population 30 June 2003	Projected population at 30 June 2008	2013	2018	2023	2028	2031	2036	2043
0-4									
Males	57	55	54	55	55	52	51	49	47
Females	54	53	52	53	52	50	49	47	45
Persons	**111**	**107**	**106**	**108**	**107**	**103**	**99**	**95**	**93**
5-9									
Males	62	57	55	54	55	55	54	51	48
Females	59	55	53	53	53	53	52	49	47
Persons	**121**	**111**	**108**	**107**	**109**	**108**	**105**	**100**	**95**
10-14									
Males	66	62	57	55	54	55	55	54	50
Females	63	59	55	54	53	54	54	52	49
Persons	**129**	**121**	**112**	**109**	**107**	**109**	**109**	**106**	**99**
15-19									
Males	68	66	62	57	55	54	55	55	52
Females	65	62	59	54	53	52	53	53	50
Persons	**133**	**128**	**121**	**111**	**108**	**106**	**107**	**108**	**103**
20-24									
Males	58	67	64	60	55	53	52	53	53
Females	55	62	59	56	51	50	49	50	50
Persons	**113**	**128**	**124**	**116**	**106**	**103**	**101**	**103**	**103**
25-29									
Males	54	56	65	62	58	53	52	50	52
Females	54	56	63	61	57	52	52	50	51
Persons	**108**	**112**	**128**	**123**	**115**	**106**	**103**	**101**	**103**
30-34									
Males	61	53	55	64	62	58	55	51	50
Females	63	55	57	64	61	58	55	52	51
Persons	**125**	**108**	**112**	**128**	**123**	**115**	**111**	**104**	**101**
35-39									
Males	65	61	52	55	63	61	58	55	50
Females	67	64	56	58	65	62	59	56	53
Persons	**131**	**125**	**108**	**112**	**128**	**123**	**118**	**111**	**103**
40-44									
Males	60	63	59	51	53	62	62	57	51
Females	63	67	64	56	58	65	64	59	54
Persons	**123**	**130**	**124**	**107**	**111**	**127**	**125**	**117**	**105**
45-49									
Males	54	59	62	58	50	53	59	61	55
Females	54	62	66	64	56	58	63	63	58
Persons	**108**	**121**	**128**	**122**	**106**	**110**	**122**	**124**	**113**
50-54									
Males	49	53	58	61	58	49	49	58	58
Females	49	54	62	66	63	55	55	63	61
Persons	**98**	**107**	**119**	**127**	**121**	**105**	**104**	**120**	**120**
55-59									
Males	46	48	52	56	60	56	52	48	59
Females	48	48	53	61	65	62	58	54	63
Persons	**94**	**96**	**105**	**117**	**124**	**119**	**109**	**102**	**123**
60-64									
Males	38	44	45	50	54	58	56	50	49
Females	40	47	47	52	59	63	62	56	56
Persons	**78**	**91**	**93**	**101**	**114**	**121**	**118**	**106**	**105**

1.14 Projected population (2003 based) by age and gender, 2003 to 2043 (continued)

Thousands

Age/gender	Estimated population 30 June 2003	Projected population at 30 June 2008	2013	2018	2023	2028	2031	2036	2043
65-69									
Males	32	35	41	43	47	51	54	53	45
Females	36	39	45	45	50	57	60	60	52
Persons	**67**	**74**	**86**	**88**	**97**	**109**	**115**	**113**	**97**
70-74									
Males	26	28	32	37	39	43	45	50	48
Females	33	33	36	42	43	47	52	57	56
Persons	**58**	**61**	**68**	**79**	**82**	**90**	**97**	**107**	**104**
75-79									
Males	19	21	23	27	32	33	35	40	44
Females	28	28	29	33	38	39	40	48	53
Persons	**48**	**49**	**53**	**59**	**70**	**72**	**76**	**87**	**97**
80-84									
Males	12	13	15	18	21	25	26	28	33
Females	21	22	23	24	27	32	33	35	43
Persons	**33**	**35**	**38**	**42**	**48**	**57**	**59**	**63**	**76**
85-89									
Males	5	7	8	9	11	13	15	17	20
Females	11	13	14	16	18	20	23	25	28
Persons	**16**	**20**	**22**	**25**	**29**	**34**	**38**	**42**	**49**
90 and over									
Males	2	2	3	4	6	7	8	11	14
Females	6	6	8	10	11	14	15	19	23
Persons	**8**	**9**	**11**	**14**	**17**	**21**	**23**	**29**	**36**
All ages									
Males	833	849	863	877	887	893	893	890	879
Females	870	886	902	918	933	944	947	949	944
Persons	**1,703**	**1,735**	**1,765**	**1,795**	**1,821**	**1,837**	**1,840**	**1,839**	**1,823**
Selected age groups									
Children (under 16)	388	365	350	345	344	341	336	323	307
16-29	327	344	348	328	308	293	290	290	288
30-44	378	363	344	348	363	365	353	331	309
45-64 male/ 45-59 female	338	368	398	416	405	391	391	396	405
Working age[1]	1,044	1,075	1,106	1,135	1,135	1,113	1,096	1,074	1,057
65-74 male/ 60-74 female	166	182	201	219	238	262	274	277	256
75 and over	104	113	124	140	164	184	196	222	258
Pensionable age[1]	271	295	309	315	342	383	408	442	459

Source: Government Actuary's Department, London

[1] Includes changes which will be made between 2010 to 2020 when the female age for pension increases from 60 to 65.

Notes to Population tables

TABLE 1.1

The mid-year population figures are estimates of the usually resident population of Northern Ireland at 30 June each year, and include members of Her Majesty's Forces stationed in Northern Ireland at that time. The population information published in this Abstract supersedes that published in earlier editions. The Mid-Year Population Estimates are generally quoted in rounded form. For example, Table 1.4 gives the population of Northern Ireland in 2004 as 1,710,320. This is because population counts from the census and subsequent updates involving births, deaths and migration cannot be precise. In general, the precision of the population estimates should be considered to be no better than to the nearest 100.

TABLES 1.1 TO 1.5

The published information includes a breakdown of the population by age and gender at Local Government District level, Health and Social Services Board, Education and Library Board, and NI level.

TABLE 1.8

The Total Period Fertility Rate (TPFR) is the average number of children that would be born to a cohort of women who experience, throughout their childbearing years, the fertility rates of the calendar year in question.

TABLE 1.10

A straight comparison of crude death rates between areas may present a misleading picture because of the differences in the gender and age structure of the respective populations. The technique of standardisation is used to address this. In general, standardisation involves a comparison of the actual number of events occurring in an area with the aggregate number expected if the age/gender specific rates in the standard population were applied to the age/gender groups of the observed population. The results are expressed either as standardised rates or as standardised mortality ratios (SMRs) where the standard rate (for Northern Ireland) equals 100.

TABLE 1.11

"Life expectancy" is the average future lifetime of a person if they are subject to the death probabilities indicated by the mortality records of the years covered.

TABLE 1.13

Estimates of total net migration are made each year as part of the general process of estimating Northern Ireland's mid-year population. These estimates are based on transfers of medical cards recorded by the National Health Service Central Registers and the Northern Ireland Central Services Agency. The estimate of migration to the Republic of Ireland is based on data from the Republic of Ireland Quarterly National Household Survey.

TABLE 1.14

Population projections show the estimated impact of certain demographic assumptions (fertility, migration and mortality) over time. The latest set of population projections is based on the 2003 mid-year population estimates for Northern Ireland.

Housing and Households

- In 2004-05, the average household size in Northern Ireland was 2.56. People living alone represented one quarter of the region's households. The proportion of NI households comprising five or more people has decreased over the past five years from 14% in 2000-01 to 10% in 2004-05.

- Households of married or co-habiting couples represented 58% of all NI households in 2004-05; lone parent households accounted for a further 14%. In the same year, 35% of NI households included dependent children. In 2004-05, a lone parent headed 29% of all families with dependent children. This compares with 24% in 1999-00.

- In 2004-05, almost a quarter of all NI household members were children aged under 16, whilst 45% were adults aged between 30 and 64. People aged 65 or over represented approximately 14% of NI household members but accounted for over two fifths (43%) of those living alone.

- Average weekly household expenditure in Northern Ireland was £407 in 2003-04. This varied significantly by composition of household. Average expenditure by pensioner households with one or two adults was £152 per week compared with £543 per week for households with children.

- **Wages and salaries made up the majority of weekly household income in all UK regions in 2003-04. The proportion of income derived from self employment was highest in Northern Ireland accounting for 13% of total weekly household income, compared with a UK average of 9%. At 12% the proportion of NI weekly household income, derived from social security benefits, was also higher than the UK average of 7%.**

- **In 2003-04, 94% of all UK households had some type of financial deposit or savings account. However, only 87% of NI households had such accounts. Similarly, at 86% Northern Ireland had the lowest proportion of households with a Direct Payment Account across all the UK regions.**

- **Over two fifths of all NI households had no savings in 2003-04. Those on lower incomes were more likely to have no savings. In 2003-04, 62% of households with weekly incomes less than £200 and 55% of households with weekly incomes of between £200 and £400 had no savings.**

- **Over three fifths of all NI households (63%) occupy relatively modern buildings (built from 1965 onwards).**

- **In 2004-05, the construction of over 14,000 dwellings was started in Northern Ireland. The majority of these new starts (93%) were in the private sector. Housing Associations accounted for all of the 1,029 public sector housing starts.**

- **Between 1999-2000 and 2004-05, the average selling price of new houses registered with the National House Building Council increased by 59% to £118,000. This increase includes rises due to inflation.**

Number of persons in household, 1999-2000 to 2004-05

2.1

Percentages and numbers

Number of persons in household	1999-00	2000-01	2001-02	2002-03	2003-04	2004-05[P]
1	*26*	*25*	*26*	*28*	*26*	*25*
2	*30*	*28*	*29*	*29*	*31*	*33*
3	*15*	*16*	*18*	*16*	*14*	*17*
4	*16*	*16*	*15*	*15*	*17*	*14*
5	*8*	*9*	*7*	*8*	*7*	*7*
≥ 6	*5*	*5*	*5*	*4*	*4*	*3*
Average household size	**2.67**	**2.72**	**2.67**	**2.58**	**2.61**	**2.56**
Sample base (all households)	3,039	2,800	2,805	2,782	2,718	2,772

Source: Continuous Household Survey, Northern Ireland Statistics and Research Agency

Household type, 1999-2000 to 2004-05

2.2

Percentages

Household type	1999-00	2000-01	2001-02	2002-03	2003-04	2004-05[P]
1 adult aged 16-59	*11*	*10*	*11*	*13*	*12*	*13*
2 adults aged 16-59	*12*	*12*	*13*	*13*	*14*	*14*
Youngest aged 0-4	*15*	*15*	*15*	*14*	*14*	*13*
Youngest aged 5-15	*20*	*22*	*19*	*20*	*19*	*19*
≥ 3 adults	*12*	*13*	*13*	*12*	*12*	*13*
2 adults with 1 or both ≥ 60	*15*	*13*	*14*	*13*	*14*	*16*
1 adult ≥ 60	*15*	*15*	*15*	*16*	*14*	*13*
Sample base (all households)	3,039	2,800	2,804	2,782	2,718	2,772

Source: Continuous Household Survey, Northern Ireland Statistics and Research Agency

2.3 Type of household, 1999-2000 to 2004-05

Percentages

Type of household	1999-00	2000-01	2001-02	2002-03	2003-04	2004-05[p]
1 person only	*26*	*26*	*26*	*28*	*26*	*25*
2 or more adults	*3*	*3*	*3*	*3*	*3*	*3*
Married/cohabiting couple						
- with dependent children[1,2]	*29*	*29*	*27*	*27*	*27*	*25*
- with non-dependent children only	*7*	*8*	*8*	*7*	*7*	*8*
- no children	*22*	*20*	*22*	*23*	*23*	*25*
Lone parent						
- with dependent children[1,2]	*8*	*10*	*10*	*8*	*9*	*10*
- with non-dependent children only	*4*	*4*	*4*	*4*	*4*	*4*
Two or more families	*1*	*1*	*1*	*1*	*1*	*1*
Sample base (all households)	3,039	2,800	2,805	2,782	2,718	2,772

Source: Continuous Household Survey, Northern Ireland Statistics and Research Agency

[1] Dependent children are persons under 16, or aged 16-18 and in full time education, in the family unit and living in the household.

[2] May also include non-dependent children.

2.4 Families with dependent children[1] by marital status, 1999-2000 to 2004-05

Percentages

Family type	1999-00	2000-01	2001-02	2002-03	2003-04	2004-05[p]
Married/ cohabiting couple[2]	*76*	*73*	*73*	*76*	*75*	*71*
Lone mother	***23***	***25***	***25***	***22***	***24***	***27***
- single	*10*	*12*	*13*	*11*	*12*	*13*
- widowed	*2*	*1*	*1*	*1*	*1*	*1*
- divorced	*4*	*5*	*5*	*4*	*4*	*5*
- separated	*7*	*7*	*6*	*6*	*7*	*8*
Lone father	*1*	*2*	*2*	*2*	*1*	*2*
All lone parents	***24***	***27***	***27***	***24***	***25***	***29***
Sample base (families with dependent children)	1,149	1,104	1,051	997	990	974

Source: Continuous Household Survey, Northern Ireland Statistics and Research Agency

[1] Dependent children are persons under 16, or aged 16-18 and in full-time education, in the family unit and living in the household.

[2] Including married women whose husbands were not defined as resident in the household.

2.5 Household members by age and household type, 2004-05P

Percentages

Age	1 adult only	2 adults aged 16-59	Youngest aged 0-4	Youngest aged 5-15	3 or more adults	2 adults either 60 or over	**All household members**
0-4	.	.	*32*	.	.	.	***6***
5-9	.	.	*13*	*17*	.	.	***8***
10-15	.	.	*6*	*27*	.	.	***9***
16-24	*3*	*14*	*7*	*12*	*30*	-	***12***
25-29	*6*	*19*	*8*	*2*	*10*	*1*	***7***
30-44	*19*	*25*	*32*	*26*	*12*	*3*	***21***
45-59	*22*	*43*	*2*	*15*	*34*	*11*	***19***
60-64	*7*	.	-	-	*6*	*24*	***5***
65-69	*9*	.	-	-	*3*	*21*	***4***
70-74	*11*	.	-	-	*2*	*17*	***4***
75 or over	*23*	.	-	-	*3*	*23*	***6***
Sample base (household members)	705	772	1,409	2,069	1,245	884	**7,065**

Source: Continuous Household Survey, Northern Ireland Statistics and Research Agency

2.6 Projected Households (2002-based) by household size, 2001 to 2025

Numbers and Percentages

Household size	2001	%	2006	%	2011	%	2016	%	2021	%	2025	%
1 person	172,200	*27*	196,100	*29*	222,100	*31*	249,100	*33*	274,200	*35*	292,900	*36*
2 person	176,700	*28*	196,000	*29*	217,200	*31*	238,200	*32*	256,000	*32*	267,800	*33*
3 person	103,900	*17*	109,100	*16*	113,700	*16*	117,200	*16*	118,700	*15*	118,900	*15*
4 person	95,500	*15*	94,800	*14*	92,700	*13*	90,200	*12*	88,200	*11*	86,500	*11*
5 person	50,000	*8*	47,300	*7*	44,000	*6*	40,600	*5*	37,900	*5*	36,000	*4*
6 person	21,900	*3*	19,700	*3*	17,300	*2*	15,100	*2*	13,300	*2*	12,100	*1*
7 or more person	8,200	*1*	5,700	*1*	3,900	*1*	2,600	*0*	1,800	*0*	1,300	*0*
All Households	**628,400**	.	**668,800**	.	**710,900**	.	**753,000**	.	**790,200**	.	**815,500**	.
Average household size	**2.65**		**2.53**		**2.42**		**2.33**		**2.25**		**2.20**	

Source: Northern Ireland Statistics and Research Agency

2.7 Average gross weekly household income and expenditure[1] by tenure, 2003-04

£s

Tenure	Income	Expenditure
Public Rented[2]	239	212
Owner occupied		
- Owned with mortgage	657	514
- Owned outright	570	403
Other[3]	320	311
All households	**520**	**407**
Sample base (all households)	616	616

Source: Northern Ireland Expenditure and Food Survey, Northern Ireland Statistics and Research Agency

[1] Average gross weekly household income and expenditure figures are rounded to the nearest pound.
[2] Rented from the Local Authority, Council or the Northern Ireland Housing Executive.
[3] Privately rented and rent free property.

2.8 Average gross weekly household income and expenditure[1] by social class of household reference person, 2003-04

£s

Social class of household reference person	Income	Expenditure
Managerial/professional	735	573
Intermediate	777	464
Routine and manual	440	391
Unclassified	238	222
All households	**520**	**407**
Sample base (all households)	616	616

Source: Northern Ireland Expenditure and Food Survey, Northern Ireland Statistics and Research Agency

[1] Average gross weekly household income and expenditure figures are rounded to the nearest pound.

2.9 Average gross weekly household income and expenditure[1] by composition of household, 2003-04

£s

Household composition	Income	Expenditure
Pensioner households with 1 or 2 adults[2]	149	152
Non pensioner adult households	506	354
Households with children	620	543
All households	**520**	**407**
Sample base (all households)	616	616

Source: Northern Ireland Expenditure and Food Survey, Northern Ireland Statistics and Research Agency

[1] Average gross weekly household income and expenditure figures are rounded to the nearest pound.

[2] A pensioner household is one in which at least three quarters of the total household income is derived from national insurance and similar pensions, including benefits paid in supplement to, or instead of, such pensions.

2.10 Average gross weekly household income and expenditure[1] by age of household reference person, 2003-04

£s

Age of household reference person	Income	Expenditure
Under 30	462	406
30 - 49	579	484
50 - 64	686	429
65 and over	242	212
All households	**520**	**407**
Sample base (all households)	616	616

Source: Northern Ireland Expenditure and Food Survey, Northern Ireland Statistics and Research Agency

[1] Average gross weekly household income and expenditure figures are rounded to the nearest pound.

Average gross weekly household income and expenditure[1] by area, 2003-04

2.11

£s

Area[2]	Income	Expenditure
Belfast District Council	431	384
East of Northern Ireland	598	428
West of Northern Ireland	455	389
All households	**520**	**407**
Sample base (all households)	616	616

Source: Northern Ireland Expenditure and Food Survey, Northern Ireland Statistics and Research Agency

[1] Average gross weekly household income and expenditure figures are rounded to the nearest pound.

[2] After those households in Belfast District Council have been excluded, households in the remaining 25 District Councils are divided depending on whether their District Council is in the East or the West of Northern Ireland (a list of the District Council split can be provided by the Northern Ireland Statistics and Research Agency).

Figure 2.1 Average gross weekly household income and expenditure by area, 2003-04

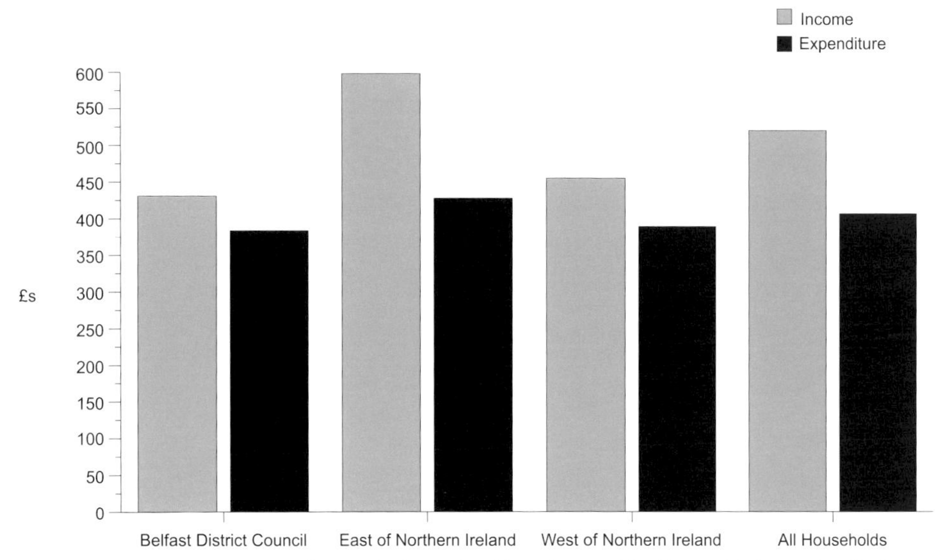

Source: Northern Ireland Expenditure and Food Survey, Northern Ireland Statistics and Research Agency

HOUSING AND HOUSEHOLDS

2.12 Average weekly household expenditure on various commodities and services[1], 2003-04

£s and percentages

Commodity or service	Average weekly household expenditure (£s)	%
Food and non-alcoholic drinks	48	*12*
Acoholic drinks, tobacco and narcotics	14	*3*
Clothing and footwear	31	*8*
Housing, fuel and power	31	*8*
Household goods and services	33	*8*
Health	4	*1*
Transport	56	*14*
Communication	12	*3*
Recreation and culture	48	*12*
Education	4	*1*
Restaurants and hotels	39	*10*
Miscellaneous goods and services	37	*9*
Total consumption expenditure	**355**	**87**
Total non-consumption expenditure	52	*13*
Total average weekly expenditure	**407**	***100***
Sample base (all households)	616	616

Source: Northern Ireland Expenditure and Food Survey, Northern Ireland Statistics and Research Agency

[1] Average weekly household expenditure figures are rounded to the nearest pound.

2.13 Sources of total weekly household income by region, 2003-04

Percentages

Government Office Region	Source of Income									Sample base (all households)
	Wages and Salaries	Self-employment Income	Investments	Tax Credits	State Retirement Pension plus any IS/MIG/PC[1]	Other pensions	Social Security disability benefits	Other Social Security benefits	Other sources	
North East	*62*	*5*	*1*	*2*	*8*	*7*	*4*	*8*	*1*	1,215
North West & Merseyside	*64*	*8*	*2*	*2*	*7*	*7*	*3*	*6*	*2*	2,936
Yorkshire & the Humber	*63*	*7*	*2*	*2*	*7*	*8*	*3*	*6*	*3*	2,200
East Midlands	*67*	*7*	*2*	*1*	*7*	*6*	*2*	*5*	*2*	1,903
West Midlands	*65*	*7*	*2*	*1*	*7*	*7*	*2*	*6*	*2*	2,208
Eastern	*65*	*10*	*2*	*1*	*6*	*7*	*2*	*4*	*3*	2,248
London	*67*	*11*	*2*	*1*	*4*	*5*	*1*	*6*	*3*	2,670
South East	*66*	*9*	*3*	*1*	*5*	*9*	*1*	*3*	*3*	3,370
South West	*62*	*9*	*2*	*1*	*7*	*9*	*2*	*5*	*3*	2,120
England	*65*	*9*	*2*	*1*	*6*	*7*	*2*	*5*	*3*	20,870
Wales	*60*	*8*	*2*	*2*	*8*	*8*	*4*	*7*	*2*	1,278
Scotland	*65*	*8*	*2*	*1*	*6*	*7*	*3*	*6*	*2*	4,795
Northern Ireland	*58*	*13*	*1*	*2*	*7*	*6*	*4*	*8*	*2*	1,917
United Kingdom	***65***	***9***	***2***	***1***	***6***	***7***	***2***	***5***	***3***	**28,860**

Source: Family Resources Survey, Department for Social Development

[1] IS = Income Support, MIG = Minimum Income Guarantee and PC = Pension Credit.

Figure 2.2 Sources of NI household income as a percentage of average gross weekly household income, 2003-04

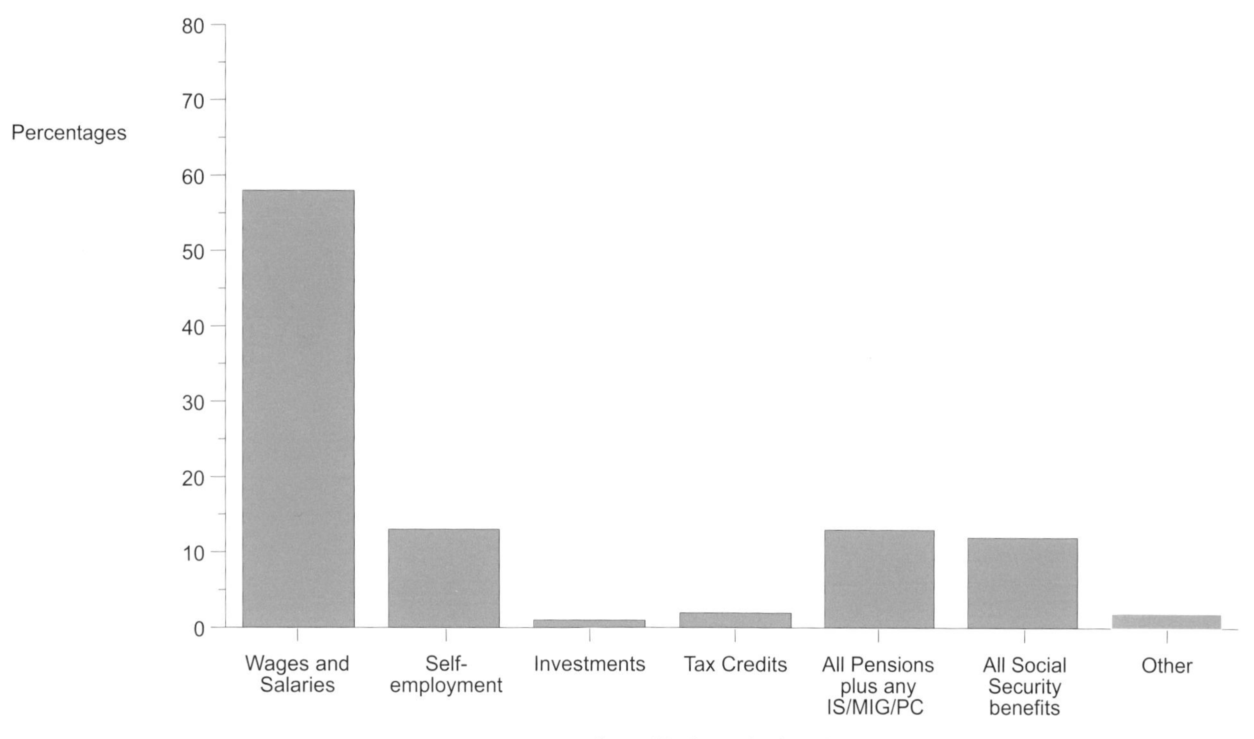

Source: Northern Ireland Family Resources Survey; Department for Social Development

Households with any type of financial deposits or savings accounts by region, 2003-04

2.14

Percentages

Government Office Region	Direct Payment Account	Any type of account	No account	Sample base (all households)
North East	*92*	*93*	*7*	1,215
North West & Merseyside	*93*	*93*	*7*	2,936
Yorkshire & the Humber	*92*	*93*	*7*	2,200
East Midlands	*90*	*91*	*9*	1,903
West Midlands	*93*	*93*	*7*	2,208
Eastern	*95*	*96*	*4*	2,248
London	*93*	*93*	*7*	2,670
South East	*97*	*97*	*3*	3,370
South West	*97*	*97*	*3*	2,120
England	*94*	*94*	*6*	20,870
Wales	*95*	*95*	*5*	1,278
Scotland	*92*	*92*	*8*	4,795
Northern Ireland	*86*	*87*	*13*	1,917
United Kingdom	***93***	***94***	***6***	**28,860**

Source: Family Resources Survey, Department for Social Development

2.15 NI household savings levels by weekly household income bands, 2003-04

Percentages

Capital	Total weekly household income band: Less than £200	£200 - less than £400	£400 - less than £600	£600 - less than £800	£800 or more	All households
No savings	*62*	*55*	*35*	*27*	*18*	*43*
Less than £1,500	*12*	*15*	*21*	*23*	*12*	*16*
£1,500 but less than £3,000	*7*	*6*	*8*	*12*	*12*	*8*
£3,000 but less than £8,000	*10*	*12*	*15*	*16*	*18*	*14*
£8,000 but less than £10,000	*2*	*2*	*3*	*4*	*6*	*3*
£10,000 but less than £16,000	*4*	*3*	*7*	*5*	*12*	*6*
£16,000 but less than £20,000	*1*	*1*	*1*	*1*	*4*	*2*
£20,000 or more	*2*	*5*	*8*	*12*	*18*	*8*
Sample base (all households)	434	633	356	239	255	1,917

Source: Family Resources Survey, Department for Social Development

2.16 Accommodation by household type, 2004-05[P]

Percentages

Accommodation	One adult aged 16-59	Two adults aged 16-59	Small family[1]	Large family[2]	Large adult household[3]	Two adults, one or both aged 60 or over	One adult aged 60 or over	**All household types**
Detached house	*21*	*36*	*36*	*54*	*53*	*49*	*24*	***39***
Semi-detached house	*20*	*31*	*29*	*21*	*20*	*24*	*21*	***24***
Terraced house	*38*	*29*	*32*	*23*	*25*	*25*	*32*	***29***
Purpose built flat or maisonette	*17*	*3*	*2*	*1*	*1*	*2*	*18*	***6***
Converted flat or maisonette/rooms	*4*	-	-	-	-	*0*	*3*	***1***
With business premises/other	*1*	-	*1*	-	-	-	*2*	***1***
Sample base (all households)	351	386	548	228	463	442	354	**2,772**

Source: Continuous Household Survey, Northern Ireland Statistics and Research Agency

[1] One or two persons aged 16 or over and one or two persons aged under 16.

[2] One or more persons aged 16 or over and three or more persons aged under 16, or three or more persons aged 16 or over and two persons aged under 16.

[3] Three or more persons aged 16 or over, with or without one person aged under 16.

Tenure, 1999-2000 to 2004-05

2.17

Percentages

Tenure	1999-00	2000-01	2001-02	2002-03	2003-04	2004-05P
Owned outright	*30*	*31*	*32*	*31*	*31*	*33*
Owned with mortgage[1]	*37*	*38*	*40*	*41*	*42*	*39*
Rented local authority (NIHE[2])	*23*	*22*	*18*	*17*	*15*	*15*
Rented other[3]	*8*	*9*	*9*	*10*	*10*	*11*
Rent free[4]	*1*	*1*	*1*	*1*	*2*	*2*
Sample base (all households)	3,039	2,800	2,805	2,781	2,717	2,769

Source: Continuous Household Survey, Northern Ireland Statistics and Research Agency

1 Includes properties being purchased through the co-ownership scheme.

2 Northern Ireland Housing Executive.

3 Includes properties which are rented from a housing association and rented privately.

4 Includes squatting and rent free.

Accommodation by tenure, 2004-05P

2.18

Percentages

Accommodation	Owner occupied		Rented		
	Owned outright	With mortgage[1]	NIHE[2]	Other[3]	**All households**
Detached house	*56*	*46*	*3*	*16*	***39***
Semi-detached house	*22*	*30*	*17*	*20*	***24***
Terraced house	*19*	*22*	*63*	*38*	***29***
Purpose built flat or maisonette	*1*	*1*	*16*	*18*	***6***
Converted flat or maisonette/rooms	-	*0*	*1*	*5*	***1***
With business premises/other	*1*	-	.	*3*	***1***
Sample base (all households)	909	1,084	424	352	**2,769**

Source: Continuous Household Survey, Northern Ireland Statistics and Research Agency

1 Includes properties being purchased through the co-ownership scheme.

2 Northern Ireland Housing Executive.

3 Includes Housing Associations, rented privately, squatting and rent free.

2.19 Persons per room by tenure, 2004-05[P]

Percentages and numbers

Persons per room	Owner occupied: Owned outright	Owner occupied: With mortgage[1]	Rented: NIHE[2]	Rented: Other[3]	**All households**
Less than 0.5	*87*	*65*	*74*	*75*	***75***
0.5 to 0.65	*8*	*23*	*15*	*16*	***16***
0.66 to 0.99	*4*	*11*	*9*	*9*	***8***
1	*1*	*1*	*1*	*1*	***1***
More than 1	-	-	*1*	*0*	**-**
Average persons per room	**0.29**	**0.41**	**0.36**	**0.35**	**0.36**
Average household size	**2.20**	**3.15**	**2.12**	**2.16**	**2.55**
Sample base (all households)	909	1,084	424	352	**2,769**

Source: Continuous Household Survey, Northern Ireland Statistics and Research Agency

1 Includes properties being purchased through the co-ownership scheme.

2 Northern Ireland Housing Executive.

3 Includes Housing Associations, rented privately, squatting and rent free.

2.20 Age of building by tenure, 2004-05[P]

Percentages

Age of building	Owner occupied: Owned outright	Owner occupied: With mortgage[1]	Rented: NIHE[2]	Rented: Other[3]	**All households**
Before 1919	*16*	*6*	*3*	*18*	***10***
1919-1944	*13*	*8*	*4*	*15*	***10***
1945-1964	*25*	*12*	*20*	*11*	***17***
1965 or later	*46*	*74*	*73*	*56*	***63***
Sample base (all households)	909	1,083	424	352	**2,768**

Source: Continuous Household Survey, Northern Ireland Statistics and Research Agency

1 Includes properties being purchased through the co-ownership scheme.

2 Northern Ireland Housing Executive.

3 Includes Housing Associations, rented privately, squatting and rent free.

2.21 Tenure by age of building, 2004-05[P]

Percentages

Tenure	Before 1919	1919-1944	1945-1964	1965 or later	All ages
Owner Occupied					
Owned outright	*50*	*44*	*47*	*24*	***33***
With mortgage[1]	*24*	*31*	*27*	*46*	***39***
Rented					
NIHE[2]	*5*	*6*	*18*	*18*	***15***
Other[3]	*22*	*20*	*8*	*11*	***13***
Sample base (all households)	288	266	480	1,734	**2,768**

Source: Continuous Household Survey, Northern Ireland Statistics and Research Agency

1 Includes properties being purchased through the co-ownership scheme.

2 Northern Ireland Housing Executive.

3 Includes Housing Associations, rented privately, squatting and rent free.

2.22 NI households' weekly housing costs by tenure, 2003-04

Percentages

	Weekly housing costs							
Tenure	Under £20	£20 but under £40	£40 but under £60	£60 but under £80	£80 but under £100	£100 but under £150	£150 or more	Sample base (all households)
Rented								
Social rented sector tenants	*1*	*14*	*70*	*14*	-	-	*0*	368
Rented privately	*22*	*5*	*17*	*21*	*22*	*9*	*4*	212
Owner Occupied								
Owned outright	*99*	*1*	-	*0*	*0*	*0*	*0*	597
With mortgage	*21*	*37*	*25*	*9*	*5*	*3*	*1*	740

Source: Family Resources Survey, Department for Social Development

2.23 Total occupied housing stock by tenure,[1,2,3] 1995 to 2005

Thousands and percentages

Year	Owner occupied	%	Northern Ireland Housing Executive	%	Housing associations	%	Private rented and other	%	**Total occupied stock**
1995	389.0	*68.6*	144.5	*25.5*	13.0	*2.3*	20.5	*3.6*	**567.0**
1996	399.0	*69.5*	139.5	*24.3*	14.0	*2.4*	22.0	*3.8*	**574.5**
1997	412.0	*70.3*	135.0	*23.0*	14.5	*2.5*	24.5	*4.2*	**586.0**
1998	424.5	*71.4*	130.5	*21.9*	15.0	*2.5*	26.0	*4.4*	**596.0**
1999	429.5	*71.5*	124.0	*20.6*	16.5	*2.8*	30.5	*5.1*	**601.0**
2000	442.5	*72.6*	118.0	*19.4*	17.5	*2.9*	31.5	*5.1*	**609.5**
2002	464.5	*74.1*	110.5	*17.6*	19.7	*3.1*	31.9	*5.1*	**626.6**
2003	477.8	*75.4*	102.8	*16.2*	20.5	*3.2*	32.4	*5.1*	**633.9**
2004	494.2	*77.1*	91.6	*14.3*	21.0	*3.3*	34.6	*5.4*	**641.4**
2005	464.8	*72.1*	96.6	*15.0*	21.3[P]	*3.3*[P]	62.3	*9.7*	**644.9**[P]

Sources: Department for Social Development; Northern Ireland Housing Executive; Rate Collection Agency; Planning Service

1 Figures do not include 'split hereditaments' where the domestic portion is less than the commercial portion i.e. flats above shops.

2 Stock totals are normally collected at December for each year but from 2002 the data are collected at 31 March for each year. There was no collection of data for December 2001 due to this change and therefore, there are no 2001 figures.

3 The changes to Owner Occupied and Private Rented & Other sectors are a result of a statistical adjustment. This adjustment was introduced to reflect the current trends in the housing market, which were highlighted in the 2001 Census and the House Condition Surveys of 2001 and 2004.

Figure 2.3 Total occupied housing stock by tenure, 1995 to 2005

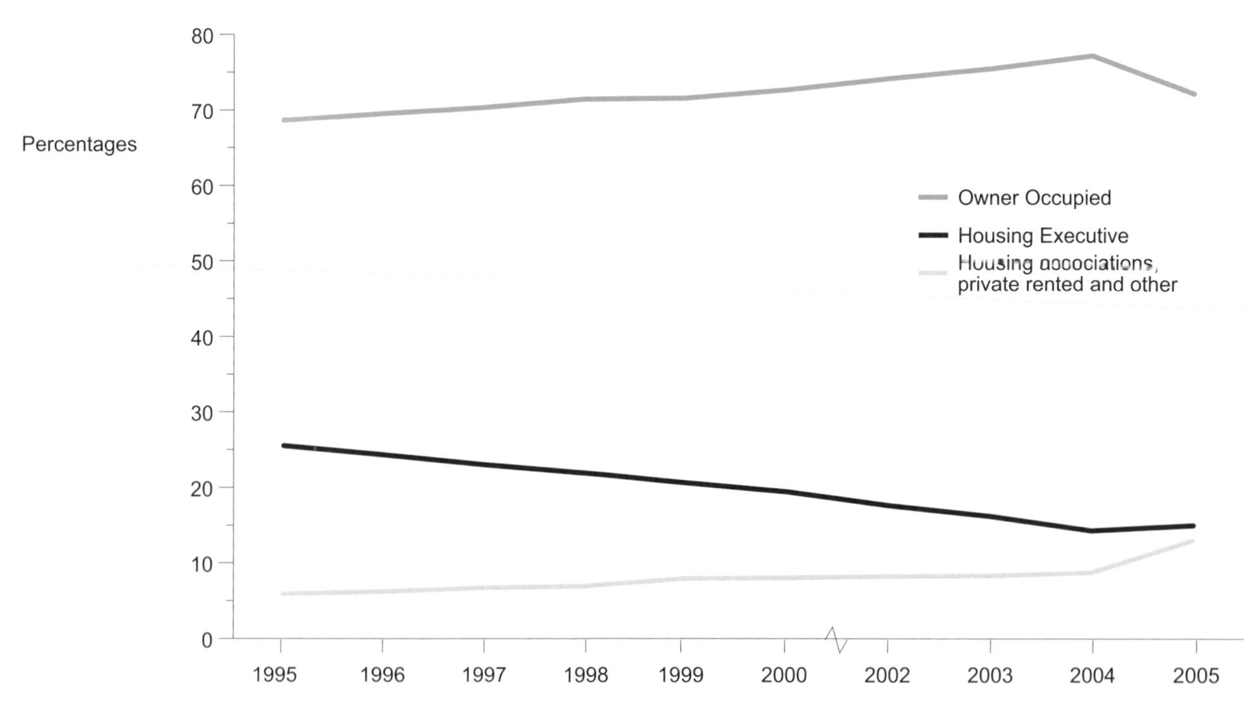

Sources: Department for Social Development; Northern Ireland Housing Executive; Rate Collection Agency; Planning Service

Sales of dwellings by Northern Ireland Housing Executive, 1999-2000 to 2004-05

2.24

Numbers

	1999-00	2000-01	2001-02	2002-03	2003-04	2004-05
Sales to tenants	4,482	5,509	4,985	5,991	5,583	3,053
Sales to non tenants	44	46	26	63	69	82
SPED cases[1]	111	69	50	102	118	86
All sales	**4,637**	**5,624**	**5,061**	**6,156**	**5,770**	**3,221**

Source: Northern Ireland Housing Executive

[1] Special Purchase of Evacuated Dwellings scheme.

New dwellings by sector, 1999-2000 to 2004-05

2.25

Numbers

Starts, completions and year	Northern Ireland Housing Executive[1]	Housing associations	**All social rented sector**[2]	Private sector[3,4]	**All sectors**
New starts					
1999-00	76	1,507	**1,583**	9,685	**11,268**
2000-01	23	885	**908**	10,418	**11,326**
2001-02	25	772	**797**	12,065	**12,862**
2002-03	0	669	**669**	11,573	**12,242**
2003-04	0	1,140	**1,140**	12,671	**13,811**
2004-05	0	1,029	**1,029**	13,199	**14,228**
Completions					
1999-00	190	1,092	**1,282**	9,067	**10,349**
2000-01	46	1,112	**1,158**	10,512	**11,670**
2001-02	29	1,386	**1,415**	12,072	**13,487**
2002-03	2	1,026	**1,028**	13,387	**14,415**
2003-04	0	560	**560**	13,951	**14,511**
2004-05	0	828	**828**	14,940	**15,768**

Sources: Department for Social Development; Northern Ireland Housing Executive; District Council Building Control Offices

[1] From 2001-02, the Northern Ireland Housing Executive (NIHE) no longer builds new dwellings. Occasionally it may still replace an isolated rural dwelling as part of its cottage improvement programme.

[2] Data for the social rented sector are provided by the NIHE and the Housing Associations Branch of the Department for Social Development.

[3] Details of new housing starts and completions for the private sector are supplied by District Council Area Building Control Offices. As of 1 January 2001, data have been captured directly from each District Council database, accounting for the marked increase in starts and completions recorded.

[4] Figures for private sector completions have been statistically adjusted to correct, as far as possible, the proven under recording of private sector completions.

National House Building Council (NHBC) registered new house sales and prices[1], 1999-2000 to 2004-05

2.26

Numbers and £s

Year	Number of Sales	Average price per house (£)
1999-00	8,453	74,000
2000-01	7,629	85,000
2001-02	6,133	89,000
2002-03	6,655	98,000
2003-04	6,486[r]	108,000
2004-05	6,800[p]	118,000[p]

Source: National House Building Council

[1] Figures relate to those sales notified to NHBC by purchasers' solicitors.

Notes to Housing and Households tables

TABLES 2.1 TO 2.5, AND 2.16 TO 2.21

The Continuous Household Survey (CHS), which began in 1983, is based on a simple random sample of the general population resident in private households in Northern Ireland.

TABLES 2.7 TO 2.12

The information presented is from the Expenditure and Food Survey (EFS) for the financial year April 2003 to March 2004.

The survey is primarily used to provide information for the Retail Prices Index; National Accounts estimates of household expendiure; the analysis of the effect of taxes and benefits, and trends in nutrition. However, the results are multi-purpose, providing an invaluable supply of economic and social data.

TABLE 2.8

From 2001, the National Statistics Socio-economic classification (NS-SEC) was adopted for all official surveys in place of Social Class based on Occupation and Socio-economic group. NS-SEC is itself based on the Standard Occupational Classification 2000 (SOC 2000) and details of employment status.

TABLE 2.12

From 2001-02, the Classification Of Individual Consumption by Purpose (COICOP) was introduced as a new coding frame for expenditure items. Under this system, mortgage interest payments are classified as non-consumption expenditure rather than a housing cost.

TABLES 2.13 TO 2.15 AND 2.22

The information presented is from the Family Resources Survey (FRS) for the financial year April 2003 to March 2004.

The survey collects detailed information on the incomes and circumstances of private households and has been carried out in Great Britain since 1992, but 2002-03 saw the introduction of Northern Ireland for the first time. The primary function of the FRS is to collect information on the resources of households, that is income received from all sources.

TABLE 2.13

For households and benefit units which include an adult over pension age, Retirement Pension (including SERPS and graduated Retirement Pension) and Income Support/Minimum Income Guarantee (MIG)/Pension Credit are shown together in one category. This is due to known reporting problems: pensioners do not always recall that they are receiving MIG and sometimes record total income under Retirement Pension.

TABLE 2.22

Total weekly housing costs include all payments for rent, mortgage, rates, structural insurance and other charges on owner occupiers relating to their property (for example ground rent and compulsory service charges).

TABLE 2.23

Tenure data for the social rented sector are sourced from the Northern Ireland Housing Executive (NIHE) and the Department for Social Development's Housing Associations Branch. The figures for the private sector, i.e. owner-occupied and private rented / other dwellings, are based on information supplied by the Rate Collection Agency, adjusted to allow for the fact that some dwellings in the owner-occupied sector are actually privately rented.

TABLE 2.24

The figures for sales of dwellings by the NIHE include sales to sitting tenants and developers, and those made under the Special Purchase of Evacuated Dwellings (SPED) scheme. The SPED scheme facilitates the purchase and resale by the NIHE of private sector properties vacated by individuals under threat of intimidation.

TABLE 2.25

Dwellings are classified as self-contained units only.

STARTS – A dwelling is counted as started on the date work begins on the laying of foundations, including 'slabbing' if required, but not including site preparation. Thus, when foundational work commences on a pair of semi-detached houses, two houses are started, and when work begins on a block of flats, all the dwellings which that block shall contain are started.

Housing Association hostels and other communal establishments are excluded from dwelling starts.

COMPLETIONS – A dwelling is regarded as completed when it becomes ready for occupation, whether occupied or not. The figures published for private sector completions have been adjusted by statistical methods to correct, as far as possible, the proven under-recording of private sector completions.

TABLE 2.26

Data for new house sales and prices are derived from transactions for new dwellings notified by solicitors to the National House Building Council (NHBC). The NHBC often experience delay in receiving returns from purchasers' solicitors. Therefore, revised figures may appear significantly different to the provisional totals supplied. While NHBC-registered builders account for a very high proportion of newly built dwellings, their coverage is less comprehensive in rural areas.

Social and Welfare

- In 2003-04, 28% of NI households were in receipt of some form of income related benefit, compared with a UK average of 22%.

- In 2005, disabled people accounted for 58% of all income support claimants in Northern Ireland. Lone parents accounted for a further 27%. The corresponding GB proportions were 53% and 36%.

- In February 2005, there were over 29,000 Jobseekers' Allowance (JSA) claimants in Northern Ireland, 77% of which were male and 23% of which were female.

- In April 2005, 54,000 families were in receipt of both Working Tax Credit and Child Tax Credit. Around 54% of those families were headed by a lone parent.

- In 2004, in both Northern Ireland and Great Britain, the majority of Incapacity Benefit recipients were being paid at the long-term rate.

- The number of NI families who received Child Benefit in 2004 was around 3% higher than in 1994. However, the number of children for whom this benefit was paid was 5% lower in 2004 than in 1994.

- The number of persons in receipt of National Insurance based Retirement Pension has increased by 7% over the period 1999 to 2004.

Households in receipt of state support benefits by region, 2003-04

3.1

Percentages

Government Office Region	Tax Credit	Child Benefit	IS/MIG/ PC[1]	Housing Benefit	Retire-ment Pension	Job-seekers' Allowance	Incapacity Benefit	Severe Disable-ment Allowance	Attendance Allowance	Invalid Care Allowance	Disability Living Allowance	In receipt of any income related benefit	In receipt of any non-income related benefit	In receipt of any benefit	Sample base (all households)
	State support received														
North East	*16*	*28*	*18*	*22*	*32*	*4*	*9*	*1*	*5*	*3*	*12*	*32*	*72*	*76*	1,215
North West & Merseyside	*17*	*29*	*15*	*16*	*31*	*2*	*7*	*1*	*4*	*2*	*11*	*25*	*70*	*72*	2,936
Yorkshire & the Humber	*17*	*28*	*13*	*16*	*30*	*3*	*6*	*1*	*4*	*2*	*9*	*25*	*68*	*72*	2,200
East Midlands	*16*	*27*	*11*	*13*	*30*	*2*	*5*	-	*4*	*2*	*8*	*20*	*66*	*68*	1,903
West Midlands	*16*	*29*	*13*	*13*	*31*	*3*	*5*	*1*	*4*	*2*	*7*	*23*	*68*	*70*	2,208
Eastern	*14*	*28*	*9*	*11*	*31*	*2*	*4*	*1*	*3*	*1*	*6*	*17*	*66*	*68*	2,248
London	*9*	*26*	*13*	*18*	*22*	*3*	*3*	*1*	*2*	*1*	*6*	*25*	*56*	*60*	2,670
South East	*12*	*28*	*8*	*9*	*31*	*2*	*3*	*1*	*2*	*2*	*5*	*15*	*65*	*67*	3,370
South West	*15*	*26*	*10*	*11*	*34*	*1*	*4*	-	*4*	*1*	*6*	*18*	*68*	*69*	2,120
England	*14*	*28*	*12*	*14*	*30*	*2*	*5*	*1*	*3*	*2*	*7*	*21*	*66*	*68*	20,870
Wales	*17*	*28*	*14*	*15*	*32*	*3*	*8*	*1*	*5*	*2*	*13*	*24*	*71*	*73*	1,278
Scotland	*15*	*26*	*15*	*19*	*30*	*3*	*7*	*1*	*4*	*2*	*10*	*27*	*67*	*71*	4,795
Northern Ireland	*19*	*36*	*19*	*18*	*27*	*5*	*8*	*1*	*6*	*4*	*15*	*28*	*74*	*78*	1,917
United Kingdom	***15***	***28***	***12***	***15***	***30***	***2***	***5***	***1***	***4***	***2***	***8***	***22***	***66***	***69***	**28,860**

Source: Family Resources Survey, Department for Social Development

[1] IS = Income Support, MIG = Minimum Income Guarantee and PC = Pension Credit.

3.2 Estimated government expenditure on certain cash benefits, 1994-95 to 2004-05

Units as indicated

Type of benefit	1994-95	1995-96	1996-97	1997-98	1998-99	1999-00	2000-01	2001-02	2002-03	2003-04	2004-05
£ million											
Retirement Pension	632	660	708	751	801	837	865	949	1,029	1,084	1,138
Sickness and Invalidity/ Incapacity Benefit[1]	310	332	331	327	325	311	309	310	314	318	320
Widow's Benefit	35	34	36	34	34	31	31	35	35	33	31
Unemployment Benefit[2]	31	30	18	.	.	.	.	.	.	.	.
Jobseekers' Allowance[3]	.	.	97	185	173	148	132	138	103	99	85
Severe Disablement Allowance	31	32	34	38	40	41	42	43	42	41	41
Income Support[4]	650	666	596	500	533	554	598	598	678	610	490
Pension Credit[5]	.	.	.	.	.	.	.	.	.	114[r]	278
Child Benefit[6]	231	238	250	252	262	288	296	304	306	309[r]	.
Family Credit[7]	62	71	83	91	98	77	.	.	.	.	.
Attendance Allowance	109	127	143	153	164	170	177	187	176	181	187
Disability Living Allowance	202	244	288	319	342	381	407	444	478	515	550
£ per head[8]											
Retirement Pension	385	400	423	445	473	495	509	562	607	639	665
Sickness and Invalidity/ Incapacity Benefit[1]	189	201	198	194	192	184	182	183	185	187	187
Widow's Benefit	21	21	21	20	20	18	18	21	21	19	18
Unemployment Benefit[2]	19	18	11	.	.	.	.	.	.	.	.
Jobseekers' Allowance[3]	.	.	58	110	102	88	78	82	61	58	50
Severe Disablement Allowance	19	20	20	23	24	24	25	25	25	24	24
Income Support[4]	396	404	356	296	315	328	352	354	400	360	286
Pension Credit[5]	.	.	.	.	.	.	.	.	.	67[r]	163
Child Benefit[6]	141	145	149	149	155	171	174	180	180	182[r]	.
Family Tax Credit[7]	38	43	49	54	58	45	.	.	.	.	.
Attendance Allowance	66	77	86	91	97	101	104	111	104	107	109
Disability Living Allowance	123	148	172	189	202	225	240	263	282	304	322

Sources: Department for Social Development; Northern Ireland Statistics and Research Agency; HM Revenue & Customs

1 Incapacity Benefit replaced Sickness and Invalidity Benefits from April 1995.
2 From October 1996 Unemployment Benefit has been replaced by contribution-based Jobseekers' Allowance.
3 Includes contribution and income-based Jobseekers' Allowance.
4 Income-based Jobseekers' Allowance replaced Income Support for the unemployed in October 1996.
5 Pension Credit replaced Minimum Income Guarantee (MIG) in October 2003 (MIG were Income Support payments made to claimants aged 60 or over).
6 Includes Child Benefit, Child Benefit (Lone Parent) and One Parent Benefit. From April 1997, One Parent Benefit was incorporated into the main Child Benefit rates. The new higher rate of Child benefit was known as Child Benefit (Lone Parent).
7 Family Credit was replaced by Working Families Tax Credit (WFTC) from October 1999. WFTC was replaced in April 2003 by the Child and Working Tax Credits (C & WTC). WFTC and C & WTC are administered by HM Revenue & Customs.
8 Based on mid-year home population estimates for 2004.

Note: The data presented in this table are not National Statistics.

Recipients of social security benefits, 1999 to 2004

3.3

Percentages

Type of benefit	Northern Ireland						Great Britain
	1999	2000	2001	2002	2003	2004	2004-05
Attendance Allowance[1]	29.6	29.7	29.4	29.1	28.7	28.1	14.9
Child Benefit[2]	42.7	42.1	35.2	35.6	36.1[r]	35.3	..
Working Families Tax Credit[3,4]	5.7	7.1	7.1	7.6	8.4	.	.
Housing Benefit[5]	26.0	24.0	20.1	20.0	20.2	19.3	16.1
Income Support[6,7]	13.1	13.3	13.6	13.5	13.7	10.0	6.3
Pension Credit[8]	.	.	.	.	.	27.9	20.3
Child Benefit Lone Parent[2]	6.8	.	.	.	.	.	.
Retirement Pension[9]	91.1	92.2	91.2	92.1	92.8	92.6	96.0
Jobseekers' Allowance (Contribution-based)[10]	0.4	0.4	0.4	0.4	0.5	0.4	0.4
Disability Living Allowance[11]	7.6	7.9	8.3	8.6	8.9	9.4	4.5
Incapacity Benefit[12]	7.0	6.9	6.8	6.8	7.0	6.8	4.1

Sources: Department for Social Development; Department of Social Security; Department for Work and Pensions

1 Total number of recipients at 31 March, except for 2001, 2004 and GB which are taken at 31 May, as a percentage of the population aged 65 and over (based on relevant mid-year estimate).

2 The total number of recipient families at December for all years except 2000 and 2001 (which are taken at September) and 2003 (which is taken at August) as a percentage of all households (1991 Census for 1998 to 2000; 2001 Census for 2001 onwards).

3 Total number of recipients at May, the 2003 figure as at February, as a percentage of all households (1991 Census for 1998 to 2000; 2001 Census for 2001 onwards). Working Families Tax Credit (WFTC) replaced Family Credit from October 1999 and is now administered by HM Revenue & Customs.

4 WFTC was replaced in April 2003 by the Working Tax Credit and Child Tax Credit. WFTC awards that terminated from 2 December 2002 were automatically extended to 6 April 2003 with no need for a renewal application. This had the effect of artificially increasing the number of families in receipt of WFTC.

5 Average number of recipients of rent rebate/allowance as a percentage of all households (1991 Census for 1998 to 2000; 2001 Census for 2001 to 2003; Demography & Methodology Branch (DMB) estimated household figures for 2004). The 2001 figure is based on recipients as at September 2001, the 2002 to 2004 figures as at August. GB figures are taken as a percentage of all households at 2003.

6 The total number of recipients at the last Friday in May as a percentage of the population aged 16 or over (mid-year estimates) for 1999 to 2003 and as a percentage of the population aged 16-59 for 2004.

7 From November 2003, Income Support figures are severely affected by the introduction of Pension Credit, which replaced Minimum Income Guarantee (MIG) on 6 October 2003 and extended Income Support entitlement to customers aged 60 and over.

8 The total number of recipients at the last Friday in May as a percentage of the population aged 60 or over (mid-year) estimates.

9 Total number of recipients (excluding graduated and non contributory pension) at September for all years except 2001 (which is taken at March), as a percentage of the population over pension age (mid-year estimates). GB figures are taken at August.

10 These figures are calculated as the total number of contribution-based recipients of Jobseekers' Allowance on the second Thursday in May as a percentage of the population of working age.

11 Disability Living Allowance figures are calculated as the total number of recipients at May as a percentage of the total population.

12 Total number of recipients as at the last Friday in May as a percentage of the population of working age. GB figure taken at the last day in May.

3.4 Number of Income Support/Pension Credit claimants receiving weekly payment[1,2], 2000 to 2005

Numbers

	Northern Ireland						Great Britain
	2000[1]	2001	2002	2003	2004	2005	2005
Pension Credit							
Recipients above State Pension age	.	.	.	.	75,020	84,480	2,470,600
Others	.	.	.	.	8,180	9,260	203,500
Total Pension Credit Recipients (aged 60 and over)	**.**	**.**	**.**	**.**	**83,200**	**93,740**	**2,674,100**
Income Support							
Retirement Pensioners	59,140	61,620	62,540	62,300	.	.	.
Others	14,760	14,900	15,060	16,520	.	.	.
All aged 60 and over[3]	**73,900**	**76,520**	**77,600**	**78,820**	**.**	**.**	**.**
Disabled	47,120	49,800	52,680	54,900	57,480	59,300	1,123,900
Lone Parent	32,600	32,580	30,680	29,920	27,700	27,220	779,600
Miscellaneous	16,980	16,260	15,540	16,540	14,760	14,700	222,400
Former MIG[4]	.	.	.	.	1,240	920	11,100
All under 60	**96,700**	**98,640**	**98,900**	**101,360**	**101,180**	**102,140**	**2,137,000**
All Income Support	**170,600**	**175,160**	**176,500**	**180,180**	**.**	**.**	**.**
Income Support under 60 plus Pension Credit	**.**	**.**	**.**	**.**	**184,380**	**195,880**	**4,811,100**

Sources: Department for Social Development; Department for Work and Pensions

[1] Northern Ireland data are extracted from the Quarterly Statistical Enquiries. The data are taken at the last Friday in February, except for 2000 which are taken at the last Friday in May.

[2] Figures exclude all unemployed claimants and Government Training Scheme cases.

[3] Pension Credit replaced Minimum Income Guarantee (MIG) in October 2003 (MIG were Income Support payments made to claimants aged 60 and over).

[4] A small number of former MIG cases did not convert to Pension Credit on 6 October 2003. These are mainly cases where the claimant is aged under 60 and the partner is over 60.

Figure 3.1 Income Support/Pension Credit recipients by client group as a percentage of all claimants, February 2005

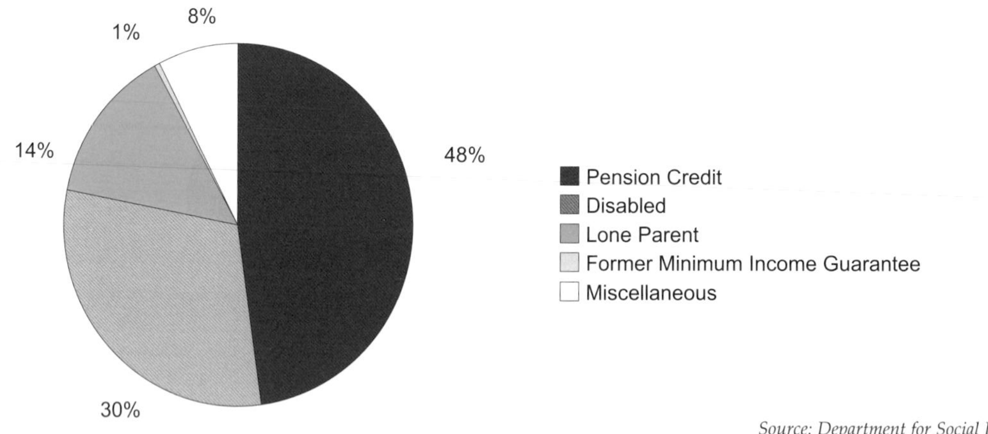

Source: Department for Social Development

3.5 Number of persons provided for by Income Support[1,2], 2000 to 2005

Numbers

	Northern Ireland						Great Britain
	2000[1]	2001	2002	2003	2004	2005	2005
Claimants	**170,600**	**175,160**	**176,500**	**180,180**	**101,180**	**102,140**	**2,137,000**
Dependants							
- Under 11	61,120	61,700	57,540	56,320	51,980	50,180	1,283,500
- 11-15 years	31,000	30,740	31,220	30,920	28,060	27,460	560,600
- Children under 16 years	**92,120**	**92,440**	**88,760**	**87,240**	**80,040**	**77,640**	**1,844,000**
- 16-17 years	7,840	7,480	7,240	7,700	7,240	8,060	124,000
- 18 years and over	1,860	1,460	1,420	1,580	1,620	1,600	26,000
All Dependants	**101,820**	**101,380**	**97,420**	**96,520**	**88,900**	**87,300**	**1,994,100**
Partners	**26,180**	**29,620**	**30,220**	**31,300**	**15,660**	**15,020**	**280,500**
Total number of persons provided for	**298,600**	**306,160**	**304,140**	**308,000**	**205,740**	**204,460**	**4,411,600**

Sources: Department for Social Development; Department for Work and Pensions

1 Northern Ireland data are extracted from the Quarterly Statistical Enquiries. The data are taken at the last Friday in February, except for 2000 which are taken at the last Friday in May.

2 Figures exclude all unemployed claimants and Government Training Scheme cases.

3.6 Average weekly Income Support and Pension Credit payment[1,2], 2000 to 2005

£s

	Northern Ireland						Great Britain
	2000[1]	2001	2002	2003	2004[3]	2005[3]	2005[3]
Pension Credit							
Recipients above State Pension age	.	.	.	.	51.68	50.82	38.09
Others	.	.	.	.	87.13	90.15	85.68
Total Pension Credit Recipients (aged 60 and over)	**.**	**.**	**.**	**.**	**55.16**	**54.70**	**41.71**
Income Support Retirement Pensioners	45.86	44.70	46.89	47.01	.	.	.
Others	83.16	83.17	90.50	89.41	.	.	.
All aged 60 and over[4]	**53.31**	**52.19**	**55.35**	**55.90**	**.**	**.**	**.**
Disabled	74.80	77.96	83.69	87.84	89.55	93.39	80.97
Lone Parent	91.20	98.52	103.55	110.52	111.95	107.59	103.01
Miscellaneous	55.42	54.98	60.30	54.62	55.90	53.70	57.16
Former MIG[5]	.	.	.	.	90.92	108.61	105.27
All under 60	**76.93**	**80.96**	**86.17**	**89.11**	**90.79**	**91.60**	**86.66**
All Income Support	**66.70**	**68.39**	**72.62**	**74.58**	**90.79**	**91.60**	**86.66**

Sources: Department for Social Development; Department for Work and Pensions

1 NI data are extracted from the Quarterly Statistical Enquiries. The data are taken at the last Friday in February, except for 2000 which are taken at the last Friday in May.
2 Figures exclude all unemployed claimants and Government Training Scheme cases.
3 The average amount of Income Support for under 60/Pension Credit award is not given, as new Pension Credit cases are being added each month with small weekly amounts.
4 Pension Credit replaced Minimum Income Guarantee (MIG) in October 2003 (MIG were Income Support payments made to claimants aged 60 or over).
5 A small number of former MIG cases did not convert to Pension Credit on 6 October 2003. These are mainly cases where the claimant is aged under 60 and the partner is over 60.

3.7 Jobseekers' Allowance (JSA) claimants analysed by gender and benefit entitlement[1], 2000 to 2005

Numbers

Gender and benefit entitlement	Northern Ireland 2000	2001	2002	2003	2004	2005	Great Britain 2005
Males							
Contribution-based JSA only	3,241	3,389	3,523	3,693	3,115	3,180	109,900
Contribution-based JSA & income-based JSA	437	328	449	340	210	130	13,900
Income-based JSA only in payment	28,451	26,004	23,603	21,447	20,640	17,990	455,400
All with benefit	**32,129**	**29,721**	**27,575**	**25,480**	**23,965**	**21,300**	**579,200**
No benefit in payment	1,926	1,862	2,063	1,892	1,790	1,490	55,800
All males	**34,055**	**31,583**	**29,638**	**27,372**	**25,755**	**22,790**	**634,900**
Females							
Contribution-based JSA only	1,551	1,433	1,345	1,370	1,245	1,090	43,100
Contribution-based JSA & income-based JSA	55	31	44	14	30	45	1,100
Income-based JSA only in payment	7,021	6,588	5,968	5,294	5,125	4,495	149,700
All with benefit	**8,627**	**8,052**	**7,357**	**6,678**	**6,400**	**5,630**	**193,900**
No benefit in payment	1,336	1,336	1,265	1,125	1,045	995	26,500
All females	**9,963**	**9,388**	**8,622**	**7,803**	**7,445**	**6,625**	**220,500**
Persons							
Contribution-based JSA only	**4,792**	**4,822**	**4,868**	**5,063**	**4,360**	**4,270**	**153,000**
Contribution-based JSA & income-based JSA	**492**	**359**	**493**	**354**	**240**	**175**	**15,000**
Income-based JSA only in payment	**35,472**	**32,592**	**29,571**	**26,741**	**25,765**	**22,485**	**605,100**
All with benefit	**40,756**	**37,773**	**34,932**	**32,158**	**30,365**	**26,930**	**733,100**
No benefit in payment	**3,262**	**3,198**	**3,328**	**3,017**	**2,835**	**2,485**	**82,300**
All Persons	**44,018**	**40,971**	**38,260**	**35,175**	**33,200**	**29,415**	**855,400**

Sources: Department for Social Development; Department for Work and Pensions

[1] Data are taken at the second Thursday of February.

Jobseekers' Allowance (JSA) claimants by Local Government District[1], February 2005 — 3.8

Numbers

Area		JSA Claimants
Belfast		6,765
Outer Belfast	Carrickfergus	595
	Castlereagh	585
	Lisburn	1,430
	Newtownabbey	1,085
	North Down	950
East of Northern Ireland	Antrim	525
	Ards	1,080
	Ballymena	660
	Banbridge	490
	Craigavon	955
	Down	1,050
	Larne	400
North of Northern Ireland	Ballymoney	320
	Coleraine	1,430
	Derry	3,525
	Limavady	670
	Moyle	345
	Strabane	1,240
West and South of Northern Ireland	Armagh	745
	Cookstown	360
	Dungannon	485
	Fermanagh	1,040
	Magherafelt	285
	Newry & Mourne	1,410
	Omagh	825
Unknown		180
Northern Ireland		**29,430**

Source: Department for Social Development

[1] The Local Government Districts are grouped using the NUTS Level 3 Classification.

Figure 3.2 JSA claimants as a percentage of working age population by UK Government Office Region, February 2005

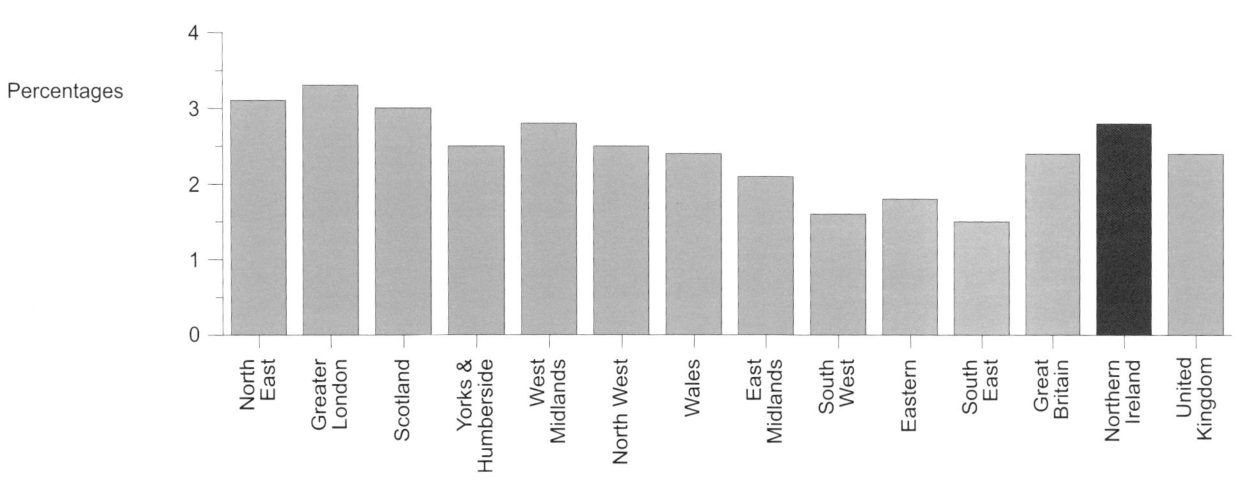

Sources: Department for Social Development; Department for Work and Pensions

3.9 In-work families receiving Child Tax Credit (CTC) or Working Tax Credit (WTC) awards; combination and level of payment by family type, 2004 to 2005

Thousands

	Northern Ireland						Great Britain					
	Couples			Singles			Couples			Singles		
	Apr 04	Dec 04	Apr 05	Apr 04	Dec 04	Apr 05	Apr 04	Dec 04	Apr 05	Apr 04	Dec 04	Apr 05
Receiving WTC & CTC	28.8	24.6	25.0	29.0	28.4	29.1	730.4	645.4	658.3	798.3	792.1	816.6
Receiving CTC	73.3	75.4	77.0	4.2	4.6	4.7	2,447.8	2,479.5	2,528.5	184.9	204.2	210.9
Receiving WTC	2.6	3.1	3.3	5.8	6.1	6.8	71.3	75.8	80.7	154.4	172.1	190.5
Receiving Neither[1]	1.5	2.9	3.0	-	-	-	52.1	99.3	103.4	0.6	1.1	1.1
Other[1]	2.9	5.9	6.3	2.2	3.8	4.1	96.2	194.8	206.8	70.6	121.9	129.8
Total	**109.2**	**111.9**	**114.5**	**41.2**	**42.9**	**44.7**	**3,398.0**	**3,494.7**	**3,577.8**	**1,208.8**	**1,291.3**	**1,349.2**

Sources: Department for Social Development; HM Revenue & Customs

[1] Claimed, and eligible for, CTC or WTC at the reference date, but with zero awards based on their circumstances at that date and their annual income reported by that date. These claimants may have positive awards based on their circumstances at other times in the year, and may finally qualify for positive annual awards based on all their circumstances in the year and their current year incomes.

Figure 3.3 Disability Living Allowance per 1,000 population by UK Government Office Region, February 2005

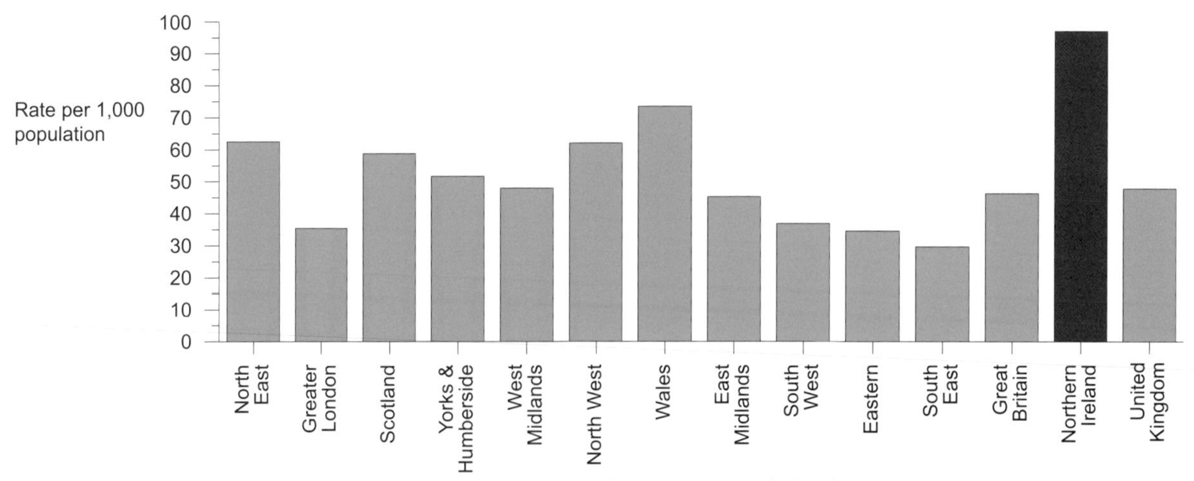

Sources: Department for Social Development; Department for Work and Pensions

SOCIAL AND WELFARE

Incapacity Benefit recipients by age and rate of benefit, 2000 to 2004

Numbers

Quarter ending	Northern Ireland						Great Britain					
	Under pension age[1]	Over pension age[1]	**All persons**	Rate of benefit IBST(L)[2]	IBST(H)[3]	IBLT[4]	Under pension age[1]	Over pension age[1]	**All persons**	Rate of benefit IBST(L)[2]	IBST(H)[3]	IBLT[4]
2000												
Feb	69,907	184	**70,091**	5,058	4,489	60,544	1,500,800	3,500	**1,504,300**	90,900	88,500	1,324,900
May	70,091	37	**70,128**	4,715	4,996	60,417	1,497,800	500	**1,498,300**	90,000	89,600	1,318,700
Aug	70,153	23	**70,176**	4,540	5,093	60,543	1,501,300	500	**1,501,800**	90,400	90,100	1,321,300
Nov	70,295	35	**70,330**	4,736	4,830	60,764	1,509,100	600	**1,509,700**	91,500	92,100	1,326,100
2001												
Feb	70,475	28	**70,503**	4,577	4,601	61,325	1,514,700	500	**1,515,200**	93,600	91,800	1,329,800
May[5]	70,343	..	**70,344**	4,412	4,790	61,142	1,515,800	400[6]	**1,516,200**	96,000	93,900	1,326,300
Aug[5]	71,333	..	**71,333**	4,598	5,092	61,643	1,511,000	100[6]	**1,511,100**	90,700	96,800	1,323,600
Nov[5]	70,904	..	**70,905**	3,922	4,992	61,991	1,503,100	600	**1,503,800**	84,300	97,600	1,321,900
2002												
Feb	69,858	19	**69,877**	3,694	4,394	61,789	1,496,600	300[6]	**1,496,900**	84,100	92,600	1,320,300
May[5]	70,872	..	**70,872**	3,618	4,364	62,890	1,513,700	700	**1,514,400**	86,300	84,600	1,343,500
Aug[5]	71,251	..	**71,252**	3,798	4,563	62,891	1,512,600	-[6]	**1,512,600**	87,100	88,000	1,337,600
Nov[5]	71,771	..	**71,771**	4,133	4,509	63,129	1,505,800	100[6]	**1,505,800**	87,900	87,700	1,330,200
2003												
Feb[5]	72,273	..	**72,274**	4,253	4,515	63,506	1,506,200	300[6]	**1,506,500**	89,300	87,800	1,329,300
May	72,921	23	**72,944**	4,312	4,851	63,781	1,504,400	200[6]	**1,504,600**	90,800	86,700	1,327,100
Aug[5]	72,208	..	**72,208**	3,803	4,953	63,452	1,496,800	200[6]	**1,497,000**	84,500	88,800	1,323,800
Nov[5]	71,974	..	**71,974**	3,643	4,650	63,681	1,494,300	300[6]	**1,494,500**	84,500	90,800	1,319,300
2004												
Feb[5]	71,685	..	**71,685**	3,492	4,251	63,942	1,486,200	400[6]	**1,486,600**	82,500	82,700	1,321,500
May[5]	71,176	..	**71,176**	3,294	4,173	63,709	1,478,400	400[6]	**1,478,800**	84,200	81,800	1,312,800
Aug	70,580	28	**70,608**	2,881	4,155	63,572	1,467,300	400[6]	**1,467,700**	81,000	81,600	1,305,100
Nov	70,425	98	**70,523**	2,911	3,999	63,613	1,456,900	100[6]	**1,457,000**	81,400	81,300	1,294,300

Sources: Department for Social Development; Department for Work and Pensions

1 Pension age = age 65 and over for men and age 60 and over for women.

2 IBST(L) = Incapacity Benefit Short Term Lower.

3 IBST(H) = Incapacity Benefit Short Term Higher.

4 IBLT = Incapacity Benefit Long Term.

5 Figures under 5 are suppressed to preserve confidentiality.

6 Figures under 500 are subject to a high degree of sampling error and should only be used as a guide to the current situation.

3.11 Families receiving Child Benefit by number of children in family, 1994 to 2004

Numbers

Number of children in family	1994	1995	1996	1997	1998	1999	2000[1]	2001[1]	2002[2]	2003[3]	2004[3]
1	82,452	83,690	84,934	85,308	..	..	87,917	88,037	89,146	93,400	93,600
2	78,892	80,074	81,080	80,990	..	..	80,321	79,908	80,221	83,900	83,400
3	40,134	40,050	39,832	39,384	..	..	37,014	35,959	35,724	37,000	37,200
4	16,090	15,688	15,396	14,974	..	..	12,949	12,285	11,828	12,500	12,200
5 or more	7,108	6,696	6,272	5,798	..	..	4,852	4,463	4,144	4,500	3,900
All families receiving Child Benefit	**224,676**	**226,198**	**227,514**	**226,454**	**225,925**	**227,025**	**223,053**	**220,652**	**221,063**	**231,300**	**230,300**
Children for whom benefit paid	463,856	463,296	462,306	456,878	452,900	449,425	437,561	428,892	426,389	446,900	441,900

Sources: Department for Social Development; HM Revenue & Customs

[1] Total recipients for 2000 and 2001 as at September.

[2] Total recipients for 2002 as at October.

[3] Total recipients for 2003 and 2004 as at August.

3.12 Recipients of National Insurance-based old age and Retirement Pensions[1], Widows' Benefits, Bereavement Allowance and Guardian's Allowance, 1999 to 2004

Numbers

Type of allowance	1999	2000	2001	2002	2003	2004
Pensions						
Males	82,626	83,972	84,857	86,488	88,100	89,674
Females on own insurance	80,212	82,427	84,837	88,026	92,243	96,536
Females on husband's insurance	38,841	39,188	39,131	39,026	38,938	38,779
Widows	33,335	31,681	30,317	28,873	27,294	25,734
All pension recipients	**235,014**	**237,268**	**239,142**	**242,413**	**246,575**	**250,723**
Widows' Benefits[2,3]	8,717	8,014	7,485	6,630	6,003	5,203
Bereavement Allowance[3]	.	.	.	913	1,350	1,460
Guardian's Allowance[4]	125	129	125	162	116	87

Sources: Department for Social Development; HM Revenue & Customs

[1] Retirement Pensions at March each year.

[2] Widow's Benefit at March each year.

[3] From 9 April 2001, male and female claimants may be eligible for Bereavement Allowance for up to 52 weeks following the death of a spouse.

[4] Guardian's Allowance at 31 December each year. HM Revenue & Customs provided figures from 2003 onwards.

Notes to Social and Welfare tables

TABLE 3.1

The information presented is from the Family Resources Survey (FRS) for the financial year April 2003 to March 2004.

This survey collects detailed information on the incomes and circumstances of private households and has been carried out in Great Britain since 1992, but 2002-03 saw the introduction of Northern Ireland for the first time. The primary function of the FRS is to collect information on the resources of households, that is income received from all sources.

TABLES 3.4 TO 3.6

Figures are based on a 5% sample of all income support claimants which is conducted on the last Friday in February, May, August and November of each year.

Pension Credit replaced Minimum Income Guarantee (MIG) for Income Support pensioners in October 2003. Pension Credit tops up any money an individual and their partner has coming in to a minimum level set by the government. It also awards them for having certain types of income and savings. There are two parts to Pension Credit:

- The Guarantee Credit, for people aged 60 and over, and;
- The Savings Credit, for people aged 65 and over.

TABLE 3.7

Figures are based on a 20% sample for Northern Ireland. GB figures are based on a 5% sample.

TABLE 3.9

The table is based on a random sample of families with Child Tax Credit (CTC) or Working Tax Credit (WTC) awards at the reference date. The sample comprises 10% of such single adults (with or without children) and 20% of such couples.

Each figure in the table is derived by weighting the relevant sample cases by the inverses of these sampling fractions (each case is further weighted so that the overall total equals an independent count of families with awards).

WTC/CTC is an annual award that has the ability to amend the amount eligible as circumstance changes are notified. Working Families Tax Credit (WFTC) was a fixed award for 26 weeks and based on circumstances at time of application.

Unlike WFTC, WTC now extends to families without children.

TABLE 3.10

Incapacity Benefit is paid to people who are assessed as being incapable of work and who meet the contribution conditions. NI data are based on a 100% sample while GB data are based on a 5% sample of all Incapacity Benefit cases.

TABLE 3.12

National Insurance pensions (contribution based State Retirement Pension) are dependent on either a person's own National Insurance contributions or the contributions paid by a spouse. The two main conditions for payment are that a person has reached State pension age (65 for men, 60 for women) and the contributions conditions are satisfied.

A widow is entitled to National Insurance Widow's Benefit if her late husband met the contribution conditions. If he fully satisfied the conditions, she will receive the standard rate of benefit, otherwise she will receive a reduced rate.

Since 9 April 2001, the system of Widows' benefits has been replaced by bereavement benefits. Bereavement benefits are available to both men and women. Bereavement Allowance in this table represents both:

- Widowed Parent's Allowance (WPA) and;
- Bereavement Allowance.

Guardian's Allowance is a National Insurance Benefit paid to someone who is bringing up a child or children whose parents have died. It is paid in addition to child benefit. One of the parents must have satisfied a residence condition before they died. In certain, very limited circumstances, it can be paid when only one parent is dead, when, for example, the other parent is missing and cannot be found, or the other parent is in prison.

4 Health and Care

- In 2004-05, 34% of males and 36% of females reported having a long-standing illness while 24% of males and 27% of females reported that they had a long-standing illness that limited their activities.

- In 2004-05, 14% of males and 17% of females interviewed had consulted a GP in the previous 14 days. Those aged 45 years and above were more likely to have consulted a GP than those aged under 45.

- The prevalence of smoking was greater among males (27%) than females (25%) in 2004-05. The percentage of people smoking has decreased from 28% in 1994-95 to 26% in 2004-05.

- In 2003-04, the waiting times for elective admission to hospital varied by specialty. For Trauma and Orthopaedics only 43% of admissions were made within 3 months and 75% within 12 months. This compared with 85% of admissions for Oral Surgery being made within 3 months and 98% within 12 months.

- Between 1998-99 and 2003-04, there was a general increase in the proportion of particular surgical procedures carried out as day cases.

- There were just under 679,000 attendances at Accident and Emergency Departments during the year 2003-04. Of these, 89% were first attendances, an increase from 85% in 1998-99. Between 1998-99 and 2003-04, the number of first attendances at Accident and Emergency Departments increased by 8%. The number of follow-up attendances generally decreased by 27% over the same period from almost 101,000 in 1998-99 to 74,000 in 2003-04.

- **There were approximately 482,000 discharges, deaths or day cases in 2003-04, 69% of which were treated as ordinary inpatients, the remainder as day cases. Between 1998-99 and 2003-04, the actual number of day cases increased by just over one third.**

- **There were around 1.48 million outpatient attendances in 2003-04, 72% of which were consultant initiated. In the same year there were almost 205,000 cases of non-attendance.**

- **Following a fall in the number of available hospital beds between 1998-99 and 2002-03, there was a slight increase in the number of beds available in 2003-04.**

- **In 2003-04, 74% of places in residential homes (excluding children's homes) were for older people. The remainder of places were for people with learning disabilities, people who were mentally ill and people who were physically disabled.**

- **At 31 March 2004, there were over 26,000 people in receipt of home help, 4,600 in receipt of meals on wheels, and 10,300 registered at statutory day care facilities.**

- **In 2004, there were 2,510 children looked after by Social Services. Of these, 61% were in foster homes while 13% were in residential homes.**

4.1 Prevalence of reported long-standing illness among adults by gender and age, 2000-01 to 2004-05

Percentages

Gender and age	Long-standing illness					Long-standing illness which limits activities				
	2000-01	2001-02	2002-03	2003-04	2004-05[p]	2000-01	2001-02	2002-03	2003-04	2004-05[p]
Males										
16-44	*18*	*19*	*20*	*19*	*17*	*11*	*13*	*12*	*12*	*10*
45-64	*43*	*42*	*42*	*42*	*45*	*33*	*31*	*32*	*30*	*33*
65-74	*59*	*67*	*66*	*59*	*56*	*42*	*49*	*45*	*41*	*41*
75 or over	*72*	*69*	*69*	*67*	*65*	*58*	*54*	*55*	*55*	*46*
All ages	***33***	***34***	***35***	***33***	***34***	***24***	***24***	***24***	***23***	***24***
Sample base (all adult males)	2,444	2,474	2,371	2,213	2,263	2,444	2,474	2,370	2,213	2,263
Females										
16-44	*21*	*21*	*22*	*21*	*22*	*15*	*14*	*15*	*14*	*15*
45-64	*44*	*42*	*45*	*45*	*42*	*34*	*32*	*32*	*33*	*30*
65-74	*57*	*60*	*60*	*67*	*59*	*44*	*45*	*47*	*49*	*44*
75 or over	*75*	*75*	*66*	*71*	*72*	*60*	*61*	*54*	*57*	*60*
All ages	***36***	***36***	***37***	***37***	***36***	***27***	***26***	***27***	***27***	***27***
Sample base (all adult females)	2,857	2,804	2,704	2,609	2,666	2,857	2,804	2,704	2,609	2,666

Source: Continuous Household Survey, Northern Ireland Statistics and Research Agency

4.2 Consultations with a National Health Service (NHS) General Practitioner in the 14 days before interview by gender and age, 2000-01 to 2004-05

Percentages

Age	Males					Females				
	2000-01	2001-02	2002-03	2003-04	2004-05[p]	2000-01	2001-02	2002-03	2003-04	2004-05[p]
16-44	*7*	*8*	*10*	*8*	*8*	*16*	*17*	*18*	*16*	*15*
45-64	*16*	*14*	*18*	*17*	*19*	*22*	*22*	*19*	*22*	*18*
65-74	*23*	*23*	*27*	*22*	*19*	*21*	*23*	*26*	*25*	*23*
75 or over	*22*	*24*	*23*	*27*	*24*	*22*	*21*	*26*	*24*	*20*
All ages	***12***	***13***	***15***	***13***	***14***	***19***	***20***	***20***	***20***	***17***
Sample base (all adults)	2,444	2,474	2,371	2,214	2,263	2,857	2,804	2,703	2,609	2,664

Source: Continuous Household Survey, Northern Ireland Statistics and Research Agency

4.3 In receipt of National Health Service (NHS) dental or hospital treatment in the 4 weeks prior to interview by gender and age, 2003-04

Percentages

	Medical treatment in the 4 weeks prior to interview		
	Visited dentist for NHS examination / treatment	Visited hospital for NHS treatment	Sample base (all individuals)
Males			
4 and under	*4*	*3*	163
5-15	*14*	*5*	451
16-29	*6*	*3*	344
30-44	*7*	*3*	508
45-59	*10*	*4*	373
60-74	*12*	*10*	291
75 and over	*8*	*15*	115
All ages	***9***	***5***	**2,245**
Females			
4 and under	*5*	*5*	174
5-15	*15*	*2*	385
16-29	*8*	*3*	416
30-44	*10*	*7*	558
45-59	*12*	*9*	414
60-74	*9*	*13*	328
75 and over	*5*	*12*	171
All ages	***10***	***7***	**2,446**
All individuals			
4 and under	***5***	***4***	**337**
5-15	***15***	***4***	**836**
16-29	***7***	***3***	**760**
30-44	***9***	***5***	**1,066**
45-59	***11***	***6***	**787**
60-74	***10***	***11***	**619**
75 and over	***6***	***13***	**286**
All ages	***9***	***6***	**4,691**

Source: Family Resources Survey, Department for Social Development

General Medical Services (GMS), 1999-2000 to 2004-05

4.4

Units as indicated

	1999-00	2000-01	2001-02	2002-03	2003-04	2004-05
GPs on Medical List (number)[1, 2]	1,054	1,058	1,061	1,076	1,076	1,078
Assistants[1]	13	12	12	13	15	13
Patients registered (000s)	1,769	1,771	1,772	1,780	1,783	1,787
Amounts paid to doctors under Health Service (£000)[3]						
Gross Cost (£000)	**78,604**	**82,471**	**84,664**	**88,194**	**96,894**[4]	**138,250**[4]

Source: Central Services Agency

[1] At mid period (1 October).

[2] From 2003, these are Unrestricted Principals and Equivalents (UPE) GPs only.

[3] These costs refer to the majority of non-cash limited services, further expenditure under GMS is allocated through Health and Social Services Boards on a cash limited basis.

[4] This increase is due to advance payments being made in relation to the New GMS Contract introduced in April 2004.

Note: The data presented in this table are not National Statistics.

General Dental Services (GDS), 1999-2000 to 2004-05

4.5

Units as indicated

	1999-00	2000-01	2001-02	2002-03	2003-04	2004-05
Dentists on Dental List[1] (number)	632	661	673	689	696	720
Claims paid						
Number (000s)	1,086	1,113	1,126	1,123	1,107	1,086
Gross cost (£000)[2]	58,712	61,237	64,454	66,201	66,910	67,294
Amount paid by patients (£000)	14,358	15,085	16,041	16,824	16,627	16,797
Net cost of exchequer (£000)[2]	44,354	46,152	48,413	49,376	50,282	50,498
Average gross cost per claim (£)[2]	54.06	55.02	57.24	58.95	60.44	61.97

Source: Central Services Agency

[1] At beginning of period.

[2] Includes treatments, capitation, continuing care and occasional treatments but excludes some elements of GDS expenditure.

Note: The data presented in this table are not National Statistics.

4.6 General Ophthalmic Services, 1999-2000 to 2004-05

Units as indicated

	1999-00	2000-01	2001-02	2002-03	2003-04	2004-05
Ophthalmic medical practitioners[1]	17	20	23	19	19	19
Ophthalmic opticians[1]	359	388	425	451	476	475
Dispensing opticians[1]	10	9	9	10	20	25
Sight tests (000s)[2]	298	296	315	322	334	334
Optical appliances supplied/vouchers (000s)[3]	158	160	165	168	169	167
Gross cost of services (£millions)	11.5	12.0	12.7	13.5	14.0	14.4

Source: Central Services Agency

1 At beginning of period.

2 Excludes sight tests carried out in the home (i.e. domiciliary visits).

3 Does not include repair/replacement spectacles.

Note: The data presented in this table are not National Statistics.

4.7 Pharmaceutical Services[1] (chemists and dispensing doctors), 1999-2000 to 2004-05

Units as indicated

	1999-00	2000-01	2001-02	2002-03	2003-04	2004-05
Number of prescription forms (000s)	13,454	13,666	14,277	14,622	15,158	15,283
Number of prescription items (000s)	23,249	23,985	24,705	25,501	26,656	27,401
Gross cost (£000)[2]	**266,535**	**278,405**	**303,489**	**327,045**	**362,401**	**382,789**
Amount paid by patients (£000)[3]	8,183	8,499	9,074	9,597	9,798	10,262
Amount paid by patients for prepayment certificates (£000)	1,617	1,803	1,977	2,206	2,336	2,456
Net cost of exchequer (£000)	256,736	268,103	292,438	315,242	350,267	370,071
Average gross cost per prescription item (£)	11.46	11.61	12.28	12.82	13.60	13.97

Source: Central Services Agency

1 All data relates to the period during which the prescription item was dispensed and not when the payment was made.

2 Gross cost is defined as net ingredient costs plus on-cost, fees and other payments.

3 Excludes amount paid by patients for pre-payment certificates.

Note: The data presented in this table are not National Statistics.

Figure 4.1 Pharmaceutical services – average gross cost per prescription item, 1994 to 2004-05

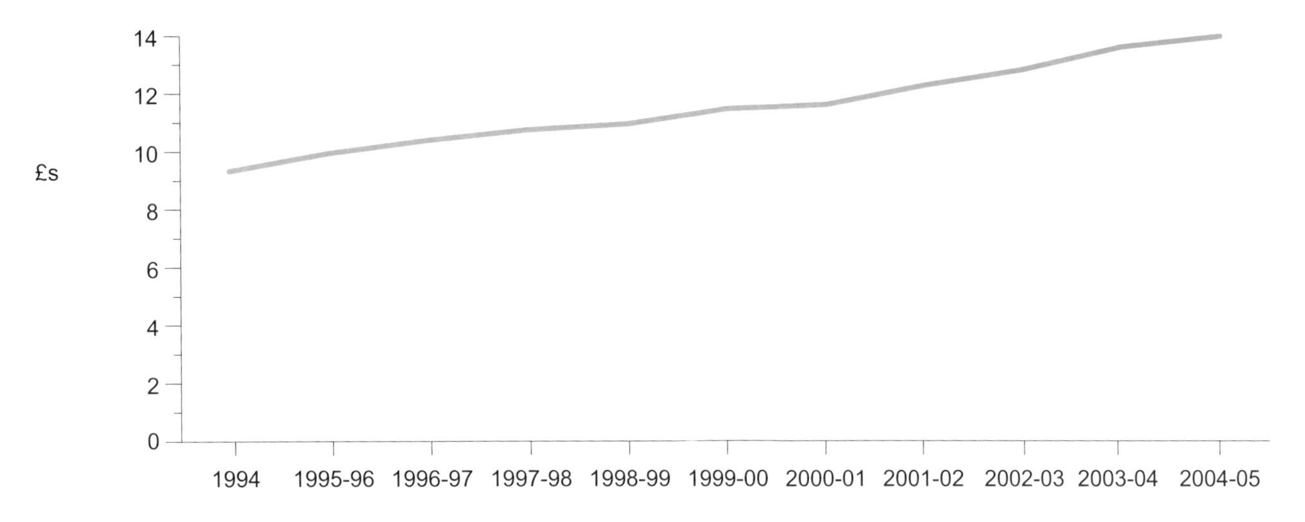

Source: Central Services Agency

4.8 Prevalence of cigarette smoking among persons aged 16 and over by gender, 1994-95 to 2004-05

Percentages

Gender	1994-95	1996-97	1998-99	2000-01	2002-03	2004-05[P]
Males	*29*	*31*	*28*	*26*	*27*	*27*
Females	*27*	*27*	*29*	*28*	*26*	*25*
All persons	***28***	***29***	***29***	***27***	***26***	***26***
Sample base (all adults)	5,382	4,801	4,570	4,402	5,176	4,038

Source: Continuous Household Survey, Northern Ireland Statistics and Research Agency

4.9 Waiting times for elective admission to hospital by selected specialty, 1998-99 to 2003-04

Percentages and numbers

Specialty, waiting times and admissions	1998-99	1999-00	2000-01	2001-02	2002-03	2003-04
General Surgery						
Seen in under 3 months	*75*	*77*	*76*	*74*	*70*	*71*
Seen in under 12 months	*94*	*95*	*95*	*95*	*93*	*93*
Number of admissions	**39,074**	**36,401**	**35,922**	**35,889**	**38,948**	**40,157**
Urology						
Seen in under 3 months	*67*	*69*	*68*	*69*	*63*	*68*
Seen in under 12 months	*95*	*96*	*95*	*95*	*91*	*94*
Number of admissions	**9,871**	**9,323**	**9,927**	**10,894**	**10,876**	**11,651**
Trauma and Orthopaedics						
Seen in under 3 months	*50*	*48*	*54*	*56*	*47*	*43*
Seen in under 12 months	*81*	*82*	*86*	*86*	*81*	*75*
Number of admissions	**8,223**	**7,903**	**7,247**	**7,357**	**7,530**	**7,782**
Ear, Nose & Throat						
Seen in under 3 months	*53*	*56*	*54*	*54*	*49*	*48*
Seen in under 12 months	*91*	*92*	*91*	*88*	*84*	*88*
Number of admissions	**15,099**	**13,822**	**12,616**	**12,224**	**12,550**	**12,340**
Ophthalmology						
Seen in under 3 months	*51*	*54*	*53*	*52*	*50*	*48*
Seen in under 12 months	*91*	*91*	*89*	*89*	*89*	*88*
Number of admissions	**12,642**	**11,888**	**12,010**	**12,630**	**13,589**	**14,712**
Oral Surgery						
Seen in under 3 months	*78*	*74*	*73*	*82*	*75*	*85*
Seen in under 12 months	*98*	*98*	*98*	*98*	*94*	*98*
Number of admissions	**2,791**	**2,765**	**2,408**	**2,792**	**3,565**	**3,655**
Plastic Surgery						
Seen in under 3 months	*62*	*64*	*68*	*67*	*68*	*64*
Seen in under 12 months	*80*	*86*	*90*	*89*	*90*	*86*
Number of admissions	**3,135**	**2,974**	**2,923**	**3,044**	**3,276**	**3,642**
Cardiac Surgery						
Seen in under 3 months	*41*	*40*	*42*	*47*	*42*	*53*
Seen in under 12 months	*85*	*88*	*82*	*87*	*88*	*94*
Number of admissions	**987**	**755**	**667**	**577**	**753**	**731**
Paediatric Surgery						
Seen in under 3 months	*43*	*60*	*61*	*58*	*60*	*52*
Seen in under 12 months	*75*	*91*	*92*	*93*	*92*	*91*
Number of admissions	**1,779**	**1,428**	**1,451**	**1,382**	**1,445**	**1,376**
Gynaecology						
Seen in under 3 months	*69*	*68*	*67*	*65*	*63*	*64*
Seen in under 12 months	*98*	*97*	*96*	*95*	*92*	*93*
Number of admissions	**17,931**	**16,479**	**16,056**	**15,490**	**15,605**	**15,793**

Source: Department of Health, Social Services and Public Safety

Day case surgery rates by type of operation, 1998-99 to 2003-04

4.10

Numbers and percentages

Type of operation and day case surgery rates	1998-99	1999-00	2000-01	2001-02	2002-03	2003-04
Arthroscopy of the knee						
Procedures carried out as day cases	732	777	618	603	472	588
% day cases	*69*	*69*	*69*	*63*	*56*	*67*
All procedures	**1,064**	**1,133**	**895**	**959**	**849**	**882**
Bronchoscopy						
Procedures carried out as day cases	1,177	1,265	1,348	1,556	1,514	1,534
% day cases	*76*	*77*	*79*	*83*	*85*	*86*
All procedures	**1,553**	**1,637**	**1,716**	**1,869**	**1,782**	**1,775**
Carpal Tunnel						
Procedures carried out as day cases	355	349	358	505	531	577
% day cases	*64*	*62*	*68*	*78*	*78*	*78*
All procedures	**558**	**561**	**523**	**646**	**682**	**740**
Cataract extraction						
Procedures carried out as day cases	4,520	5,106	5,496	6,073	6,553	7,591
% day cases	*72*	*78*	*80*	*84*	*86*	*89*
All procedures	**6,248**	**6,509**	**6,834**	**7,188**	**7,664**	**8,512**
Circumcision						
Procedures carried out as day cases	535	446	465	532	545	530
% day cases	*70*	*74*	*78*	*82*	*82*	*76*
All procedures	**763**	**605**	**593**	**652**	**663**	**694**
Correction of squint						
Procedures carried out as day cases	248	275	240	250	256	277
% day cases	*43*	*52*	*52*	*53*	*57*	*62*
All procedures	**577**	**525**	**464**	**473**	**451**	**447**
Cystoscopy						
Procedures carried out as day cases	4,706	4,389	4,803	5,129	5,001	5,761
% day cases	*83*	*83*	*84*	*85*	*85*	*86*
All procedures	**5,678**	**5,261**	**5,699**	**6,023**	**5,857**	**6,669**
Endoscopy of gastric intestinal tract						
Procedures carried out as day cases	22,045	23,123	24,979	27,340	28,586	30,922
% day cases	*91*	*92*	*92*	*93*	*93*	*94*
All procedures	**24,141**	**25,188**	**27,022**	**29,380**	**30,588**	**32,984**
Inguinal hernia repair						
Procedures carried out as day cases	533	549	667	883	974	932
% day cases	*24*	*27*	*32*	*43*	*42*	*42*
All procedures	**2,235**	**1,997**	**2,060**	**2,063**	**2,292**	**2,203**
Laparoscopic sterilisation						
Procedures carried out as day cases	1,868	1,667	1,531	1,418	1,240	1,213
% day cases	*78*	*78*	*80*	*79*	*80*	*83*
All procedures	**2,410**	**2,137**	**1,917**	**1,795**	**1,546**	**1,462**
Varicose veins						
Procedures carried out as day cases	432	562	423	456	526	564
% day cases	*26*	*36*	*35*	*47*	*40*	*35*
All procedures	**1,646**	**1,549**	**1,192**	**978**	**1,318**	**1,626**
Ganglion excision						
Procedures carried out as day cases	324	319	251	294	291	271
% day cases	*85*	*85*	*82*	*88*	*88*	*87*
All procedures	**380**	**374**	**307**	**336**	**332**	**313**
Operations on nasal septum/turbinate						
Procedures carried out as day cases	308	270	248	268	262	291
% day cases	*19*	*20*	*20*	*25*	*23*	*24*
All procedures	**1,643**	**1,349**	**1,243**	**1,070**	**1,141**	**1,198**

Source: Department of Health, Social Services and Public Safety

4.11 Attendance at Accident and Emergency Departments[1], 1998-99 to 2003-04

Numbers

	1998-99	1999-00	2000-01	2001-02	2002-03	2003-04
First attendances	562,258	574,503	580,535	584,350	584,062	605,001
Follow-up attendances[2]	100,788	101,086	92,119	88,432	75,597	73,997
All attendances	**663,046**	**675,589**	**672,654**	**672,782**	**659,659**	**678,998**

Source: Department of Health, Social Services and Public Safety

[1] Excludes planned consultant clinics held in Accident and Emergency Departments.

[2] A follow-up attendance is any reattendance which does not involve appointments with a consultant or a member of his/her firm.

Figure 4.2 Attendance at Accident and Emergency Departments, 1993-94 to 2003-04

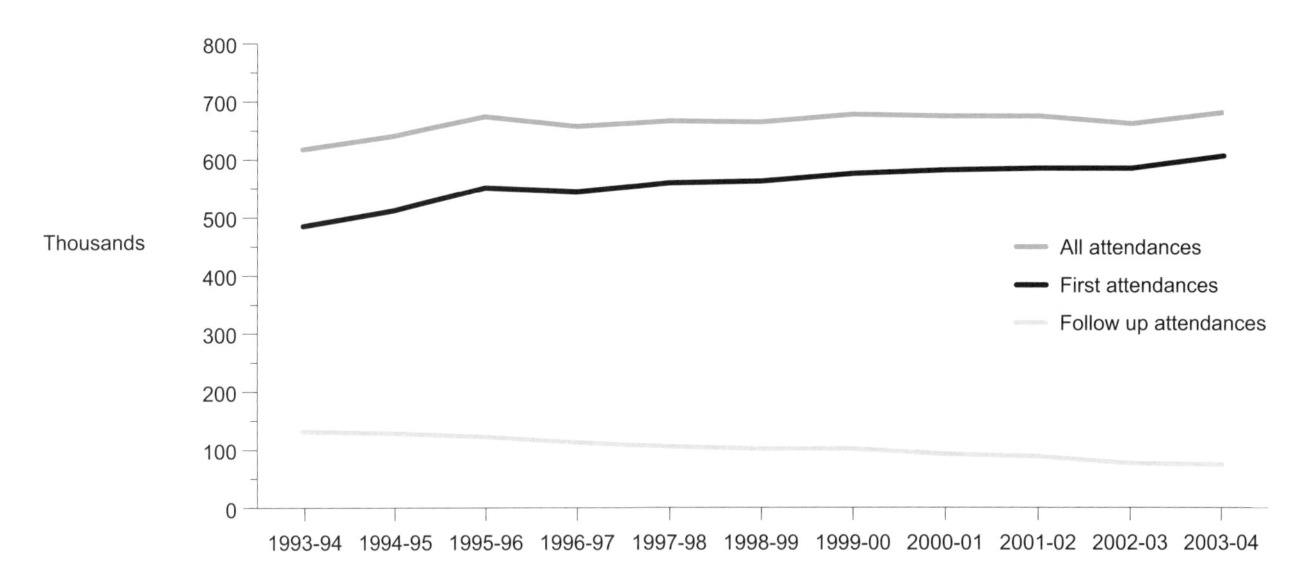

Source: Department of Health, Social Services and Public Safety

4.12 Inpatient discharges and deaths by Programme of Care and day cases, 1998-99 to 2003-04

Numbers

Programme of Care	1998-99	1999-00	2000-01	2001-02	2002-03	2003-04
Acute services	256,032	255,797	258,792[r]	254,765	254,079[r]	258,052
Maternity and child health	53,593	51,018	48,660	48,749	48,467	49,632
Elderly care	12,622	12,210	12,344	11,809	11,814	12,480
Mental health	9,973	10,482	10,488	10,366	10,035	9,146
Learning disability	2,548	2,567	2,652[r]	2,446	2,364	2,366
All discharges and deaths	**334,768**	**332,074**	**332,936**[r]	**328,135**	**326,759**[r]	**331,676**
Day cases	111,760	118,941	123,693[r]	130,068	138,605	150,772
Total Inpatient discharges and deaths and day cases	**446,528**	**451,015**	**456,629**[r]	**458,203**	**465,364**[r]	**482,448**

Source: Department of Health, Social Services and Public Safety

Outpatient activity by type of attendance and non-attendance, 1998-99 to 2003-04

Numbers

Type of attendance/ non-attendance	1998-99	1999-00	2000-01	2001-02	2002-03	2003-04
Attendances						
- Referrals	400,121	409,964	413,431	413,123	407,576	408,689
- Consultant initiated	1,027,773	1,025,354	1,027,711	1,045,077	1,054,387 r	1,073,252
All attendances	**1,427,894**	**1,435,318**	**1,441,142**	**1,458,200**	**1,461,963** r	**1,481,941**
Non-attendances						
- Referrals	46,637	49,255	50,414	49,439	47,045	48,135
- Consultant initiated	168,818	167,388	165,964	162,374	156,925	156,674
All non-attendances	**215,455**	**216,643**	**216,378**	**211,813**	**203,970**	**204,809**
Clinic sessions	88,731	91,790	94,050	96,345	99,358	105,632

Source: Department of Health, Social Services and Public Safety

Available beds by Programme of Care, 1998-99 to 2003-04

Numbers

Programme of Care	1998-99	1999-00	2000-01	2001-02	2002-03	2003-04
Acute services	4,303	4,246	4,230	4,252	4,267	4,396
Maternity and child health	819	795	746	716	696	670
Elderly care	1,656	1,596	1,587	1,553	1,511	1,532
Mental health	1,317	1,344	1,349	1,280	1,223	1,162
Learning disability	723	659	658	617	604	585
All available beds	**8,818**	**8,640**	**8,570**	**8,418**	**8,301**	**8,345**

Source: Department of Health, Social Services and Public Safety

Figure 4.3 Available beds by Programme of Care, 1993-94 to 2003-04

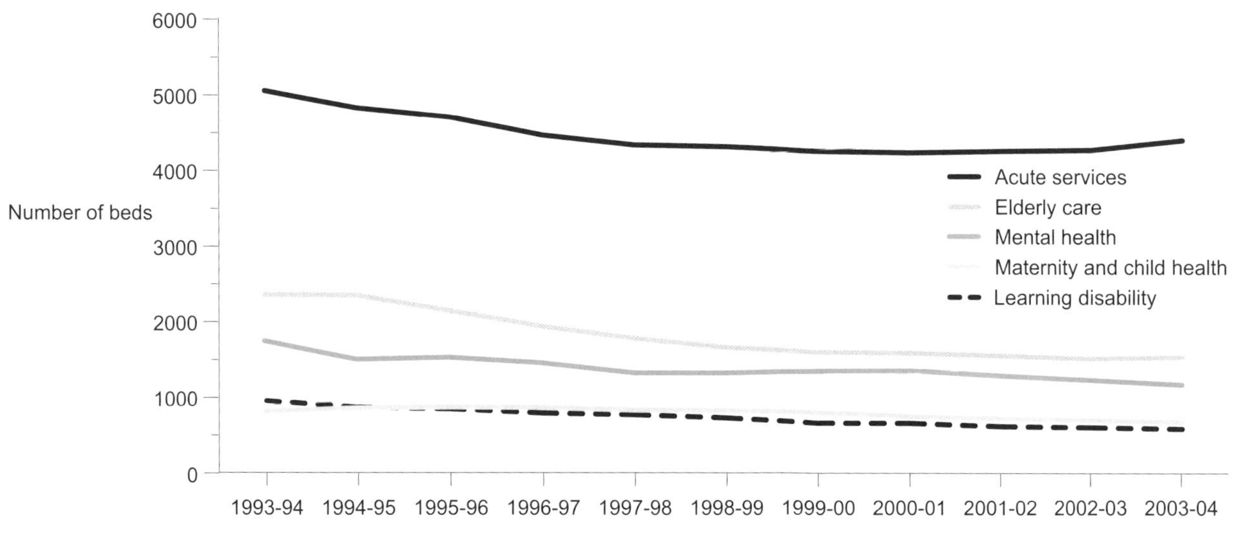

Source: Department of Health, Social Services and Public Safety

4.15 Available places in residential homes, 1998-99 to 2003-04

Numbers

Places in homes	1998-99	1999-00	2000-01	2001-02	2002-03	2003-04
Older persons						
Statutory homes	1,730	1,714	1,704	1,681	1,634	1,635
Voluntary homes	900	871	860	843	854	819
Private homes	2,059	1,525	1,587	1,508	1,605	1,573
Dual Registered homes[1]	..	407	428	564	613	597
All homes	**4,689**	**4,517**	**4,579**	**4,596**	**4,706**	**4,624**
Average occupied places in statutory homes	1,549	1,610	1,600	1,575	1,519	1,495
Learning disabled persons						
Statutory homes	340	325	319	285	265	233
Voluntary homes	496	461	508	525	520	502
Private homes	344	351	348	353	330	338
Dual Registered homes[1]	..	5	5	5	5	16
All homes	**1,180**	**1,142**	**1,180**	**1,168**	**1,120**	**1,089**
Average occupied places in statutory homes	317	306	291	260	250	202
Mentally ill persons						
Statutory homes	202	201	194	217	204	191
Voluntary homes	263	263	249	270	291	197
Private homes	186	136	135	135	117	96
Dual Registered homes[1]	..	22	26	23	25	41
All homes	**651**	**622**	**604**	**645**	**637**	**525**
Average occupied places in statutory homes	160	163	155	182	170	158
Physically disabled persons						
Statutory homes	0	0	0	0	0	0
Voluntary homes	65	37	37	47	47	37
Private homes	5	5	8	8	0	0
Dual Registered homes[1]	..	0	0	0	0	7
All homes	**70**	**42**	**45**	**55**	**47**	**44**
Average occupied places in statutory homes	0	0	0	0	0	0

Source: Department of Health, Social Services and Public Safety

[1] Residential places only.

Persons receiving domiciliary and day care services, 1999 to 2004

4.16

Numbers

Type of service	1999	2000	2001	2002	2003	2004
Home help	28,115	27,844	27,401	26,948	26,339	26,408
Meals on wheels	4,374	4,702	4,092	4,178	4,657	4,650
Registered at day care facilities[1]	9,464	10,451	10,487	10,586	10,403	10,287

Source: Department of Health, Social Services and Public Safety

[1] Statutory day care only.

Children's services, 1999 to 2004

4.17

Numbers

Service provided	1999	2000	2001	2002	2003	2004
Children looked after						
- In residential homes	260	285	273	299	296	325
- In foster care	1,506	1,611	1,528	1,513	1,577	1,529
- Placed with family/other accommodation	558	526	613	641	573	656
All children looked after	**2,324**	**2,422**	**2,414**	**2,453**	**2,446**	**2,510**
Children on child protection register	1,463	1,480	1,414	1,531	1,608	1,417
Child protection registrations[1]	1,093	1,067	970	1,080	1,102	962

Source: Department of Health, Social Services and Public Safety

[1] During financial year.

4.18 Number of deaths by cause and gender, 1994 to 2004

Numbers

Gender and cause of death	1994	1995	1996	1997	1998	1999	2000	2001	2002	2003	2004[p]
Males											
Ischaemic heart disease	2,205	2,175	2,049	2,064	1,996	1,936	1,771	1,693	1,569	1,533	1,524
Cerebrovascular disease	627	627	597	635	593	619	527	581	579	579	542
Other circulatory diseases	480	522	509	467	481	475	465	489	528	452	450
All circulatory diseases	**3,312**	**3,324**	**3,155**	**3,166**	**3,070**	**3,030**	**2,763**	**2,763**	**2,676**	**2,564**	**2,516**
Chronic lower respiratory disease	371	363	428	366	380	440	372	345	301	375	364
Other respiratory diseases	713	770	801	756	767	899	956	546	505	553	535
All respiratory diseases	**1,084**	**1,133**	**1,229**	**1,122**	**1,147**	**1,339**	**1,328**	**891**	**806**	**928**	**899**
Cancer (malignant neoplasms)	**1,854**	**1,841**	**1,903**	**1,846**	**1,921**	**1,793**	**1,755**	**1,934**	**1,908**	**1,914**	**1,937**
Motor vehicle traffic accidents	119	104	92	111	96	98	106	91	91	75	97
Suicides	107	91	99	95	95	103	130	119	132	104	96
Undetermined	10	14	15	13	18	24	10	13	10	8	9
Other external causes of death	252	250	194	185	179	185	159	148	197	185	205
All external causes of death	**488**	**459**	**400**	**404**	**388**	**410**	**405**	**371**	**430**	**372**	**407**
All other causes of death	**624**	**725**	**731**	**706**	**795**	**892**	**877**	**1,048**	**1,128**	**1,142**	**1,176**
All causes	**7,362**	**7,482**	**7,418**	**7,244**	**7,321**	**7,464**	**7,128**	**7,007**	**6,948**	**6,920**	**6,935**
Females											
Ischaemic heart disease	1,963	1,911	1,807	1,700	1,658	1,632	1,463	1,455	1,379	1,310	1,253
Cerebrovascular disease	1,111	1,063	1,056	1,012	1,009	1,060	942	950	994	952	892
Other circulatory diseases	625	631	615	628	630	700	608	661	680	622	603
All circulatory diseases	**3,699**	**3,605**	**3,478**	**3,340**	**3,297**	**3,392**	**3,013**	**3,066**	**3,053**	**2,884**	**2,748**
Chronic lower respiratory disease	260	304	285	322	307	326	295	291	306	336	317
Other respiratory diseases	1,054	1,219	1,235	1,221	1,173	1,496	1,396	793	771	818	753
All respiratory diseases	**1,314**	**1,523**	**1,520**	**1,543**	**1,480**	**1,822**	**1,691**	**1,084**	**1,077**	**1,154**	**1,070**
Cancer (malignant neoplasms)	**1,741**	**1,650**	**1,720**	**1,743**	**1,727**	**1,759**	**1,786**	**1,762**	**1,744**	**1,843**	**1,820**
Motor vehicle traffic accidents	56	38	30	42	34	36	33	21	30	19	35
Suicides	31	31	25	25	31	18	33	22	30	28	32
Undetermined	3	11	4	5	6	9	12	4	11	4	9
Other external causes of death	110	125	139	117	110	138	104	127	136	127	160
All external causes of death	**200**	**205**	**198**	**189**	**181**	**199**	**212**	**174**	**207**	**178**	**236**
All other causes of death	**798**	**845**	**884**	**912**	**987**	**1,027**	**1,073**	**1,420**	**1,557**	**1,483**	**1,545**
All causes	**7,752**	**7,828**	**7,800**	**7,727**	**7,672**	**8,199**	**7,775**	**7,506**	**7,638**	**7,542**	**7,419**

Source: Northern Ireland Statistics and Research Agency

Mortality rates by cause of death and gender, 1994 to 2004

4.19

Rates per 100,000 population

Gender and cause of death	1994	1995	1996	1997	1998	1999	2000	2001	2002	2003	2004
Males											
Ischaemic heart disease	*275*	*271*	*253*	*253*	*244*	*237*	*216*	*205*	*189*	*184*	*182*
Cerebrovascular disease	*78*	*78*	*74*	*78*	*72*	*76*	*64*	*70*	*70*	*70*	*65*
Other circulatory diseases	*60*	*65*	*63*	*57*	*59*	*58*	*57*	*59*	*64*	*54*	*54*
All circulatory diseases	***413***	***413***	***389***	***388***	***375***	***370***	***337***	***335***	***323***	***308***	***301***
Chronic lower respiratory disease	*46*	*45*	*53*	*45*	*46*	*54*	*45*	*42*	*36*	*45*	*44*
Other respiratory diseases	*89*	*96*	*99*	*93*	*94*	*110*	*117*	*66*	*61*	*66*	*64*
All respiratory diseases	***135***	***141***	***152***	***138***	***140***	***164***	***162***	***108***	***97***	***111***	***107***
Cancer (malignant neoplasms)	***231***	***229***	***235***	***226***	***235***	***219***	***214***	***235***	***230***	***230***	***232***
Motor vehicle traffic accidents	*15*	*13*	*11*	*14*	*12*	*12*	*13*	*11*	*11*	*9*	*12*
Suicides	*13*	*11*	*12*	*12*	*12*	*13*	*16*	*14*	*16*	*12*	*11*
Undetermined	*1*	*2*	*2*	*2*	*2*	*3*	*1*	*2*	*1*	*1*	*1*
Other external causes of death	*31*	*31*	*24*	*23*	*22*	*23*	*19*	*18*	*24*	*22*	*25*
All external causes of death	***61***	***57***	***49***	***50***	***47***	***50***	***49***	***45***	***52***	***45***	***49***
All other causes of death	***78***	***90***	***90***	***87***	***97***	***109***	***107***	***127***	***136***	***137***	***141***
All causes	***918***	***931***	***915***	***888***	***894***	***912***	***869***	***850***	***838***	***831***	***829***
Females											
Ischaemic heart disease	*233*	*226*	*212*	*199*	*193*	*190*	*170*	*168*	*159*	*151*	*143*
Cerebrovascular disease	*132*	*126*	*124*	*118*	*117*	*123*	*109*	*110*	*115*	*109*	*102*
Other circulatory diseases	*74*	*75*	*72*	*73*	*73*	*81*	*70*	*76*	*78*	*72*	*69*
All circulatory diseases	***439***	***427***	***409***	***390***	***384***	***394***	***349***	***354***	***352***	***332***	***314***
Chronic lower respiratory disease	*31*	*36*	*33*	*38*	*36*	*38*	*34*	*34*	*35*	*39*	*36*
Other respiratory diseases	*125*	*144*	*145*	*143*	*137*	*174*	*162*	*92*	*89*	*94*	*86*
All respiratory diseases	***156***	***180***	***179***	***180***	***172***	***212***	***196***	***125***	***124***	***133***	***122***
Cancer (malignant neoplasms)	***207***	***195***	***202***	***204***	***201***	***204***	***207***	***204***	***201***	***212***	***208***
Motor vehicle traffic accidents	*7*	*4*	*4*	*5*	*4*	*4*	*4*	*2*	*3*	*2*	*4*
Suicides	*4*	*4*	*3*	*3*	*4*	*2*	*4*	*3*	*3*	*3*	*4*
Undetermined	*0*	*1*	*0*	*1*	*1*	*1*	*1*	*0*	*1*	*0*	*1*
Other external causes of death	*13*	*15*	*16*	*14*	*13*	*16*	*16*	*15*	*16*	*15*	*18*
All external causes of death	***24***	***24***	***23***	***22***	***21***	***23***	***25***	***20***	***24***	***20***	***27***
All other causes of death	***95***	***100***	***104***	***107***	***115***	***119***	***124***	***164***	***179***	***170***	***177***
All causes	***921***	***926***	***916***	***903***	***893***	***953***	***901***	***868***	***880***	***867***	***849***

Source: Northern Ireland Statistics and Research Agency

Notes to Health and Care tables

TABLE 4.1, 4.2, AND 4.8

The Continuous Household Survey, which began in 1983, is based on a simple random sample of the general population resident in private households in Northern Ireland.

TABLE 4.3

The information presented is from the Family Resources Survey (FRS) for the financial year April 2003 to March 2004.

This survey collects detailed information on the incomes and circumstances of private households and has been carried out in Great Britain since 1992, but 2002-03 saw the introduction of Northern Ireland for the first time. The primary function of the FRS is to collect information on the resources of households, that is income received from all sources.

TABLE 4.9

The table refers to waiting times for people going into hospital for treatment in ten specialties. People who need urgent treatment are admitted very quickly - immediately in most cases. Other people, whose need is not quite so urgent, are placed on the waiting list. This table does not include all inpatient specialties (a specialty is a particular branch of medicine or surgery; information is recorded against the specialty of the treating consultant). These specialties were chosen because historically they have had the longest waiting times.

TABLE 4.11

Accident and Emergency Departments provide services for patients who arrive with urgent problems, generally without appointment. A follow-up attendance is any reattendance which does not involve appointments with a consultant or a member of his/her firm.

TABLE 4.12 AND TABLE 4.14

Programmes of Care are divisions of health care into which activity and finance data are assigned. They provide a common framework by which to plan and monitor the health service. There are nine Programmes of Care in total – only those relevant to hospital activity are included in the table. Available beds refer to hospital beds in wards open overnight.

TABLE 4.12

The number of hospital discharges and deaths are shown according to Programme of Care for those patients admitted with the intention of staying overnight. Day cases are patients who do not require the use of a hospital bed overnight.

TABLE 4.13

An outpatient is a patient who attends a clinic to see a consultant, a member of his/her firm, or a locum for such a member. This table shows the number of outpatient attendances, non-attendances and clinic sessions in each financial year. A consultant initiated outpatient attendance is an attendance initiated by the consultant or a member of his/her staff; a referral is an attendance that has not been initiated by the consultant in charge of the clinic or his/her staff. Most referrals are seen as a consequence of a GP written referral request. Other sources of referral include self-referrals and requests from other consultants and staff in Accident and Emergency Departments.

TABLE 4.15

Residential homes refer to accommodation staffed 24 hours a day, providing board and general care to residents. Such premises are provided for vulnerable persons who require supervision in circumstances where nursing care would normally be inappropriate.

Statutory homes are those provided by Health and Social Services Trusts under the provisions of the Health and Personal Social Services (Quality, Improvement and Regulation) (NI) Order 2003. Voluntary homes and private homes are those registered as homes for persons in need, in accordance with the Health and Personal Social Services (Quality, Improvement and Regulation) (NI) Order 2003.

Voluntary organisation means any association carrying on or proposing to carry on activities otherwise than for the purpose of gain by the association or by individuals thereof. Dual registered homes are homes registered to provide both residential care and nursing care. Only residential places within such homes are included in the table.

Data relate to the average number of available places during the year. Average occupied places are only collected for statutory homes.

TABLE 4.16

The table shows the total number of persons either receiving home help or meals on wheels or registered at statutory day care facilities at 31 March each year. Some clients who receive home help as part of a domiciliary care package have been excluded from the totals. Day care facilities include adult training/social education/resource centres, workshops and day centres. Data for day centres may include some clients who have been allocated to more than one Programme of Care.

TABLE 4.17

A child is looked after by a Trust if he/she is in their care or if he/she is provided with accommodation for a continuous period of more than 24 hours by the Trust in exercise of its Social Services function.

A Child Protection Register must be maintained by each Trust, listing every child in the Trust who has been abused or is considered to be at risk of abuse, and who is currently the subject of a child protection plan.

Unless otherwise stated, figures relate to the position at 31 March each year.

5 Education and Training

- Compared with England and Wales, higher proportions of NI pupils achieved two or more A levels and five or more GCSEs at grades A*-C in 2003/04. A lower proportion of NI pupils achieved no GCSE passes in the same year.

- In 2004/05, there were just over 337,000 pupils in NI grant-aided and independent schools. The number of pupils in nursery and post-primary schools in 2004/05 was higher than in 1994/95, whilst the number of primary school pupils has been declining since 1995/96.

- There were just under 19,000 full-time teachers in NI grant-aided and independent schools in 2004/05.

- Pupil:teacher ratios are lowest in special schools (5.8) and highest in nursery schools (25.7). Compared with England, Northern Ireland had a lower pupil:teacher ratio in 2004/05 for both primary and secondary schools.

- In 2003/04, higher education students accounted for 11% of all students in Further Education Colleges, up from 6% in 1993/94.

- Between 2001/02 and 2003/04, there was a 5% increase in the number of NI domiciled students at UK Higher Education Institutions. During the same period, the number of students studying Higher Education courses at NI Institutions also increased by around 5%.

- **The most popular subject areas for NI domiciled students who achieved undergraduate qualifications in 2003/04 were: Subjects Allied to Medicine (20%), Business and Administrative Studies (16%), and Social Studies (10%). The most popular subject areas for NI domiciled students who achieved postgraduate qualifications in 2003/04 were: Education (34%), Subjects Allied to Medicine and Business and Administrative Studies (both 11%).**

- **Of those students for whom Destinations data was returned in 2002/03, 67% of NI domiciled undergraduate qualifiers entered employment. The corresponding UK proportion was 71%, while 45% of students at ROI institutions entered employment. In the same period, 85% of NI domiciled postgraduate qualifiers entered employment, compared with 86% of UK domiciled and 77% of postgraduate qualifiers at ROI institutions.**

- **In 2003/04, among students enrolled on vocational courses at NI Further Education Colleges, the most popular Science subjects were: Mathematical and Computing Sciences (46%), and Architecture, Building and Planning (20%). The most popular Arts subjects were: Business and Administrative Studies (43%), and Creative Arts and Design (19%).**

Highest qualifications of school leavers by gender[1,2], 1992/93 to 2003/04

5.1

Numbers

Gender and qualification level	1992/93	1993/94	1994/95	1995/96	1996/97	1997/98	1998/99	1999/00	2000/01	2001/02	2003/04
Males											
2 or more 'A' levels (or equivalent)[3]	3,031	3,158	3,288	3,236	3,588	3,642	3,654	3,708	3,916	3,949	4,507
1 'A' level	318	341	314	249	257	249	214	177	197	196	254
5 or more GCSE grades A*-C (or equivalent)[4]	1,534	1,771	2,133	2,178	2,462	2,419	2,469	2,456	2,357	2,328	2,283
1-4 GCSE grades A*-C (or equivalent)[4]	3,245	3,309	3,095	3,472	3,256	3,254	3,132	2,977	2,904	2,890	2,819
Other grades (1+ D-G)[5]	2,186	2,413	2,767	2,790	2,534	2,368	2,673	2,685	2,444	2,413	2,262
No GCSEs	1,006	963	946	657	1,020	908	839	893	1,003	1,035	951
All male leavers	**11,320**	**11,955**	**12,543**	**13,054**[6]	**13,117**	**12,840**	**12,981**	**12,896**	**12,821**	**12,811**	**13,076**
Females											
2 or more 'A' levels (or equivalent)[3]	3,799	4,002	4,262	4,524	4,768	5,224	5,278	5,216	5,489	5,810	6,337
1 'A' level	397	357	344	337	272	240	211	184	227	270	237
5 or more GCSE grades A*-C (or equivalent)[4]	1,971	2,209	2,629	2,686	2,622	2,722	2,683	2,519	2,405	2,128	1,948
1-4 GCSE grades A*-C (or equivalent)[4]	2,765	2,850	2,676	2,893	2,729	2,606	2,464	2,379	2,301	2,221	2,245
Other grades (1+ D-G)[5]	1,478	1,521	1,670	1,619	1,638	1,540	1,473	1,469	1,460	1,353	1,319
No GCSEs	586	461	409	291	571	457	331	416	459	411	488
All female leavers	**10,996**	**11,400**	**11,990**	**12,620**[6]	**12,600**	**12,789**	**12,440**	**12,183**	**12,341**	**12,193**	**12,574**
Persons											
2 or more 'A' levels (or equivalent)[3]	**6,830**	**7,160**	**7,550**	**7,760**	**8,356**	**8,866**	**8,932**	**8,924**	**9,405**	**9,759**	**10,844**
1 'A' level	**715**	**698**	**658**	**586**	**529**	**489**	**425**	**361**	**424**	**466**	**491**
5 or more GCSE grades A*-C (or equivalent)[4]	**3,505**	**3,980**	**4,762**	**4,864**	**5,084**	**5,141**	**5,152**	**4,975**	**4,762**	**4,456**	**4,231**
1-4 GCSE grades A*-C (or equivalent)[4]	**6,010**	**6,159**	**5,771**	**6,365**	**5,985**	**5,860**	**5,596**	**5,356**	**5,205**	**5,111**	**5,064**
Other grades (1+ D-G)[5]	**3,664**	**3,934**	**4,437**	**4,409**	**4,172**	**3,908**	**4,146**	**4,154**	**3,904**	**3,766**	**3,581**
No GCSEs	**1,592**	**1,424**	**1,355**	**948**	**1,591**	**1,365**	**1,170**	**1,309**	**1,462**	**1,446**	**1,439**
All school leavers	**22,316**	**23,355**	**24,533**	**25,674**[6]	**25,717**	**25,629**	**25,421**	**25,079**	**25,162**	**25,004**	**25,650**

Source: Department of Education

1 Excludes special and independent schools.

2 As a result of technical problems with new software installed in schools, 2002/03 School Leavers statistics are not available.

3 Includes Advanced General National Vocational Qualifications.

4 Includes General Certificate of Secondary Education (GCSE) grades A*-C only and Intermediate General National Vocational Qualifications.

5 Includes General Certificate of Secondary Education (GCSE) grades D-G only and Foundation General National Vocational Qualifications.

6 Includes leavers for whom qualification data were missing. Qualification data were missing for 472 males and 270 females.

Figure 5.1 Highest qualifications of school leavers, 1992/93 to 2003/04

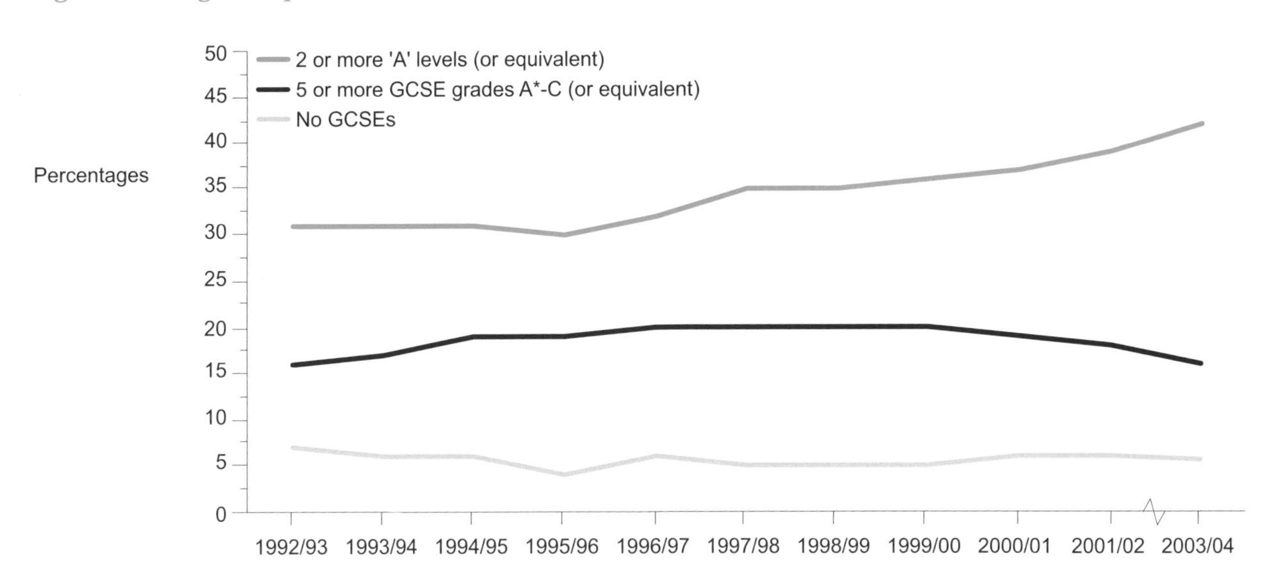

Source: Department of Education

5.2 School performance comparisons: Northern Ireland[1], England and Wales, 1998/99 to 2003/04

Percentages

Qualification level and region	1998/99	1999/00[2]	2000/01[2]	2001/02[3]	2002/03[3]	2003/04[3]
2 or more 'A' levels[4]						
Northern Ireland	92	93	93	95	95	96
England	86	87	89	93	93	94
Wales	91	92	93	94	94	95
5 or more GCSEs (A*-C)[5]						
Northern Ireland	56	57	57	59	59	60
England	48	49	50	52	53	54
Wales	48	49	50	50	51	51
5 or more GCSEs (A*-G)[5]						
Northern Ireland	87	87	87	87	87	88
England	88	89	89	89	89	89
Wales	83	85	85	85	85	85
No GCSEs[5]						
Northern Ireland	3	4	4	4	4	4
England	6	6	5	5	5	5
Wales	8	8	8	8	7	7

Sources: Department of Education; Department for Education and Skills; National Assembly for Wales

[1] Excludes special and independent schools in Northern Ireland.

[2] 'A' Level figures for 1999/00 and 2000/01 for Northern Ireland are from the University of Bath GCE Database. All other 'A' Level figures for Northern Ireland are taken from the Summary of Annual Examination Results.

[3] From 2001/02 onwards, 'A' Level figures for Northern Ireland, England and Wales include Advanced Vocational Certificates of Education (VCEs). Also included in this section are those pupils aged 17 in Wales and year 14 in Northern Ireland who obtained 'AS' Levels and who did not sit the 'A2' Modules of these subjects. In this respect 2 'AS' Levels are equivalent to 1 'A' Level.

[4] 'A' Level figures are expressed as a percentage of pupils in the final year of an 'A' Level course in Northern Ireland; as a percentage of all 16-18 year olds in schools entered for at least one 'A' Level in summer of the academic year in England; and as a percentage of all candidates entered for 2 or more 'A' Levels in Wales.

[5] GCSE figures are expressed as a percentage of pupils in year 12 in Northern Ireland, and as a percentage of 15 year olds in England and Wales.

Pupils in schools and children in pre-school education centres, 1994/95 to 2004/05

5.3

Numbers

	1994/95	1995/96	1996/97	1997/98	1998/99	1999/00	2000/01	2001/02	2002/03	2003/04	2004/05
Pre-school education centres[1]	.	.	.	.	**1,945**	**3,407**	**3,957**	**5,340**	**5,804**	**5,913**	**5,952**
Grant-aided schools											
Nursery	5,334	5,411	5,496	5,533	5,501	5,952	5,965	6,093	6,269	6,238	6,121
Primary	186,642	187,336	186,809	184,466	181,714	178,956	177,629	176,340	174,151	171,561	169,422
Secondary	89,534	90,426	90,746	90,858	91,752	92,603	92,979	92,760	92,645	92,047	90,085
Grammar											
- preparatory	3,596	3,451	3,399	3,378	3,189	3,023	2,818	2,699	2,651	2,606	2,576
- secondary	60,502	61,150	61,997	62,236	62,192	62,361	62,574	62,743	63,102	63,347	63,364
Special	4,562	4,648	4,680	4,681	4,675	4,688	4,674	4,710	4,879	4,834	4,669
Hospital schools	203	176	178	197	180	173	171	246	236	298	317
All grant-aided schools	**350,373**	**352,598**	**353,305**	**351,349**	**349,203**	**347,756**	**346,810**	**345,591**	**343,933**	**340,931**	**336,554**
Independent schools	**941**	**1,044**	**925**	**1,213**	**1,346**	**1,243**	**1,255**	**1,072**	**948**	**835**	**802**

Source: Department of Education

[1] Voluntary and private centres funded under the Pre-school Education Expansion Programme, which began in 1998/99.

Full-time teachers in grant-aided and independent schools by type of school, 1994/95 to 2004/05

5.4

Numbers

Type of school	1994/95	1995/96	1996/97	1997/98	1998/99	1999/00	2000/01	2001/02	2002/03	2003/04[1]	2004/05[1]
Grant-aided schools											
Nursery	168	169	170	169	166	176	177	176	183	188	185
Primary	8,402	8,441	8,407	8,323	8,114	8,010	7,888	7,873	7,779	7,688	7,581
Secondary	6,124	6,227	6,236	6,108	6,111	6,168	6,268	6,236	6,187	6,129	6,099
Grammar											
- preparatory	169	169	173	161	161	154	147	138	132	135	130
- secondary	3,652	3,720	3,787	3,790	3,811	3,834	3,896	3,891	3,881	3,925	3,909
Special	622	651	678	659	668	709	719	705	724	729	717
Hospital schools	26	25	25	26	25	24	23	24	23	24	22
All grant-aided schools	**19,163**	**19,402**	**19,476**	**19,236**	**19,056**	**19,075**	**19,118**	**19,043**	**18,909**	**18,818**	**18,643**
Independent schools	**87**	**83**	**96**	**120**	**111**	**117**	**116**	**100**	**101**	**88**	**83**

Source: Department of Education

[1] Since 2003/04, the teacher figures were compiled on a new, improved basis - the figures for Nursery, Primary, Secondary and Special Schools were extracted from the Teachers' Payroll System and sent to schools to be verified. These figures are not comparable with previous years.

5.5 Pupil:teacher ratios in grant-aided schools by type of school, 1994/95 to 2004/05

Ratios

Type of school	1994/95	1995/96	1996/97	1997/98	1998/99	1999/00	2000/01	2001/02	2002/03	2003/04[1]	2004/05[1]
Nursery	*24.8*	*24.1*	*23.8*	*24.5*	*23.7*	*25.3*	*24.4*	*24.4*	*24.1*	*25.2*	*25.7*
Primary	*21.2*	*20.7*	*20.5*	*20.4*	*20.6*	*20.4*	*20.2*	*19.9*	*19.7*	*20.0*	*20.0*
Secondary	*14.3*	*14.1*	*14.0*	*14.2*	*14.3*	*14.1*	*13.9*	*13.8*	*13.8*	*14.1*	*13.8*
Grammar											
- preparatory	*19.8*	*18.3*	*18.0*	*18.7*	*17.3*	*17.5*	*16.6*	*16.9*	*17.2*	*17.0*	*17.3*
- secondary	*16.2*	*16.0*	*16.0*	*15.8*	*15.7*	*15.6*	*15.4*	*15.3*	*15.3*	*15.2*	*15.2*
Special	*7.0*	*6.7*	*6.5*	*6.8*	*6.5*	*6.2*	*5.9*	*5.9*	*6.0*	*5.9*	*5.8*
All grant-aided schools[2]	***17.6***	***17.3***	***17.1***	***17.1***	***17.2***	***16.9***	***16.7***	***16.5***	***16.4***	***16.6***	***16.5***

Source: Department of Educatio

[1] Since 2003/04, the teacher figures used for pupil:teacher ratios calculation were compiled on a new, improved basis - the figures for Nursery, Primary, Secondary and Special Schools were extracted from the Teachers' Payroll System and sent to schools to be verified. These figures are not comparable with previous years.

[2] Excludes hospital schools.

Figure 5.2 Pupil:teacher ratios in grant-aided schools by type of school, 2004/05

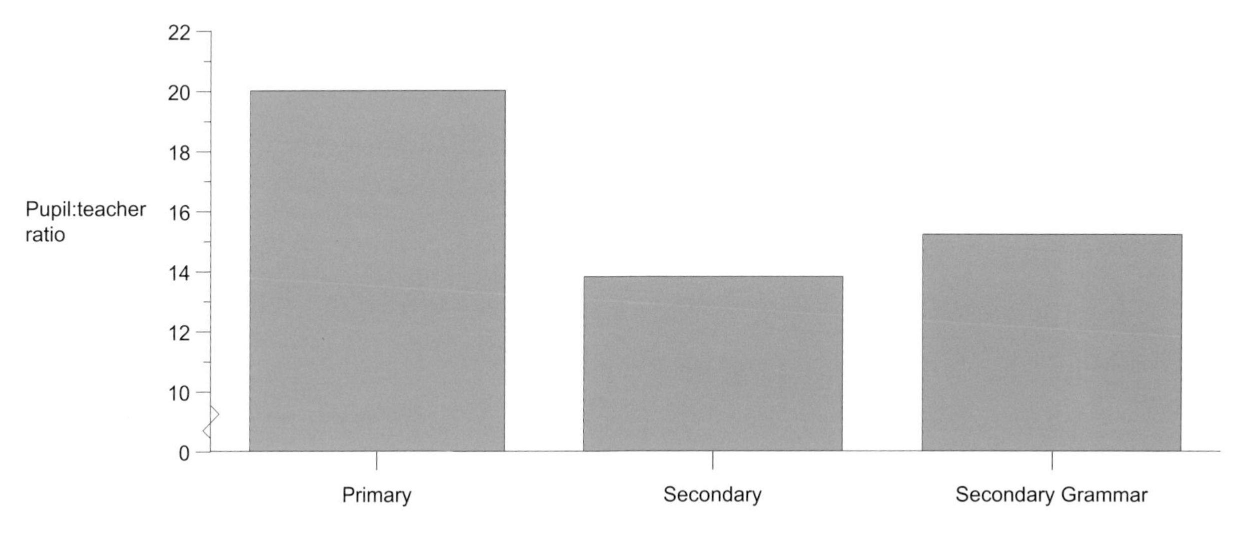

Source: Department of Education

5.6 Pupil:teacher ratios in Northern Ireland, Republic of Ireland and England by type of school, 2004/05

Ratios

Type of school	Northern Ireland	Republic of Ireland[1]	England
Primary[2]	*20.0*	*18.0*	*22.5*[P]
Secondary[3,4,5]	*14.3*	*15.4*	*16.8*[P]

Sources: Department of Education; Department of Education and Science; Department for Education and Skills

[1] Figures for the Republic of Ireland refer to 2002/03.

[2] Includes Special Schools in the Republic of Ireland.

[3] Includes Grammar Schools.

[4] Teachers and students in sixth form colleges are not included in the figure for England.

[5] Figures for the Republic of Ireland are for full-time teachers only and do not include full-time equivalent of part-time teachers for ratio calculations.

Figure 5.3 Pupil:teacher ratios in grant-aided schools by type of school and region/country, 2004/05

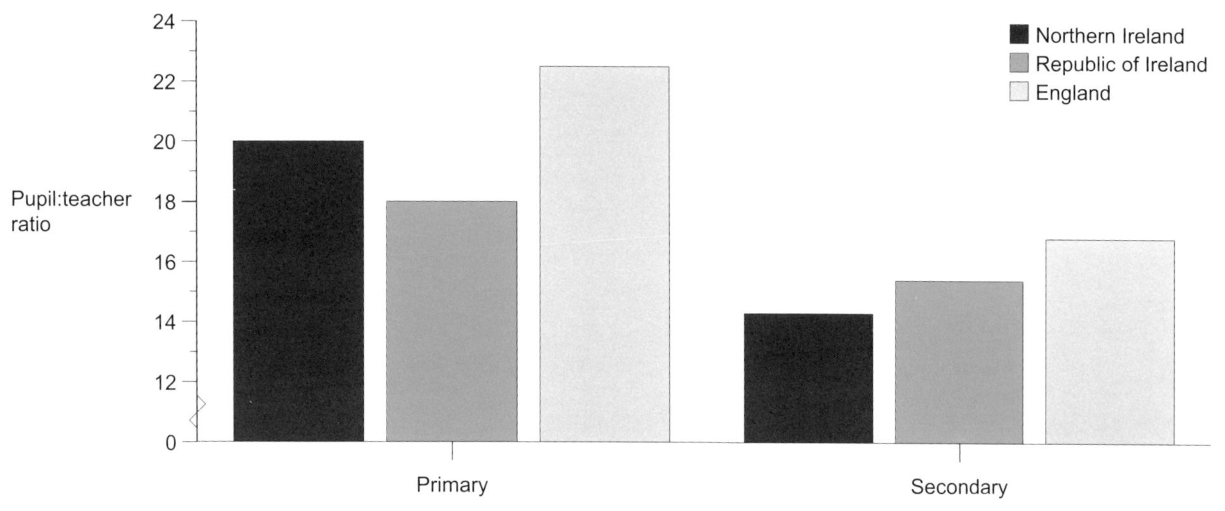

Sources: Department of Education; Department of Education and Science; Department for Education and Skills

5.7 Number of schools and pre-school education centres, 1994/95 to 2004/05

Numbers

	1994/95	1995/96	1996/97	1997/98	1998/99	1999/00	2000/01	2001/02	2002/03	2003/04	2004/05
Pre-school education centres[1]	.	.	.	.	**190**	**268**	**305**	**360**	**363**	**383**	**365**
Grant-aided schools											
Nursery	91	91	91	91	91	95	95	96	100	100	99
Primary	938	923	920	920	916	917	902	899	897	892	894
Secondary	161	165	167	166	165	166	166	164	164	163	162
Grammar											
- preparatory[2]	(25)	(25)	(25)	(25)	(24)	(24)	(22)	(21)	(20)	(19)	(18)
- secondary	71	71	71	72	72	72	72	71	71	70	70
Special	47	47	47	47	47	50	48	48	47	47	45
Hospital schools	3	3	3	3	3	3	3	3	3	3	3
All grant-aided schools	**1,311**	**1,300**	**1,299**	**1,299**	**1,294**	**1,303**	**1,286**	**1,281**	**1,282**	**1,275**	**1,273**
Independent schools	**20**	**21**	**19**	**22**	**22**	**22**	**27**	**25**	**22**	**17**	**17**

Source: Department of Education

[1] Voluntary and private centres funded under the Pre-School Education Expansion Programme, which began in 1998/99.

[2] Figures shown in brackets are included in the Grammar secondary totals.

5.8 Enrolments[1] in NI Further Education Colleges by gender and full-time/part-time status and lecturers employed by full-time/part-time status, 1993/94 to 2003/04

Numbers

Status and gender	1993/94	1994/95	1995/96	1996/97	1997/98	1998/99	1999/00	2000/01	2001/02	2002/03[2]	2003/04[3]
Male students											
Full-time											
Higher	839	1,141	1,256	1,438	1,421	1,350	1,539	1,635	1,773	1,687	1,624
Further	10,468	10,447	10,485	11,057	11,380	10,711	10,764	11,789	12,089	12,273	12,962
Part-time											
Higher	2,102	2,020	2,097	2,414	2,763	2,729	3,086	3,237	3,195	3,005	2,983
Further	21,137	19,057	18,537	18,824	18,884	19,389	20,733	20,811	21,402	19,786	25,576
All males											
Higher	**2,941**	**3,161**	**3,353**	**3,852**	**4,184**	**4,079**	**4,625**	**4,872**	**4,968**	**4,692**	**4,607**
Further	**31,605**	**29,504**	**29,022**	**29,881**	**30,264**	**30,100**	**31,497**	**32,600**	**33,491**	**32,059**	**38,538**
Female students											
Full-time											
Higher	742	1,230	1,699	1,895	1,880	1,908	1,870	1,941	1,968	1,675	1,813
Further	11,076	10,857	10,494	10,643	10,287	9,885	9,955	9,177	9,333	9,191	10,391
Part-time											
Higher	1,372	1,745	2,397	2,966	3,884	3,892	4,888	5,207	5,613	5,206	5,058
Further	33,787	32,756	32,848	35,865	35,170	36,436	36,544	37,512	37,043	34,203	40,430
All females											
Higher	**2,114**	**2,975**	**4,096**	**4,861**	**5,764**	**5,800**	**6,758**	**7,148**	**7,581**	**6,881**	**6,871**
Further	**44,863**	**43,613**	**43,342**	**46,508**	**45,457**	**46,321**	**46,499**	**46,689**	**46,376**	**43,394**	**50,821**
Lecturers employed[4, 5]											
Full-time	2,209	2,171	2,156	2,144	2,064	2,867	2,031	1,814	1,815	1,770	2,212
Part-time	2,562	3,205	3,154	2,780	2,647	1,974	3,086	3,266	3,113	3,096	3,099
All lecturers	**4,771**	**5,376**	**5,310**	**4,924**	**4,711**	**4,841**	**5,117**	**5,080**	**4,928**	**4,866**	**5,311**

Source: Department for Employment and Learning

1 Enrolments on vocational courses on 1 November in each academic year.

2 From 1993/94 to 2001/02, figures include students and lecturers from the Northern Ireland Hotel and Catering College. On 1 August 2002, the college merged with the University of Ulster. From 2002/03, therefore, data includes only the remaining 16 Further Education colleges.

3 In 2003/04, a new Management Information System (MIS) was implemented across the 16 Further Education colleges. For some courses a different reporting methodology is used, therefore caution should be exercised when comparing 2003/04 data with previous years.

4 All lecturing staff employed in the Further Education colleges in Northern Ireland on 1 November of that year, including those on temporary contracts of employment.

5 From 1998/99 associate lecturers are classed as full-time regardless of hours worked.

Enrolments on Higher Education courses by type of enrolment and region of Institution[1], 2001/02 to 2003/04

5.9

Numbers

Type of enrolment	NI domiciles at UK Institutions[2]			All domiciles at NI Institutions		
	2001/02	2002/03	2003/04	2001/02	2002/03	2003/04
First Degree						
Full-time	33,353	35,179	36,955	24,761	26,829	28,570
Part-time	5,278	5,233	7,561	5,199	5,080	5,384
All first degrees	**38,631**	**40,412**	**44,516**	**29,960**	**31,909**	**33,954**
Other undergraduate						
Full-time	6,391	6,026	5,035	6,434	6,056	5,019
Part-time	17,764	16,974	16,275	14,892	14,160	14,926
All other undergraduates	**24,155**	**23,000**	**21,310**	**21,326**	**20,216**	**19,945**
All undergraduate						
Full-time	**39,744**	**41,205**	**41,990**	**31,195**	**32,885**	**33,589**
Part-time	**23,042**	**22,207**	**23,836**	**20,091**	**19,240**	**20,310**
All undergraduates	**62,786**	**63,412**	**65,826**	**51,286**	**52,125**	**53,899**
Postgraduate						
Full-time	4,025	4,085	4,087	4,188	4,194	4,077
Part-time	6,982	7,111	7,226	7,249	7,502	7,694
All postgraduates	**11,007**	**11,196**	**11,313**	**11,437**	**11,696**	**11,771**
All enrolment types						
Full-time	**43,769**	**45,290**	**46,077**	**35,383**	**37,079**	**37,666**
Part-time	**30,024**	**29,318**	**31,062**	**27,340**	**26,742**	**28,004**
All enrolments	**73,793**	**74,608**	**77,139**	**62,723**	**63,821**	**65,670**

Sources: Department for Employment and Learning; Higher Education Statistics Agency

[1] The figures in this table have been revised from those previously published. This is due to a change from a census count to a full year count of students.

[2] Includes NI domiciled students enrolled on Higher Education courses at Higher Education institutions in the UK and Higher Education courses at NI Further Education colleges. It excludes NI domiciled students enrolled on Higher Education courses at GB Further Education colleges and at ROI institutions.

5.10 Northern Ireland domiciled students gaining Higher Education qualifications at UK Higher Education Institutions, 2003/04

Numbers

Postgraduate[3] qualifications	Higher degrees[1]			Other postgraduate[2]			**All postgraduate**		
	Male	Female	**All persons**	Male	Female	**All persons**	**Male**	**Female**	**All persons**
Medicine & Dentistry	30	20	**50**	5	5	**10**	**40**	**25**	**60**
Subjects Allied to Medicine	50	115	**160**	40	230	**270**	**90**	**345**	**435**
Biological Sciences	45	65	**110**	10	30	**40**	**55**	**95**	**150**
Veterinary Science	0	0	**0**	0	0	**0**	**0**	**0**	**5**
Agriculture & Related Subjects	20	15	**35**	5	10	**20**	**25**	**30**	**55**
Physical Sciences	50	35	**85**	5	5	**10**	**55**	**40**	**95**
Mathematical Sciences	5	5	**10**	0	0	**5**	**10**	**5**	**10**
Computer Sciences	105	65	**170**	55	30	**85**	**160**	**95**	**255**
Engineering & Technology	75	20	**90**	15	5	**25**	**90**	**25**	**115**
Architecture, Building & Planning	25	15	**40**	60	50	**110**	**85**	**60**	**150**
Social Studies	70	115	**185**	10	50	**65**	**80**	**165**	**245**
Law	35	30	**65**	85	130	**215**	**115**	**160**	**275**
Business & Administrative Studies	170	190	**360**	40	60	**100**	**215**	**250**	**460**
Mass Communication & Documentation	15	50	**70**	10	25	**30**	**25**	**75**	**100**
Languages	35	45	**80**	5	10	**15**	**40**	**55**	**95**
Historical & Philosophical Studies	35	25	**65**	5	5	**10**	**40**	**35**	**75**
Creative Arts & Design	20	20	**40**	10	10	**15**	**30**	**30**	**60**
Education	45	80	**125**	345	885	**1,230**	**390**	**965**	**1,355**
Combined	10	5	**15**	15	10	**20**	**25**	**15**	**40**
All postgraduate qualifications	**845**	**910**	**1,755**	**720**	**1,545**	**2,270**	**1,565**	**2,460**	**4,025**

Undergraduate qualifications	First degree[4]			Other undergraduate[5]			**All undergraduate**		
	Male	Female	**All persons**	Male	Female	**All persons**	**Male**	**Female**	**All persons**
Medicine & Dentistry	140	210	**345**	0	25	**25**	**140**	**230**	**375**
Subjects Allied to Medicine	190	985	**1,170**	75	1,335	**1,415**	**265**	**2,320**	**2,585**
Biological Sciences	230	460	**690**	35	35	**65**	**260**	**495**	**755**
Veterinary Science	10	10	**20**	0	0	**0**	**10**	**10**	**20**
Agriculture & Related Subjects	25	75	**100**	5	0	**10**	**30**	**75**	**105**
Physical Sciences	140	150	**290**	10	5	**15**	**150**	**150**	**305**
Mathematical Sciences	50	85	**135**	10	5	**15**	**60**	**90**	**150**
Computer Sciences	455	190	**645**	190	90	**280**	**645**	**280**	**925**
Engineering & Technology	425	100	**530**	55	15	**65**	**480**	**115**	**595**
Architecture, Building & Planning	270	100	**370**	10	5	**15**	**280**	**105**	**385**
Social Studies	285	615	**900**	95	250	**345**	**380**	**860**	**1,245**
Law	160	240	**400**	5	0	**5**	**165**	**245**	**405**
Business & Administrative Studies	595	1,015	**1,610**	150	250	**400**	**745**	**1,265**	**2,005**
Mass Communication & Documentation	75	125	**195**	5	5	**5**	**75**	**125**	**205**
Languages	125	375	**495**	55	60	**115**	**180**	**435**	**610**
Historical & Philosophical Studies	190	225	**415**	25	35	**60**	**215**	**260**	**475**
Creative Arts & Design	215	350	**565**	50	110	**160**	**265**	**460**	**725**
Education	85	455	**540**	40	35	**75**	**125**	**490**	**615**
Combined	45	45	**90**	20	20	**40**	**65**	**65**	**125**
All undergraduate qualifications	**3,705**	**5,805**	**9,510**	**835**	**2,270**	**3,105**	**4,540**	**8,075**	**12,615**

Sources: Department for Employment and Learning; Higher Education Statistics Agency

[1] Higher degrees include doctorates, masters degrees and higher bachelor degrees.

[2] Other postgraduate includes postgraduate diplomas, certificates and professional qualifications, PGCEs and Institutional postgraduate credits.

[3] Postgraduate courses are those leading to higher degrees, diplomas and certificates (including PGCEs and professional qualifications) which usually require a first degree as an entry qualification.

[4] First degrees include first degrees, first degrees with qualified teacher status, enhanced first degrees, first degrees obtained concurrently with a diploma and intercalated first degrees.

[5] Other undergraduate includes all Higher Education courses not included above, i.e. foundation degrees, HNC and undergraduate certificates.

Destinations of full-time NI domiciled and UK domiciled leavers from UK Institutions and first destinations of students who graduated from Higher Education courses at ROI institutions in 2002/03[1]

5.11

Numbers and percentages

	NI domiciled at UK Institutions				
	Undergraduate		Postgraduate		**Total**
Entered employment	4,871	*67.3*	1,479	*84.7*	**6,350**
Undertaking study or training	1,544	*21.3*	133	*7.6*	**1,677**
Not available for employment, study or training	315	*4.4*	41	*2.3*	**356**
Assumed to be unemployed	371	*5.1*	55	*3.1*	**426**
Other	132	*1.8*	39	*2.2*	**171**
All graduates	**7,233**	***100.0***	**1,747**	***100.0***	**8,980**
	UK domiciled at UK Institutions				
	Undergraduate		Postgraduate		**Total**
Entered employment	140,938	*71.0*	33,192	*85.8*	**174,130**
Undertaking study or training	32,499	*16.4*	2,868	*7.4*	**35,367**
Not available for employment, study or training	9,868	*5.0*	958	*2.5*	**10,826**
Assumed to be unemployed	13,135	*6.6*	1,429	*3.7*	**14,564**
Other	1,926	*1.0*	232	*0.6*	**2,158**
All graduates	**198,366**	***100.0***	**38,679**	***100.0***	**237,045**
	Students at ROI Institutions				
	Undergraduate		Postgraduate		**Total**
Entered employment	9,778	*44.8*	4,239	*77.0*	**14,017**
Undertaking study or training	10,366	*47.5*	691	*12.6*	**11,057**
Not available for employment, study or training	1,025	*4.7*	314	*5.7*	**1,339**
Assumed to be unemployed	658	*3.0*	260	*4.7*	**918**
Other	0	*0.0*	0	*0.0*	**0**
All graduates	**21,827**	***100.0***	**5,504**	***100.0***	**27,331**

Sources: Higher Education Statistics Agency; Higher Education Authority

[1] The reference date for first destinations data for UK (including NI) students is 15 January 2004, whereas for students at ROI institutions the reference date is 30 April 2004. The ROI data refers to the Higher Education Authority sector (i.e. the seven universities, two teacher training colleges, the National College of Art and Design and the Royal College of Surgeons), the Technological Sector (i.e. Institutes of Technology) and other designated affiliates.

5.12 Enrolments[1] on vocational courses at NI Further Education Colleges by subject group, gender and full-time/part-time status, 2003/04

Numbers

	Males			Females			All persons		
	Full-time	Part-time	**All males**	Full-time	Part-time	**All females**	**Full-time**	**Part-time**	**All persons**
Science Subjects									
Mathematical & Computing Sciences	1,951	5,377	**7,328**	645	8,977	**9,622**	**2,596**	**14,354**	**16,950**
Engineering & Technology	2,508	3,781	**6,289**	84	323	**407**	**2,592**	**4,104**	**6,696**
Architecture, Building & Planning	4,196	2,961	**7,157**	70	215	**285**	**4,266**	**3,176**	**7,442**
Allied to Medicine	83	376	**459**	1,725	2,174	**3,899**	**1,808**	**2,550**	**4,358**
Agriculture & Related	37	454	**491**	121	710	**831**	**158**	**1,164**	**1,322**
Physical Sciences	17	135	**152**	32	180	**212**	**49**	**315**	**364**
Medicine & Dentistry	0	0	**0**	0	36	**36**	**0**	**36**	**36**
Biological Sciences	6	1	**7**	4	24	**28**	**10**	**25**	**35**
All Science enrolments	**8,798**	**13,085**	**21,883**	**2,681**	**12,639**	**15,320**	**11,479**	**25,724**	**37,203**
Arts Subjects									
Business & Administrative Studies	1,768	4,845	**6,613**	2,983	10,383	**13,366**	**4,751**	**15,228**	**19,979**
Creative Arts & Design	823	721	**1,544**	2,817	4,550	**7,367**	**3,640**	**5,271**	**8,911**
Social Studies	167	552	**719**	1,565	4,114	**5,679**	**1,732**	**4,666**	**6,398**
Education	826	2,589	**3,415**	336	3,254	**3,590**	**1,162**	**5,843**	**7,005**
Languages etc.	0	1,403	**1,403**	0	1,988	**1,988**	**0**	**3,391**	**3,391**
Mass Communication & Documentation	518	102	**620**	291	101	**392**	**809**	**203**	**1,012**
Humanities	0	0	**0**	0	0	**0**	**0**	**0**	**0**
All Arts enrolments	**4,102**	**10,212**	**14,314**	**7,992**	**24,390**	**32,382**	**12,094**	**34,602**	**46,696**
Other Subjects									
Combined & General	**1,686**	**5,262**	**6,948**	**1,531**	**8,459**	**9,990**	**3,217**	**13,721**	**16,938**
All enrolments	**14,586**	**28,559**	**43,145**	**12,204**	**45,488**	**57,692**	**26,790**	**74,047**	**100,837**

Source: Department for Employment and Learning

[1] Enrolments on vocational courses on 1 November 2003.

Notes to Education and Training tables

TABLE 5.1

The data are from the Annual School Leavers Survey. This survey covers all school leavers in Northern Ireland and collects data on their highest level of qualification and post school destination.

TABLE 5.2

The figures are taken from the annual Summary of Annual Examination Results survey. The survey covers all post primary schools with pupils in the last year of compulsory education. They relate mainly to public examination achievements.

TABLE 5.3

The figures are taken from the annual school census. The census covers all schools in Northern Ireland and collects a wide range of data relating to pupils.

TABLE 5.4, 5.5 AND 5.6

Prior to 2003/04 the figures for nursery, primary, secondary (non-grammar), and special schools were extracted from the computerised teachers' payroll system, whilst the figures for grammar schools were obtained from a statistical return completed by the schools. Since 2003/04, the grammar school figures continued to be obtained from a statistical return completed by the schools, but each nursery, primary, secondary (non-grammar) and special school has been sent a list of teachers from the computerised teachers' payroll system and asked to verify the data. Data, since 2003/04, in tables 5.4, 5.5 and 5.6 is compiled on this new (verified) basis.

The pupil:teacher ratio is the number of full-time equivalent pupils divided by the number of full-time equivalent teachers.

TABLES 5.8 AND 5.12

The statistics in these tables have been derived from the Further Education Statistical Record (FESR), a computerised return consisting of an individual record for each enrolment on a vocational course in Northern Ireland Further Education Colleges.

TABLES 5.9, 5.10 AND 5.11

Domicile is defined as the location of permanent residency immediately prior to commencing study.

TABLE 5.10

A procedure of apportionment is used where students are undertaking a split programme of study, covering more than one subject area. Where this is the case, the headcount is divided in a way that reflects the pattern of the split programme. Due to some students being apportioned between different subject areas, individual figures have been rounded and the sum of numbers in each row or column may not match the total shown.

To prevent the identification of individuals, figures are rounded to the nearest 5, with 0, 1 and 2 rounded to 0.

TABLE 5.11

Destinations of leavers from Higher Education data for UK students are collected by the Higher Education Statistics Agency (HESA). The Destination of leavers from Higher Education population includes all students reported to HESA for the period 1 August 2002 to 31 July 2003 as obtaining relevant qualifications and whose study was primarily full-time (including sandwich students and those writing up theses). The information supplied regarding the destinations of graduates relates only to those who responded to the survey and not to the total number of students graduating.

Data for ROI students were supplied by the Higher Education Authority (HEA).

Of those students for whom Destinations data were expected, 84.5% of full-time NI domiciled students and 80.4% of full-time UK domiciled students had data returned to HESA. The response rate for ROI students was 59.0%.

6 Crime and Justice

- Between 2003-04 and 2004-05, the overall level of recorded crime in Northern Ireland decreased by around 8%.
- The percentage of crimes cleared by the police in Northern Ireland increased slightly from 27% in 2003-04 to 28% in 2004-05. In England and Wales, the clearance rate rose from 23% to 26% over the same period.
- There were almost one third fewer armed robberies in Northern Ireland in 2004-05 than in 2003-04. However, as a result of the December 2004 robbery of the Northern Bank Headquarters, the total amount of money stolen in 2004-05 was the highest ever recorded at almost £30 million.
- In recent years the number of shooting and bombing incidents peaked during 2001-02. Since then, the number of such incidents has been gradually falling. During 2004-05, four people died as a result of the security situation. This is the lowest figure recorded over the period 1969 to 2004-05.
- In 2003, there were over 16,000 convictions in magistrates courts for motoring offences. This was the highest number of such convictions over the period 1998 to 2003. The number of juvenile convictions for theft has generally decreased over the period 1998 to 2003, whilst the numbers of convictions for criminal damage and offences against the state have generally increased.

- For both males and females in 2003, the highest levels of convictions per 10,000 population for indictable and summary offences were amongst those aged 18-21, whilst the highest rates for motoring offences were amongst those aged 22-24.

- In 2003, immediate custody accounted for over half of all disposals at the Crown Court, whilst fines accounted for over two thirds of all disposals at the magistrates' courts.

- Over the period 1998 to 2003 the proportion of juvenile disposals accounted for by 'immediate custody' has fallen from 17% to 7%. Over the same period the proportion awarded Probation or Supervision orders has fallen from 34% to 26%, whilst the proportion of conditional discharges has generally risen from 25% to 33%.

- In 2004-05, there were high levels of seizures of Cocaine and LSD, both Class A drugs.

- In both the High Court and County Courts there has been a general fall in the proportion of divorces granted on the grounds of 'adultery' over the period 1993 to 2003. At the same time there has been a general increase in the proportion classified as 'other grounds'.

- Between 1999-2000 and 2004-05, total awards relating to criminal injury amounted to almost £268 million and criminal damage claims to almost £87 million. The number and value of awards made under criminal damage claims were much lower in 2004-05 than in 1999-00.

6.1 Notifiable offences recorded by the police by offence type[1], rates per 1,000 population and clearance rates, 2002-03 to 2004-05

Units as indicated

Offence type	2002-03 Recorded	2002-03 Clearance rate (%)	2003-04 Recorded	2003-04 Clearance rate (%)	2004-05 Recorded	2004-05 Clearance rate (%)
Northern Ireland						
Offences against the person	28,455	*51.4*	28,982	*57.0*	29,339	*53.1*
Sexual offences	1,469	*46.6*	1,780	*50.8*	1,686	*46.0*
Burglary	18,659	*9.9*	16,389	*12.2*	13,388	*14.8*
of which:						
- burglary in a dwelling	10,125	*9.7*	8,944	*11.1*	7,302	*13.4*
- burglary in a building other than a dwelling	8,409	*9.0*	7,317	*12.1*	5,965	*15.2*
Robbery	2,497	*13.4*	1,973	*14.4*	1,487	*16.7*
Theft	41,911	*14.0*	35,691	*15.9*	31,097	*17.4*
of which:						
- theft from motor vehicles	7,140	*3.4*	7,506	*4.6*	5,371	*4.4*
- theft/unauthorised taking of motor vehicles	8,410	*11.1*	5,369	*15.8*	4,456	*16.9*
Fraud and forgery	8,801	*28.4*	6,273	*32.4*	5,198	*36.0*
Criminal damage	36,571	*13.0*	32,402	*15.2*	31,432	*14.4*
Offences against the state	1,771	*33.4*	1,292	*41.6*	1,185	*45.9*
Other notifiable offences	2,362	*67.4*	3,171	*71.0*	3,312	*72.8*
of which:						
- drugs trafficking offences	291	*69.8*	405	*77.5*	375	*83.5*
- drugs non-trafficking offences	1,633	*67.7*	2,184	*70.5*	2,247	*71.8*
All offences	**142,496**	***23.0***	**127,953**	***27.4***	**118,124**	***28.2***
Rate per 1,000 population	*84.0*	.	*75.2*	.	*69.1*	.
England and Wales						
All offences (thousands)	**5,899**	***24.0***	**5,935**	***23.0***	**5,563**	***26.0***
Rate per 1,000 population	*113.3*	.	*113.1*	.	*105.1*	.

Sources: Police Service of Northern Ireland; Home Office

[1] Figures are recorded according to the National Crime Recording Standard, which was introduced on 1 April 2002.

Figure 6.1 Notifiable offences recorded by the police, rate per 1,000 population, 2002-03 to 2004-05

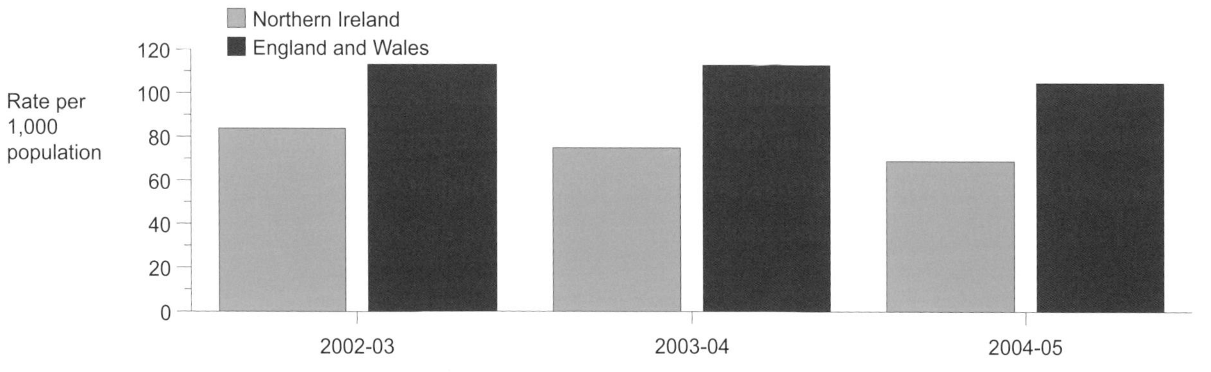

Sources: Police Service of Northern Ireland; Home Office

CRIME AND JUSTICE

Figure 6.2 Notifiable offences recorded by the police, percentage clearance rates, 2002-03 to 2004-05

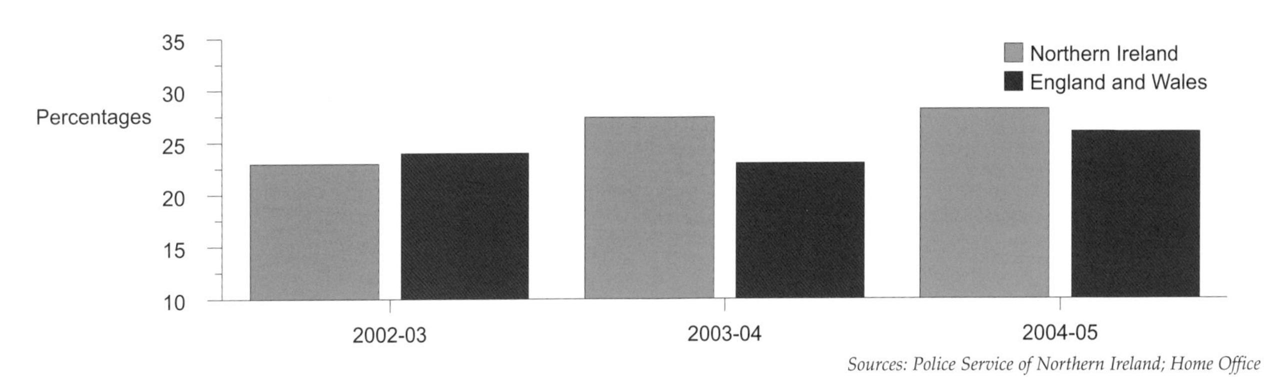

Sources: Police Service of Northern Ireland; Home Office

6.2 Security situation statistics, 1969 to 2004-05

Units as indicated

Year	Shooting incidents (number)	Bombings[1] Incidents (number)	Bombings[1] Devices used (number)	Firearms found (number)	Explosives found (kg)	Armed robberies[2] (number)	Armed robberies Amount (£000s)
1969[3]	73	..	10	14	102	..	..
1970	213	..	170	324	305	..	..
1971	1,756	..	1,515	716	1,246	489	304
1972	10,631	..	1,853	1,259	18,819	1,931	795
1973	5,019	..	1,520	1,313	17,426	1,317	612
1974	3,208	..	1,113	1,236	11,848	1,353	576
1975	1,803	..	635	820	4,996	1,325	572
1976	1,908	..	1,192	736	9,849	889	545
1977	1,081	..	535	563	1,728	676	447
1978	755	..	633	393	956	493	233
1979	728	..	564	300	905	504	568
1980	642	..	400	203	821	467	497
1981	1,142	..	529	357	3,419	689	855
1982	547	..	332	288	2,298	693	1,392
1983	424	..	367	166	1,706	718	830
1984	334	..	248	187	3,871	710	702
1985	238	..	215	173	3,344	542	656
1986	392	..	254	174	2,443	839	1,207
1987	674	..	384	206	5,885	955	1,900
1988	538	..	458	489	4,728	742	1,389
1989	566	..	420	246	1,377	604	1,079
1990	557	236	286	179	1,969	492	1,729
1991	499	312	368	164	4,167	607	1,673
1992	506	318	371	194	2,167	739	1,666
1993	476	257	289	196	3,944	643	1,515
1994	348	207	222	178	1,285	555	1,709
1995	50	2	2	118	5	421	838
1996	125	17	25	98	1,677	405	2,840
1997	225	78	93	105	1,258[r]	401	1,810
1997-98[4]	245	73	91	97	662[r]	396	1,845
1998-99	187	123	229	104	778	367	1,028
1999-00	131	66	86	110	240	432	1,687
2000-01	331	177	206	134	99	509	2,180
2001-02	358	318	407	96	96	636	7,405
2002-03	348	178	226	129	20	676	2,991
2003-04	207	71	80	148	92	485	3,034
2004-05	167	48	51	81	27	343	29,925

Source: Police Service of Northern Ireland

1 Includes explosions and defusings. An individual incident may involve more than one explosive device. Incidents involving petrol bombs, incendiaries or hoax devices are excluded.

2 Where a firearm is used or the impression of a firearm is given. Figures include attempts.

3 Statistics for 1969 are for the period August to December only.

4 From 1997-98 figures are produced on a financial year basis.

Deaths and injuries as a result of the security situation, 1969 to 2004-05

Numbers

	Deaths					Injuries				
Year	RUC/ PSNI[1]	Regular army	UDR/ RIR[2]	Civilians	**All deaths**	RUC/ PSNI[1]	Regular army	UDR/ RIR[2]	Civilians	**All injuries**
1969[3]	1	0	0	13	**14**	711	54	0	..	**765**
1970	2	0	0	23	**25**	191	620	0	..	**811**
1971	11	43	5	115	**174**	315	381	9	1,887	**2,592**
1972	17	105	26	322	**470**	485	542	36	3,813	**4,876**
1973	13	58	8	173	**252**	291	525	23	1,812	**2,651**
1974	15	30	7	168	**220**	235	453	30	1,680	**2,398**
1975	11	14	6	216	**247**	263	151	16	2,044	**2,474**
1976	23	14	15	245	**297**	303	242	22	2,162	**2,729**
1977	14	15	14	69	**112**	183	172	15	1,017	**1,387**
1978	10	14	7	50	**81**	302	127	8	548	**985**
1979	14	38	10	51	**113**	165	132	21	557	**875**
1980	9	8	9	50	**76**	194	53	24	530	**801**
1981	21	10	13	57	**101**	332	112	28	878	**1,350**
1982	12	21	7	57	**97**	99	80	18	328	**525**
1983	18	5	10	44	**77**	142	66	22	280	**510**
1984	9	9	10	36	**64**	267	64	22	513	**866**
1985	23	2	4	26	**55**	415	20	13	468	**916**
1986	12	4	8	37	**61**	622	45	10	773	**1,450**
1987	16	3	8	68	**95**	246	92	12	780	**1,130**
1988	6	21	12	55	**94**	218	211	18	600	**1,047**
1989	9	12	2	39	**62**	163	175	15	606	**959**
1990	12	7	8	49	**76**	214	190	24	478	**906**
1991	6	5	8	75	**94**	139	197	56	570	**962**
1992	3	4	2	76	**85**	148	302	18	598	**1,066**
1993	6	6	2	70	**84**	147	146	27	504	**824**
1994	3	1	2	56	**62**	170	120	6	529	**825**
1995	1	0	0	8	**9**	370	8	5	554	**937**
1996	0	1	0	14	**15**	459	53	2	905	**1,419**
1997	4	1	0	17	**22**	357	136	14	730	**1,237**
1997-98[4]	4	0	0	29	**33**	394	133	10	728	**1,265**
1998-99	1	1	0	42	**44**	452	47[r]	17	1,168	**1,684**
1999-00	0	0	0	7	**7**	356	17	16	489	**878**
2000-01	0	0	0	18	**18**	461	26	1	617	**1,105**
2001-02	0	0	0	17	**17**	931	53	12	648	**1,644**
2002-03	0	0	0	15	**15**	384	30	37	674	**1,125**
2003-04	0	0	0	7	**7**	108	12	1	644	**765**
2004-05	0	0	0	4	**4**	127	14	1	539	**681**

Source: Police Service of Northern Ireland

1 Includes Royal Ulster Constabulary Reserve/Police Service of Northern Ireland Reserve.

2 Ulster Defence Regiment/Royal Irish Regiment.

3 Statistics for 1969 deaths are for the period August to December only.

4 From 1997-98 figures are produced on a financial year basis.

Figure 6.3 Deaths as a result of the security situation, 1971 to 2004-05

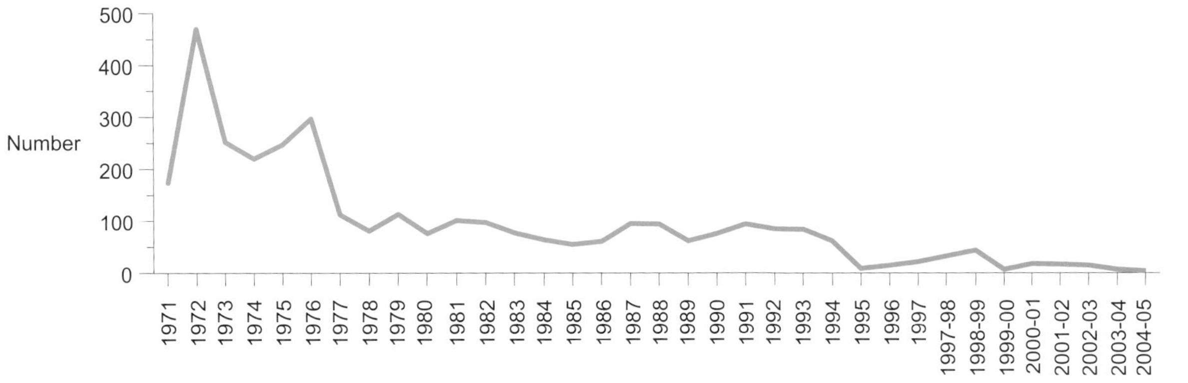

Source: Police Service of Northern Ireland

6.4 Strength of Police Service of Northern Ireland (PSNI)/Royal Ulster Constabulary (RUC)[1] by gender and full-time/part-time status, 1995 to 2004-05

Numbers

	1995	1996	1997	1998	1998-99[2]	1999-00	2000-01	2001-02	2002-03[3]	2003-04[3]	2004-05[3]
PSNI/RUC Regulars											
Males	7,541	7,531	7,562	7,580	7,534	7,406	6,916	6,058	5,908	6,027	5,940
Females	899	897	923	925	962	987	978	918	1,032	1,185	1,293
PSNI/RUC Full-Time Reserve											
Males	2,787	2,778	2,727	2,716	2,607	2,453	2,269	1,985	1,631	1,437	1,250
Females	151	151	255	259	255	235	224	199	173	135	116
PSNI/RUC Part-Time Reserve											
Males	953	949	860	842	791	746	690	644	592	546	574
Females	528	524	464	457	426	406	382	357	337	318	369

Source: Police Service of Northern Ireland

1 The Royal Ulster Constabulary became the Police Service of Northern Ireland on 4 November 2001.

2 From 1998-99 onwards, figures are at 31 March of the final year shown.

3 From 2002-03 onwards, figures exclude those on secondments and those student officers who have yet to graduate.

6.5 Persons convicted at the Crown Court by offence group, 1998 to 2003

Numbers

Offence group	1998	1999	2000	2001	2002	2003
Violence against the person	255	219	305	237	260	327
Sexual offences	79	50	87	74	54	69
Burglary	48	45	57	33	45	68
Robbery	129	113	106	112	134	178
Theft	85	74	94	98	53	73
Fraud and forgery	51	42	51	91	41	29
Criminal damage	78	33	53	28	36	48
Offences against the State	31	23	40	25	42	76
Drug offences	177	163	225	173	116	121
Other offences	84	29	87	62	76	132
All offences	**1,017**	**791**	**1,105**	**933**	**857**	**1,121**

Source: Northern Ireland Office

6.6 Persons convicted at Magistrates' Courts by offence group, 1998 to 2003

Numbers

Offence group	1998	1999	2000	2001	2002	2003
Violence against the person	1,341	1,480	1,553	1,384	1,530	1,638
Sexual offences	49	40	43	38	30	39
Burglary	599	658	646	463	550	534
Robbery	5	16	16	9	18	14
Theft	2,257	1,921	2,017	1,733	1,642	1,730
Fraud and forgery	375	434	352	307	321	285
Criminal damage	965	898	1,007	889	921	986
Offences against the State	167	155	134	133	173	198
Drug offences	411	418	424	297	299	377
Other indictable[1]	285	345	10	15	9	14
All indictable[2]	**6,454**	**6,365**	**6,202**	**5,268**	**5,493**	**5,815**
Summary[3]	4,047	3,594	3,951	3,702	3,427	3,464
Motoring[4]	15,363	15,774	15,360	14,447	14,323	16,275
All offences	**25,864**	**25,733**	**25,513**	**23,417**	**23,243**	**25,554**

Source: Northern Ireland Office

1 1998 and 1999 figures include dangerous driving.

2 From 2000, includes 'indictable-only' motoring offences.

3 Excludes motoring offences.

4 Prior to 2000, includes all motoring offences (except for Note 1 above). From 2000, includes 'triable-either-way' and summary offences only.

6.7 Juvenile[1] convictions at all courts by offence group, 1998 to 2003

Numbers

Offence group	1998	1999	2000	2001	2002	2003
Violence against the person	97	73	77	66	82	75
Sexual offences	12	12	4	1	6	5
Burglary	108	117	125	73	77	89
Robbery	4	7	15	8	14	10
Theft	304	227	254	244	212	173
Fraud and forgery	4	10	2	9	3	7
Criminal damage	139	102	143	152	132	162
Offences against the State	11	12	8	10	20	26
Drug offences	16	11	10	11	7	18
Other indictable[2]	4	6	0	1	0	1
All indictable[3]	**699**	**577**	**638**	**575**	**553**	**566**
Summary[4]	187	163	180	203	194	174
Motoring[5]	98	97	82	102	89	94
All offences	**984**	**837**	**900**	**880**	**836**	**834**

Source: Northern Ireland Office

1 Juveniles are aged 10-16 years inclusive.

2 1998 and 1999 figures include dangerous driving.

3 From 2000, includes 'indictable-only' motoring offences.

4 Excludes motoring offences.

5 Prior to 2000, includes all motoring offences (except for Note 2 above). From 2000, includes 'triable-either-way' and summary offences only.

6.8 Persons convicted at all courts by gender, age group and conviction rate, 2003

Numbers and rates

Gender and age group	Number				Rate per 10,000 population			
	Indictable[1]	Summary[2]	Motoring[3]	**All offences**	Indictable[1]	Summary[2]	Motoring[3]	**All offences**
Males aged								
10-16	474	146	90	**710**	*50*	*16*	*10*	***76***
17	310	162	219	**691**	*222*	*116*	*157*	***495***
18-21	1,778	805	2,650	**5,233**	*349*	*158*	*520*	***1,026***
22-24	844	376	1,768	**2,988**	*254*	*113*	*531*	***897***
25-29	826	358	2,297	**3,481**	*154*	*67*	*429*	***651***
30-34	641	341	1,948	**2,930**	*104*	*56*	*317*	***477***
35-39	453	304	1,657	**2,414**	*70*	*47*	*257*	***374***
40-44	313	239	1,220	**1,772**	*52*	*40*	*204*	***296***
45-59	322	245	1,842	**2,409**	*22*	*16*	*124*	***162***
60 and over	48	25	345	**418**	*4*	*2*	*26*	***31***
Unknown	0	4	13	**17**	-	-	-	-
All males	**6,009**	**3,005**	**14,049**	**23,063**	***84***	***42***	***197***	***323***
Females aged								
10-16	92	28	4	**124**	*10*	*3*	*0*	***14***
17	31	17	15	**63**	*23*	*13*	*11*	***47***
18-21	156	80	204	**440**	*32*	*16*	*42*	***91***
22-24	99	41	247	**387**	*31*	*13*	*77*	***121***
25-29	111	65	387	**563**	*20*	*12*	*71*	***103***
30-34	97	69	390	**556**	*15*	*11*	*62*	***88***
35-39	78	80	371	**529**	*12*	*12*	*56*	***79***
40-44	68	65	277	**410**	*11*	*10*	*44*	***65***
45-59	75	53	350	**478**	*5*	*3*	*23*	***32***
60 and over	3	4	42	**49**	*0*	*0*	*2*	***3***
Unknown	0	7	6	**13**	-	-	-	-
All females	**810**	**509**	**2,293**	**3,612**	***11***	***7***	***30***	***48***
All persons	**6,819**	**3,514**	**16,342**	**26,675**	***46***	***24***	***111***	***181***

Source: Northern Ireland Office

[1] Includes 'indictable-only' motoring offences.

[2] Excludes motoring offences.

[3] Includes 'triable-either-way' and summary motoring offences.

Convictions at all courts by gender, offence group and disposal, 2003

6.9

Numbers

Gender and offence group	Immediate custody	Suspended custody	Supervision in the community	Fine	Conditional discharge	Other	**All disposals**
Males							
Violence against the person	357	325	254	588	161	65	**1,750**
Sexual offences	56	23	20	5	3	0	**107**
Burglary	291	81	145	22	43	2	**584**
Robbery	142	24	15	0	1	0	**182**
Theft	347	245	288	363	205	10	**1,458**
Fraud and forgery	32	58	27	107	19	2	**245**
Criminal damage	195	137	224	174	186	22	**938**
Offences against the State	42	69	64	54	27	7	**263**
Drug offences	76	51	52	235	39	3	**456**
Other offences	7	7	3	9	0	0	**26**
All indictable offences[1]	**1,545**	**1,020**	**1,092**	**1,557**	**684**	**111**	**6,009**
Summary[2]	173	289	228	1,066	313	936	**3,005**
Motoring[3]	418	396	302	12,511	205	217	**14,049**
All offences	**2,136**	**1,705**	**1,622**	**15,134**	**1,202**	**1,264**	**23,063**
Females							
Violence against the person	14	34	52	56	42	17	**215**
Sexual offences	0	1	0	0	0	0	**1**
Burglary	0	4	8	1	5	0	**18**
Robbery	5	1	4	0	0	0	**10**
Theft	26	54	89	78	91	7	**345**
Fraud and forgery	0	23	20	11	15	0	**69**
Criminal damage	8	7	22	14	38	7	**96**
Offences against the State	1	3	1	0	5	1	**11**
Drug offences	3	7	4	17	10	1	**42**
Other offences	0	0	1	1	1	0	**3**
All indictable offences[1]	**57**	**134**	**201**	**178**	**207**	**33**	**810**
Summary[2]	6	29	55	150	99	170	**509**
Motoring[3]	4	30	30	2,133	42	54	**2,293**
All offences	**67**	**193**	**286**	**2,461**	**348**	**257**	**3,612**
All persons							
Violence against the person	**371**	**359**	**306**	**644**	**203**	**82**	**1,965**
Sexual offences	**56**	**24**	**20**	**5**	**3**	**0**	**108**
Burglary	**291**	**85**	**153**	**23**	**48**	**2**	**602**
Robbery	**147**	**25**	**19**	**0**	**1**	**0**	**192**
Theft	**373**	**299**	**377**	**441**	**296**	**17**	**1,803**
Fraud and forgery	**32**	**81**	**47**	**118**	**34**	**2**	**314**
Criminal damage	**203**	**144**	**246**	**188**	**224**	**29**	**1,034**
Offences against the State	**43**	**72**	**65**	**54**	**32**	**8**	**274**
Drug offences	**79**	**58**	**56**	**252**	**49**	**4**	**498**
Other offences	**7**	**7**	**4**	**10**	**1**	**0**	**29**
All indictable offences[1]	**1,602**	**1,154**	**1,293**	**1,735**	**891**	**144**	**6,819**
Summary[2]	**179**	**318**	**283**	**1,216**	**412**	**1,106**	**3,514**
Motoring[3]	**422**	**426**	**332**	**14,644**	**247**	**271**	**16,342**
All offences	**2,203**	**1,898**	**1,908**	**17,595**	**1,550**	**1,521**	**26,675**

Source: Northern Ireland Office

[1] Includes 'indictable-only' motoring offences.

[2] Excludes motoring offences.

[3] Includes summary and 'triable-either-way' motoring offences.

6.10 Disposals at Magistrates' Courts and the Crown Court by type of disposal, 1993 to 2003

Numbers

Court and disposal type	1993	1994	1995	1996	1997	1998	1999	2000	2001	2002	2003
Magistrates' Court											
Prison[1]	1,027	945	1,046	1,003	989	996	1,278	1,356	1,048	1,107	1,133
Custody Probation Order[1]	.	.	.	.	.	.	.	.	.	.	7
Young offenders' centre	575	499	483	443	430	326	243	191	209	288	395
Training school	125	193	169	147	148	136	13	.	.	.	.
Juvenile Justice Centre[2]	.	.	.	.	.	.	22	78	72	58	48
All immediate custody	**1,727**	**1,637**	**1,698**	**1,593**	**1,567**	**1,458**	**1,556**	**1,625**	**1,329**	**1,453**	**1,583**
Prison suspended	1,529	1,558	1,674	1,722	1,506	1,025	1,080	1,247	1,215	1,278	1,407
Young offenders' centre suspended	447	447	385	444	461	139	104	93	77	100	201
Attendance centre	94	89	101	91	66	55	14	20	37	84	91
Probation/supervision order[3]	881	1,017	1,137	1,134	1,155	1,473	1,246	1,096	1,070	1,005	974
Community service order	536	551	547	591	561	622	678	726	587	643	623
Combination order	.	.	.	.	.	38	7	48	24	36	96
Fine[4]	25,166	24,390	22,726	20,614	21,313	17,956	18,076	17,716	16,439	15,968	17,546
Recognizance	858	961	1,001	1,203	1,267	1,134	1,089	1,357	810	912	1,091
Conditional discharge	2,021	1,830	1,928	1,679	1,597	1,538	1,439	1,286	1,559	1,497	1,526
Absolute discharge	690	661	608	509	424	303	223	242	209	163	201
Other	13	17	10	15	8	123	221	57	61	104	215
All disposals	**33,962**	**33,158**	**31,815**	**29,595**	**29,925**	**25,864**	**25,733**	**25,513**	**23,417**	**23,243**	**25,554**
Crown Court											
Prison[1]	555	471	533	469	475	520	386	521	407	410	238
Custody Probation Order[1]	.	.	.	.	.	.	.	.	.	.	331
Young offenders' centre	130	87	76	106	111	63	67	32	42	23	51
Training school	2	5	6	0	4	2	0	.	.	.	.
Juvenile Justice Centre[2]	.	.	.	.	.	.	0	0	0	2	0
All immediate custody	**687**	**563**	**615**	**575**	**590**	**585**	**453**	**553**	**449**	**435**	**620**
Prison suspended	211	277	265	253	220	199	185	313	262	220	240
Young offenders' centre suspended	37	43	63	71	60	49	41	48	37	35	50
Attendance centre	0	1	0	0	0	0	0	0	0	1	0
Probation/supervision order[3]	73	58	60	49	47	70	43	68	48	49	63
Community service order	48	59	60	54	37	33	24	29	45	25	27
Combination order	.	.	.	.	.	13	6	7	5	18	34
Fine[4]	33	23	27	39	40	25	20	40	38	32	49
Recognizance	5	16	0	7	10	7	0	4	11	12	8
Conditional discharge	19	15	64	30	31	23	17	38	36	20	24
Absolute discharge	3	2	1	0	1	6	0	3	0	6	1
Other	6	1	2	3	3	7	2	2	2	4	5
All disposals	**1,122**	**1,058**	**1,157**	**1,081**	**1,039**	**1,017**	**791**	**1,105**	**933**	**857**	**1,121**

Source: Northern Ireland Office

1 Custody-probation orders cannot be separately identified from 'prison' sentences from 1998 to 2002. Thus, during this period, figures for 'prison' include custody-probation orders.

2 The Juvenile Justice Centre order replaced the training school order from 31 January 1999.

3 Supervision orders were abolished with the introduction of the Criminal Justice (Children) NI Order 1998.

4 From 2000, fine incorporates 'fine plus disqualification' and 'fine plus penalty points'.

Juvenile[1] sentencing by type of disposal, 1998 to 2003

6.11

Numbers

Type of disposal	1998	1999	2000	2001	2002	2003
Prison[2]	2	5	8	3	2	1
Custody Probation Order[2]	.	.	.	.	.	3
Young offenders' centre	35	48	15	7	6	7
Training school	130	12	.	.	.	.
Juvenile Justice Centre[3]	.	18	73	66	57	46
All immediate custody	**167**	**83**	**96**	**76**	**65**	**57**
Prison suspended	0	3	3	1	0	0
Young offenders' centre suspended	24	18	10	4	3	14
Attendance centre	31	10	20	36	80	89
Probation/supervision order[4]	337	274	300	290	248	216
Community service order	35	37	44	24	42	49
Combination order[2]	2	0	3	1	2	6
Fine[5]	84	128	86	98	87	80
Recognizance	38	27	43	45	34	31
Conditional discharge	250	241	283	290	263	273
Absolute discharge	12	9	9	15	10	12
Other	4	7	3	0	2	7
All juvenile disposals	**984**	**837**	**900**	**880**	**836**	**834**

Percentages

Type of disposal	1998	1999	2000	2001	2002	2003
Prison[2]	.	*1*	*1*	*0*	*0*	*0*
Custody Probation Order[2]	.	.	.	.	.	*0*
Young offenders' centre	*4*	*6*	*2*	*1*	*1*	*1*
Training school	*13*	*1*	.	.	.	.
Juvenile Justice Centre[3]	.	*2*	*8*	*8*	*7*	*6*
All immediate custody	***17***	***10***	***11***	***9***	***8***	***7***
Prison suspended	*0*	*0*	*0*	*0*	*0*	*0*
Young offenders' centre suspended	*2*	*2*	*1*	*0*	*0*	*2*
Attendance centre	*3*	*1*	*2*	*4*	*10*	*11*
Probation/supervision order[4]	*34*	*33*	*33*	*33*	*30*	*26*
Community service order	*4*	*4*	*5*	*3*	*5*	*6*
Combination order[2]	-	-	-	-	-	*1*
Fine[5]	*9*	*15*	*10*	*11*	*10*	*10*
Recognizance	*4*	*3*	*5*	*5*	*4*	*4*
Conditional discharge	*25*	*29*	*31*	*33*	*31*	*33*
Absolute discharge	*1*	*1*	*1*	*2*	*1*	*1*
Other	*0*	*1*	*0*	*0*	*0*	*1*

Source: Northern Ireland Office

[1] Juveniles are aged 10-16 years inclusive.

[2] Custody-probation orders cannot be separately identified from prison sentences from 1998 to 2002. Thus, during this period, figures for 'prison' include custody-probation orders.

[3] The Juvenile Justice Centre order replaced the training school order from 31 January 1999.

[4] Supervision orders were abolished with the introduction of the Criminal Justice (Children) NI Order 1998.

[5] From 2000, fine incorporates 'fine plus disqualification' and 'fine plus penalty points'.

6.12 Average prison population by gender, prisoner type and age, 1994 to 2004

Numbers

Gender, prisoner type and age	1994	1995	1996	1997	1998	1999	2000	2001	2002	2003	2004
Male prisoners											
Remand											
Aged under 21	106	72	69	70	71	75	69	62	81	97	105
Aged 21 or over	321	240	249	288	291	286	232	198	250	280	328
Age unknown	0	0	0	0	0	0	0	0	0	0	1
All male remand	**427**	**312**	**318**	**358**	**362**	**361**	**301**	**260**	**331**	**377**	**434**
Fine defaulter											
Aged under 21	4	5	5	6	7	8	5	4	3	4	5
Aged 21 or over	23	23	19	23	22	23	15	17	13	15	17
All male defaulters	**27**	**28**	**24**	**29**	**29**	**31**	**20**	**21**	**16**	**19**	**22**
Immediate custody											
Young offenders' centre	133	118	115	104	114	103	78	58	73	80	86
Young prisoners	91	87	66	57	44	27	22	17	20	22	30
Adult prisoners	1,179	1,177	1,076	1,044	921	695	618	533	557	633	666
All male immediate custody	**1,403**	**1,382**	**1,257**	**1,205**	**1,079**	**825**	**718**	**608**	**650**	**735**	**782**
Non-criminal	1	5	11	10	10	6	6	5	5	7	8
All males	**1,858**	**1,727**	**1,610**	**1,602**	**1,480**	**1,223**	**1,045**	**894**	**1,002**	**1,138**	**1,246**
Female prisoners											
Remand											
Aged under 21	5	2	2	3	4	4	2	1	1	2	4
Aged 21 or over	7	3	6	5	7	5	8	5	9	6	8
All female remand	**12**	**5**	**8**	**8**	**11**	**10**	**10**	**6**	**11**	**8**	**12**
Fine defaulter											
Aged under 21	1	0	0	0	0	0	0	0	0	0	0
Aged 21 or over	2	1	0	1	1	2	2	1	1	1	2
All female defaulters	**3**	**1**	**0**	**1**	**1**	**2**	**2**	**1**	**1**	**1**	**2**
Immediate custody											
Young offenders' centre	4	6	4	3	1	1	1	1	3	2	2
Young prisoners	3	2	1	0	0	0	0	0	0	0	0
Adult prisoners	19	21	16	18	14	8	10	7	9	10	10
All female immediate custody	**26**	**29**	**21**	**21**	**15**	**9**	**11**	**8**	**11**	**12**	**12**
Non-criminal	0	0	0	0	0	0	0	1	1	1	1
All females	**41**	**35**	**29**	**30**	**27**	**21**	**23**	**16**	**24**	**22**	**27**
All prisoners											
Remand	**439**	**317**	**326**	**366**	**373**	**371**	**311**	**266**	**341**	**385**	**446**
Fine defaulter	**30**	**29**	**24**	**30**	**30**	**33**	**22**	**22**	**17**	**20**	**24**
Immediate custody	**1,429**	**1,411**	**1,278**	**1,226**	**1,094**	**834**	**729**	**616**	**662**	**747**	**794**
Non-criminal	**1**	**5**	**11**	**10**	**10**	**6**	**6**	**6**	**6**	**8**	**10**
All prisoners	**1,899**	**1,762**	**1,639**	**1,632**	**1,507**	**1,244**	**1,068**	**910**	**1,026**	**1,160**	**1,274**

Source: Northern Ireland Office

6.13 Drugs seizures and arrests, 2000-01 to 2004-05

Units as indicated

Class and type of drug		2000-01	2001-02	2002-03	2003-04	2004-05
Class A						
Cocaine	gms powder	1,701.4	3,399.9	3,023.9	11,470.9	21,331.6
	wraps	0	4	12	6	24
'Crack' Cocaine	gms powder	43.1	66.5	50.0	9.2	0.0
Ecstasy	tablets	410,671	127,368	605,188	222,888	351,296
	gms powder	498.0	232.8	1.1	72.1	43.4
	capsules	11	2	25	20	4
LSD	doses	117	122	4	0	1,134
	microdots	201	0	1	6	7,012
Opiates (inc Heroin)	gms	3,131.6	102.1	346.0	189.9	5.1
	tablets	1,670	51	41	3	57
	ampoules	203	4	1	20	0
	mls	121.0	366.0	428.5	163.6	202.2
	wraps	16	69	1	2	0
Class B						
Amphetamines	kilos powder	3.9	8.8	27.6	17.3	79.1
	wraps (powder)	16	26	24	35	24
	tablets	458	118	11	58	32
Barbiturates	tablets	0	0	0	0	0
Class C						
Cannabis[1]	kilos (resin)	384.4	417.2	709.5	2,204.2	933.0
	kilos (herbal)	21.6	49.0	27.7	32.8	19.7
	plants	210	141	202	1,173	574
	joints	253	273	169	212	208
Arrests		**1,266**	**990**	**1,295**	**1,754**	**1,356**

Source: Police Service of Northern Ireland

[1] Prior to the 29 January 2004, cannabis was classified as a class B drug.

CRIME AND JUSTICE

6.14 Magistrates' Court: civil business orders made, 1994 to 2004

Numbers

	1994	1995	1996	1997	1998	1999	2000	2001	2002	2003	2004
Adult orders made											
Domestic	2,225	2,106	2,088	1,634	1,522	1,218	1,036	1,023	780	651	564
Varying and arrears	1,595	1,590	1,411	1,698	873	936	708	797	858	966	350
Debts and ejectments	21,413	13,512	18,650	20,567	18,743	15,751	17,731	15,174	16,975	16,648	17,118
Licensing	5,053	4,835	4,540	3,628	893	680	591	535	1,179	600	471
Personal protection and exclusion[1]	.	6,645	6,570	6,494	6,206	1,665	.	.	.	.	.
Non-molestation and occupation orders[2]	.	.	.	.	.	3,862	4,704	5,246	4,377	4,343	3,816
Other	6,450	457	564	720	561	485	713	395	434	1,057	1,247
All adult orders	**36,736**	**29,145**	**33,823**	**34,741**	**28,798**	**24,597**	**25,483**	**23,170**	**24,603**	**24,267**[3]	**23,566**
Juvenile orders made	**502**	**494**	**497**	**24**	**0**	**0**	**0**	**0**	**0**	**0**	**0**
Children orders made[4]	**.**	**.**	**63**	**2,838**	**3,975**	**4,977**	**5,163**	**4,128**	**4,392**	**4,262**	**4,412**

Source: Northern Ireland Court Service

1 Included in 'Other' to 1994.

2 Protection and exclusion orders were replaced by non-molestation and occupation orders as of 1 April 1999.

3 Includes two orders where the type was not recorded.

4 The Children (Northern Ireland) Order 1995 came into effect on 4 November 1996. Figures refer to free-standing cases only and excludes cases dismissed or withdrawn.

6.15 County Court: civil bills, small claims and criminal injury appeals entered and disposed of, 1993 to 2003

Numbers

	1993	1994	1995	1996	1997	1998	1999	2000	2001	2002	2003
Civil Bills											
Entered	16,040	15,608	15,304	13,562	13,450	13,198	16,066	16,500	15,195	12,171	11,427
Disposed of by County Court Judge[1]	7,162	7,729	7,353	6,968	8,182	8,508	9,196	9,137	9,758	7,479	6,433
Disposed of by District Judge[1]	4,260	3,289	4,101	2,949	2,636	2,238	1,835	1,973	2,351	2,948	2,544
Other disposals disposed of by District Judge[2]	..	3,697	3,178	2,690	2,833	3,540	3,569	4,158	3,945	3,328	3,172
Summary Civil Bills[1,3]											
Disposed of	2,549	2,034	1,521	2,377	3,389	3,054	3,226	3,309	2,943	2,654	2,321
Small Claims[1]											
Entered	15,006	14,497	14,421	14,842	12,105	11,568	11,511	10,770	13,591	15,454	10,261
Disposed of	16,187	15,083	16,939	15,532	12,617	11,606	12,155	10,730	12,521	14,765	10,194
Criminal Injury appeals											
Entered	4,497	4,088	3,387	3,021	3,366	3,736	3,812	3,346	3,683	3,582	2,722
Disposed of	3,815	4,201	3,975	3,719	3,365	3,362	3,409	3,819	3,288	3,237	3,151

Source: Northern Ireland Court Service

1 On 1 September 1993, the jurisdiction of County Court Judges and District Judges was raised. The value of cases which could be dealt with by civil bill and by small claim was increased.

2 Attributed to County Court or District Judge prior to 1994.

3 Includes default civil bills entered from 1 October 1995.

6.16 Divorces: decrees nisi granted by court type and facts proved, 1993 to 2003

Numbers

	1993	1994	1995	1996	1997	1998	1999	2000	2001	2002	2003
High Court[1]											
Adultery	157	133	115	113	118	159	122	96	121	95	89
Behaviour	268	303	300	301	311	375	317	299	321	273	306
Desertion	9	8	5	7	7	11	3	8	2	5	1
Separation											
(2 years and consent)	566	604	556	484	502	569	489	476	491	457	527
Separation (5 years)	288	316	326	326	283	363	297	331	300	243	304
Other grounds	1	2	24	18	27	40	46	39	60	57	67
All divorces	**1,289**	**1,366**	**1,326**	**1,249**	**1,248**	**1,517**	**1,274**	**1,249**	**1,295**	**1,130**	**1,294**
County Court											
Adultery	66	71	67	63	67	72	62	48	44	44	33
Behaviour	139	145	152	175	218	201	139	151	178	130	123
Desertion	10	11	7	6	8	6	5	4	4	2	1
Separation											
(2 years and consent)	552	590	627	586	632	669	514	594	658	599	568
Separation (5 years)	326	337	355	332	348	418	318	307	410	382	328
Other grounds	2	0	1	8	11	21	81	103	26	167	269
All divorces	**1,095**	**1,154**	**1,209**	**1,170**	**1,284**	**1,387**	**1,119**	**1,207**	**1,320**	**1,324**	**1,322**
All Courts	**2,384**	**2,520**	**2,535**	**2,419**	**2,532**	**2,904**	**2,393**	**2,456**	**2,615**	**2,454**	**2,616**

Source: Northern Ireland Court Service

1 Excludes Judicial Separation and Nullity.

6.17 Criminal injury claims, 1999-2000 to 2004-05

Numbers and £ millions

Applications and outcomes	1999-00	2000-01	2001-02	2002-03	2003-04	2004-05
Claims received	12,094	13,939	14,589	10,463	8,272	6,709
Withdrawn/abandoned	1,927	2,190	2,350	2,526	3,472	1,759
Number denied	2,231	2,508	2,549	4,815	6,203	7,018
Awards made	6,748	7,143	7,705	7,604	6,530	4,725
Value of awards (£ millions)	37.3	40.9	45.8	52.2	49.9	41.4

Source: The Compensation Agency

6.18 Criminal damage claims, 1999-2000 to 2004-05

Numbers and £ millions

Applications and outcomes	1999-00	2000-01	2001-02	2002-03	2003-04	2004-05
Claims received	4,239	2,046	1,863	1,675	1,026	928
Withdrawn/abandoned	414	420	473	442	306	206
Number denied	949	661	821	743	774	580
Awards made	1,451	910	858	1,034	504	271
Value of awards (£ millions)	22.8	18.8	20.6	10.5	7.0	6.8

Source: The Compensation Agency

6.19 Queen's Bench: cases set down and disposed of, 1993 to 2003

Numbers

	1993	1994	1995	1996	1997	1998	1999	2000	2001	2002	2003
Set down	3,605	2,267	2,128	2,202	1,869	1,780	1,996	1,897	2,322	2,162	2,231
Disposed of	5,108	5,167	2,805	2,047	2,269	1,914	1,923	2,095	2,094	2,033	2,044
Default judgements[1]	2,519	1,609	1,056	866	850	880	860	901	956	869	1,056

Source: Northern Ireland Court Service

[1] Includes disposals under orders 14 and 37.

6.20 Chancery Division writs and originating summonses, 1993 to 2003

Numbers

	1993	1994	1995	1996	1997	1998	1999	2000	2001	2002	2003
Mortgages	1,728	1,372	1,220	1,151	1,158	1,579	1,863	1,717	1,604	1,625	1,710
Other land and property	127	109	103	132	138	130	142	118	129	167	149
Trusts and trustees	13	33	26	29	34	23	32	18	17	19	21
Probates	17	14	9	18	22	27	34	19	33	26	35
Business/trade/industry	52	52	59	52	64	74	75	51	31	24	34
Miscellaneous	33	35	35	29	25	38	41	66	77	51	88
All categories	**1,970**	**1,615**	**1,452**	**1,411**	**1,441**	**1,871**	**2,187**	**1,989**	**1,891**	**1,912**	**2,037**

Source: Northern Ireland Court Service

CRIME AND JUSTICE

6.21 Appeals by court type, cases set down and disposed of, 1993 to 2003

Numbers

	1993	1994	1995	1996	1997	1998	1999	2000	2001	2002	2003
Court of Appeal											
Criminal set down	180	98	120	81	80	57	61	64	67	59	73
Disposed of	149	150	122	78	89	72	53	69	67	53	57
Civil set down	70	63	47	69	64	59	67	54	70	89	86
Disposed of	74	87	51	61	73	54	69	34	74	77	79
Queen's Bench											
Set down	445	523	458	388	318	339	387	369	440	395	372
Disposed of	403	652	589	424	289	281	271	339	434	359	262
County Court											
Set down	4,432	3,901	3,770	3,645	3,271	2,963	2,482	2,262	2,709	2,467	2,454
Disposed of[1]	4,345	3,907	3,647	3,942	3,178	2,969	2,451	2,216	2,606	2,467	2,439

Source: Northern Ireland Court Service

[1] Includes non-court disposals, cases withdrawn and cases abandoned from 1995 onwards.

6.22 Coroners' workload, 1993 to 2002

Numbers

	1993	1994	1995	1996	1997	1998	1999	2000	2001	2002
Deaths reported	3,077	3,119	3,274	3,278	3,275	3,537	3,668	3,615	3,752	3,563
Cases disposed	2,968	3,134	3,188	3,321	3,135	3,230	3,583	3,458	3,489	3,499
Inquests held	488	587	530	481	451	390	375	303	198	230

Source: Northern Ireland Court Service

Notes to Crime and Justice tables

TABLE 6.3

The Ulster Defence Regiment (UDR) became operational on 1 April 1970. On 1 July 1992, the Royal Irish Rangers and the Ulster Defence Regiment were amalgamated to form the Royal Irish Regiment (RIR). Figures for 1992 and subsequent years relate to RIR (Home Service) personnel only.

TABLES 6.5 TO 6.11

In England and Wales, the classification of offences recorded by the police is based on a list of 'notifiable offences' which must be notified to the Home Office by the various police forces. A similar list of offences exists in Northern Ireland for classifying the more serious offences which are the subject of court proceedings.

While certain of the most serious offences, i.e. indictable-only offences, must always be heard in the Crown Court; and the less serious offences, known as summary offences, must always be tried in a magistrates' court; there is a third category of offences known as 'triable-either-way' offences which can be either tried summarily in a magistrates' court or on indictment in the Crown Court. Unless stated otherwise, the triable-either-way offences are included with the indictable offences. Only the principal offence, that is, the most serious, is counted in the tables of police and court statistics.

In Northern Ireland, the classification systems used for both offences recorded by the police and court proceedings are broadly similar to those in use in England and Wales. The same terminology is applied, although some differences do occur, largely because of differences in legislation. Offences are said to be 'cleared up' or 'detected' if a person is charged, summonsed or cautioned for the offence; if the offence is attributable to a person below the age of criminal responsibility (ten years of age); if the offence is 'taken into consideration' by the court when sentencing an offender found guilty of another charge; or if the person known or suspected to be guilty of the offence cannot be prosecuted or cautioned (for example, because the person has died).

Up until 29 August 2005, in Northern Ireland, juveniles were all offenders aged between 10 and 16 years inclusive, however, from 30 August 2005, 17 year olds are now included within the remit of the youth court, as is the case in England and Wales.

TABLE 6.12

Figures are annual averages and are based on all types of prisoners (remand, immediate custody, fine default and non-criminal prisoners). Prisoners temporarily absent on home leave or in hospital are also included. Immediate custody

Young Offenders' Centre prisoners are those aged under 21 years sentenced to less than four years in prison. Young prisoners are those aged under 21 years sentenced to more than four years in prison.

Adult prisoners are those aged 21 years and over irrespective of length of sentence. Non-criminal prisoners are typically detained for offences such as violation of Immigration Act requirements and contempt of court.

TABLE 6.14

The Magistrates' Courts have jurisdiction to make orders relating to a range of civil business such as maintenance and affiliation, arrears of payments under maintenance and affiliation orders, debts and ejectments, and licensing of premises.

TABLE 6.15

In civil cases of lesser complexity and value than those heard in the High Court, it is possible to bring an action in the County Court where costs and fees are less. This can be done by means of a civil bill or, in the instance of cases with the least value, a small claim. Fees for small claims are lower than for civil bills. District Judges can hear defended civil bills up to a value of £3,000.

County Courts also deal with undefended debt claims by way of default judgement, which does not require judicial involvement. Prior to 1995, the County Court worked on the basis of two and three month cycles of work. Cases were entered for hearing in a cycle on the basis that they were ready for trial and disposed of when a decision was made or if the case was withdrawn. Because a case could be entered for hearing during a cycle and then adjourned to the next cycle at the request of the parties involved, cases may be entered several times during the year, inflating the number of civil bill entries. From 1992 onwards, it has been possible to identify the number of civil bills entered for the first time.

TABLE 6.16

Divorces can be heard in the Family Division of the High Court, or (if uncontested) in the County Court. There are a number of facts which, if proved, are grounds for a divorce. These include adultery, unreasonable behaviour, desertion, separation for a period of two years (if both parties consent), and separation for a period of five years (even if both parties do not consent).

There are a number of other grounds for divorce, and cases where more than one of the facts listed above are proved, are included in the category 'other grounds'.

TABLES 6.14 TO 6.16 AND 6.19 TO 6.21

There are three tiers of court in Northern Ireland: Supreme Court (including Court of Appeal, High Court and Crown Court), County Court and magistrates' court. Apart from the Court of Appeal, each has initial jurisdiction over particular types of case. They may also hear appeals against the decisions of lower court tiers.

The magistrates' courts deal with less serious criminal cases and simple civil business, while the County Court hears more complex civil cases. The Crown Court deals with more serious criminal cases, while the High Court hears the most complex civil cases. The High Court has a number of Divisions: Queen's Bench, Chancery, Admiralty and Family, each of which handle a particular kind of work.

The Court of Appeal deals with appeals against decisions of the Crown Court and of the High Court. The jurisdictional limit of the County Court was raised on 1 November 1992 and 1 September 1993.

TABLE 6.19

Queen's Bench Division is a branch of the High Court, dealing mostly with personal liability in a wide range of matters, for example, debt, injury and libel.

Cases are set down for hearing when they are ready for trial and disposed of when a decision is made or when the case is withdrawn.

Default judgements are made by the court office without judicial involvement if no defence is made against the claim of the plaintiff. Judgements made by masters under Order 14 and Order 37 are also included here.

TABLE 6.22

There is currently one full time Coroner and six part-time Coroners in Northern Ireland. When a Coroner considers it necessary to hold an inquest into a particular death, he/she may direct a post mortem examination. This may be followed by the holding of a formal inquest that may either be presided over by the Coroner only or by a Coroner with the assistance of a jury.

Economy, Commerce and Industry

- The Gross Value Added (GVA) estimate for Northern Ireland for 2003 was £22,085 million. This represented a GVA per capita of £12,971, which was 81.2% of the UK average.

- The two largest industries within the service sector, Distribution Wholesale & Retail and Business Services and Finance, both showed ouput growth of 5% or more, as did 'Other Services'. However, output from the Transport Storage & Communication and Hotels and Restaurants industries decreased over the same period.

- 2004 output from the production industries was slightly lower than the base year, 2001. The overall output decrease was made up from a large fall in the output of the electricity, gas and water industries, a slight rise in manufacturing output and strong growth in the relatively smaller mining and quarrying industries. Within the manufacturing industries, 2004 output from leather, textiles amd textile products was over 30% lower than in 2001.

- Over the period 1999 to 2004, growth in manufacturing productivity in Northern Ireland has been strong relative to the UK average. The NI 2004 index of manufacturing productivity was 32 percentage points higher than in 1999, compared with a 21 percentage point growth in the UK index over the same period.

- Of the 67,400 Value Added Tax (VAT) and Pay As You Earn (PAYE) businesses in Northern Ireland in 2005, over half (53%) were sole proprietors, and 88% employed less than 10 employees.

- In terms of the number of enterprises, agriculture dominates the economy in rural and border Local Government Districts (LGDs). Services, especially retail businesses, predominate in urban LGDs such as Belfast.

- In two out of the four years between 2000 and 2003, Northern Ireland had higher rates of VAT de-registrations than registrations.

- There were 687 foreign owned businesses operating in Northern Ireland during 2004, representing an increase of three fifths since 1999. Much of this growth can be attributed to the increase in the number of Republic of Ireland owned companies operating in Northern Ireland. There has also been relatively strong growth in the number of companies from Northern European economies such as Sweden, Denmark and the Netherlands, although the total number of such companies remains small relative to all foreign owned companies in Northern Ireland.

Gross Value Added (GVA) at basic prices[1] by type of income, industry and per head of population, 1998 to 2003

7.1

Units as indicated

GVA	1998	1999	2000	2001	2002	2003
By type of income (£ millions)						
Compensation of employees	10,150	10,786	11,528	12,311	12,988	13,737
Other income (gross operating surplus/ mixed income)	7,101	7,281	7,387	7,517	7,850	8,347
By industry (£ millions)						
Agriculture, hunting, forestry and fishing	660	471	421	390	471	..
Mining and quarrying of energy producing materials	10	11	14	14	13	..
Other Mining and quarrying	78	84	88	90	79	..
Manufacturing	3,541	3,727	3,867	3,875	3,805	..
Electricity, gas and water supply	419	399	385	369	361	..
Construction	1,054	1,186	1,319	1,455	1,589	..
Wholesale and retail trade (including motor trade)	2,087	2,277	2,395	2,562	2,671	..
Hotels and Restaurants	501	542	582	616	648	..
Transport, storage and communication	966	1,025	1,112	1,149	1,210	..
Financial intermediation	559	513	545	562	790	..
Real estate, renting and business activities	2,200	2,435	2,664	2,952	3,131	..
Public administration and defence[2]	1,990	2,020	2,043	2,097	2,165	..
Education	1,276	1,323	1,363	1,437	1,534	..
Health and social work	1,512	1,601	1,703	1,799	1,931	..
Other services	694	736	775	825	886	..
FISIM[3]	-298	-284	-360	-364	-447	..
Gross Value Added (£ millions)	**17,251**	**18,067**	**18,915**	**19,828**	**20,838**	**22,085**
GVA per head (£s)	10,282	10,761	11,239	11,737	12,282	12,971
GVA as % of UK	*2.3*	*2.3*	*2.3*	*2.3*	*2.3*	*2.3*
GVA per head as % of UK	*80.3*	*80.7*	*81.1*	*80.7*	*80.4*	*81.2*

Source: Office for National Statistics

1 The basic price valuation includes the costs of production and taxes (less subsidies) on production but excludes taxes (less subsidies) on products.

2 Public administration, national defence and compulsory social security.

3 Financial Intermediation Services Indirectly Measured.

ECONOMY, COMMERCE AND INDUSTRY

7.2 Gross Disposable Household Income (GDHI)[1] by component, 1998 to 2003

£ millions

Component	1998	1999	2000	2001	2002	2003
Primary resources						
Operating Surplus/Mixed Income	2,290	2,402	2,511	2,728	2,941	3,145
Compensation of employees	10,250	10,848	11,596	12,321	12,911	13,495
Property Income	2,453	2,348	2,532	2,633	2,431	2,527
A. Primary resources total	**14,992**	**15,598**	**16,640**	**17,682**	**18,283**	**19,168**
Primary uses						
Property income	844	783	872	862	852	886
B. Primary uses total	**844**	**783**	**872**	**862**	**852**	**886**
C. Balance of primary incomes, gross (A-B)	**14,148**	**14,815**	**15,768**	**16,820**	**17,431**	**18,281**
Secondary resources						
Inputed social contributions/Social benefits other than social benefits in kind	4,690	4,948	5,368	5,615	5,833	6,035
Other current transfers	988	980	1,099	1,117	1,279	1,383
D. Secondary resources total	**5,678**	**5,928**	**6,467**	**6,732**	**7,112**	**7,418**
Secondary uses						
Current taxes on income, wealth etc	2,000	2,126	2,292	2,441	2,477	2,587
Social contributions/Social benefits	3,024	3,234	3,407	3,439	3,656	3,891
Other current transfers	625	599	675	674	762	818
E. Secondary uses total	**5,649**	**5,959**	**6,374**	**6,553**	**6,895**	**7,296**
F. Balance of secondary income (D-E)	**29**	**-31**	**92**	**178**	**217**	**122**
G. Gross Disposable Income (C+F)	**14,177**	**14,784**	**15,860**	**16,998**	**17,648**	**18,403**

Source: Office for National Statistics

[1] Household income includes income received by households and non-profit institutions serving households.

7.3 Output of the service industries (experimental), 2001 to 2004

Index (2002 = 100)

Weight and year	All Service Industries	Distribution - Wholesale & Retail	Hotels & Restaurants	Transport Storage & Communication	Business Services & Finance	Other Services
Weights	**1000.0**	401.3	59.6	134.7	318.1	86.2
2001	**99.6**	94.4	101.6	101.8	103.4	100.0
2002	**100.0**	100.0	100.0	100.0	100.0	100.0
2003	**101.3**	103.3	93.6	98.9	100.2	104.6
2004	**104.1**	105.3	90.0	98.9	106.4	107.9

Source: Northern Ireland Index of Services (experimental), Department of Enterprise, Trade and Investment

Figure 7.1 Output of the service industries (experimental), 2001 to 2004

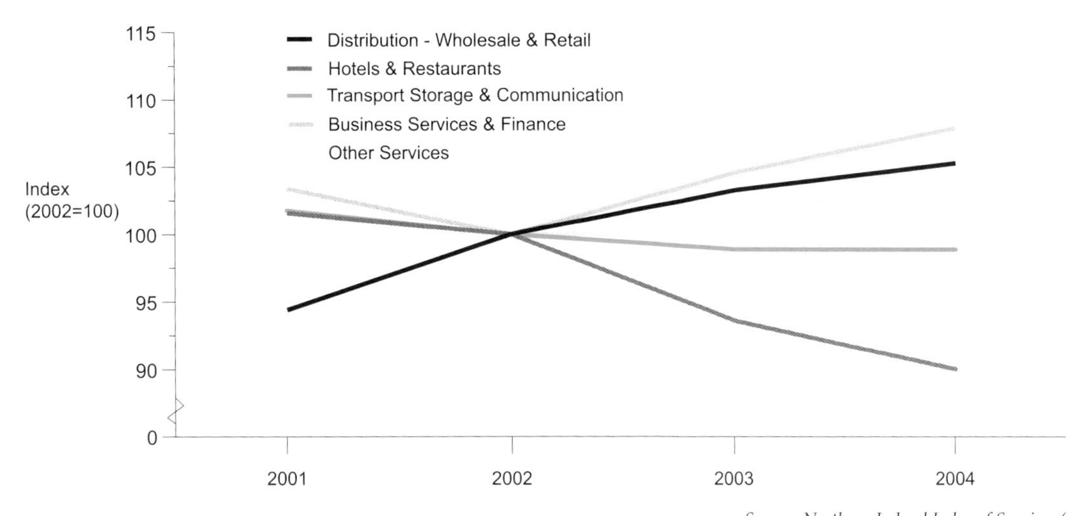

Source: Northern Ireland Index of Services (experimental), Department of Enterprise, Trade and Investment

7.4

Output of the production industries, 1999 to 2004

Index (2001 = 100)

Weight and year	**Production Industries**	Mining & Quarrying	Electricity, Gas & Water	**Manu-facturing**	Manufacturing: Food, Drink & Tobacco	Leather, Textiles & Textile Products	Chemicals & Chemical Products	Basic & Fabricated Metals	Engineering & Allied Industries	Total Other Manu-facturing
Weights	**1,000.0**	13.2	124.0	**862.9**	272.9	61.6	53.1	34.2	296.5	144.7
1999	**90.0**	84.4	108.8	**87.8**	86.4	114.9	104.8	69.5	80.7	93.7
2000	**97.3**	99.3	109.0	**95.8**	89.3	112.7	93.6	80.0	100.7	98.9
2001	**100.0**	100.0	100.0	**100.0**	100.0	100.0	100.0	100.0	100.0	100.0
2002	**95.2**	105.9	82.2	**96.9**	101.6	86.8	102.9	94.3	92.1	100.9
2003	**97.8**	117.3	84.8	**99.3**	102.0	79.2	106.8	101.0	94.7	109.3
2004	**99.7**	122.9	89.4	**100.9**	101.3	68.8	102.8	115.6	95.1	121.1

Source: Northern Ireland Index of Production, Department of Enterprise, Trade and Investment

Figure 7.2 Output of the production industries, 1999 to 2004

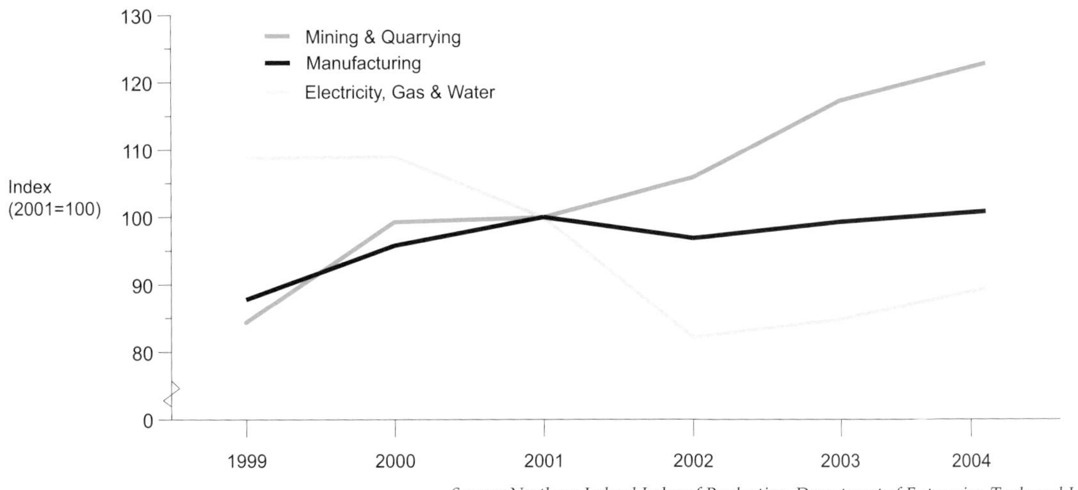

Source: Northern Ireland Index of Production, Department of Enterprise, Trade and Investment

7.5 Index of manufacturing productivity[1], 1999 to 2004

Year	1999	2000	2001	2002	2003	2004
Northern Ireland	84.2	92.5	100.0	102.0	112.2	116.5
United Kingdom	88.8	94.5	97.6	100.0	104.9	110.2

Sources: Department of Enterprise, Trade and Investment; Office for National Statistics

[1] Please note that the base years for these indices are different and comparisions should be made only on the basis of percentage change over time.

7.6 Northern Ireland Annual Business Inquiry Results, Turnover and Gross Value Added (GVA) Information, 2000 to 2003

£ million

Standard Industrial Classification	Description	2000 Total Turnover	2000 GVA at Basic Prices	2001 Total Turnover	2001 GVA at Basic Prices	2002 Total Turnover	2002 GVA at Basic Prices	2003 Total Turnover	2003 GVA at Basic Prices
C	Mining & Quarrying	158.3	53.6	221.1	74.9	224.2	69.8	271.2	78.2
D	Manufacturing	13,824.9	4,041.9	13,634.9	3,879.5	13,100.2	3,612.4	13,497.7	3,762.3
E	Electricity, Gas and Water Supply	1,021.1	420.9	976.0	661.3	1,080.5	369.3	1,057.8	391.8
F	Construction	3,365.1	928.1	3,995.5	1,314.8	4,314.7	1,486.3	4,376.2	1,532.8
G	Wholesale and Retail	14,416.6	2,652.9	14,972.4	2,832.8	15,062.1	2,838.1	16,091.5	3,169.0
H	Hotels and restaurants	814.4	298.2	942.6	371.6	1,125.5	460.7	1,154.5	480.7
I	Transport, storage and communication	2,409.7	1,112.9	2,161.4	1,063.2	2,467.9	1,261.7	2,271.3	1,119.9
K	Real estate, renting and business activities	2,339.9	1,602.8	2,710.2	1,771.4	2,250.6	1,565.9	2,510.8	1,639.5
O	Other community, social and personal service activities	824.5	291.1	952.4	208.7	1,365.9	553.0	1,420.8	575.3
NI	**Total of above**	**39,174.5**	**11,402.4**	**40,566.5**	**12,178.3**	**40,991.6**	**12,217.4**	**42,651.8**	**12,749.5**

Source: Northern Ireland Annual Business Inquiry, Department of Enterprise, Trade and Investment

Value Added Tax (VAT) and Pay As You Earn (PAYE) businesses in Northern Ireland by employee sizeband, 2002 to 2005

7.7

Numbers

Employee sizeband	2002	2003	2004	2005
0[1]	27,875	24,855	24,670	25,795
1-9	30,895	31,720	32,630	33,685
10-19	3,720	3,945	3,840	4,100
20-49	2,125	2,255	2,245	2,320
50-99	675	730	720	790
100-199	375	375	360	365
200-249	65	65	60	65
250+	265	290	290	285
All	**65,995**	**64,230**	**64,815**	**67,405**

Source: Inter Departmental Business Register, Department of Enterprise, Trade and Investment

[1] This sizeband includes sole proprietors and partnerships, holding companies and those that are not yet trading, for example, if a factory is under construction.

Value Added Tax (VAT) and Pay As You Earn (PAYE) businesses in Northern Ireland by legal status, 2002 to 2005

7.8

Numbers

Legal Status	2002	2003	2004	2005
Company	11,880	12,390	13,595	15,350
Sole Proprietor	37,595	35,715	35,155	35,685
Partnership	13,365	12,995	12,865	13,135
Public Corporation	20	20	15	20
Central Government	120	120	120	125
Local Authority	110	115	115	110
Non profit making organisation	2,900	2,870	2,950	2,980
All	**65,995**	**64,230**	**64,815**	**67,405**

Source: Inter Departmental Business Register, Department of Enterprise, Trade and Investment

7.9 Number of Value Added Tax (VAT)-registered enterprises by broad industry group and Local Government District, 2004

Numbers

Local Government District	Agriculture	Production	Construction	Motor Trades	Wholesale	Retail	Hotels and Catering	Transport	Post and Telecom	Finance	Property and Business	Education	Health	Public Admin. & other services	All
Antrim	510	125	245	75	85	135	85	110	25	0	170	5	10	45	**1,630**
Ards	560	190	325	105	145	270	135	70	10	5	250	5	10	80	**2,160**
Armagh	1,170	190	300	105	160	220	115	160	5	0	165	0	10	40	**2,645**
Ballymena	900	145	350	115	110	225	100	70	5	5	205	5	5	50	**2,290**
Ballymoney	530	65	190	60	50	105	40	50	5	0	80	0	5	15	**1,190**
Banbridge	750	105	315	60	80	135	80	75	5	5	120	0	10	40	**1,775**
Belfast	20	410	480	185	500	1,070	540	180	45	50	2,070	30	60	390	**6,035**
Carrickfergus	70	65	85	35	40	85	50	20	5	0	85	5	0	25	**575**
Castlereagh	90	105	190	55	110	135	50	30	5	10	210	5	10	55	**1,065**
Coleraine	565	105	225	95	85	220	135	55	10	0	220	5	10	60	**1,785**
Cookstown	840	155	250	85	85	125	70	75	0	0	115	0	5	25	**1,830**
Craigavon	440	205	335	120	145	295	120	90	10	5	270	10	10	80	**2,130**
Derry	325	170	330	65	130	305	160	60	10	5	320	5	5	80	**1,975**
Down	740	130	445	90	115	265	155	40	5	0	215	5	10	75	**2,290**
Dungannon	1,215	260	310	105	115	230	100	100	5	5	185	5	10	45	**2,695**
Fermanagh	1,860	135	335	125	90	295	135	65	10	5	180	5	20	70	**3,330**
Larne	360	45	100	35	35	105	50	65	5	0	75	5	5	30	**915**
Limavady	400	65	225	40	40	100	60	25	0	0	80	0	0	20	**1,065**
Lisburn	585	290	475	160	280	295	135	120	15	5	450	15	10	135	**2,965**
Magherafelt	785	175	495	75	70	150	70	80	10	0	140	0	5	20	**2,080**
Moyle	370	20	100	20	30	70	50	15	0	0	30	0	5	10	**720**
Newry & Mourne	1,070	270	565	145	210	345	185	195	5	5	290	5	20	90	**3,405**
Newtownabbey	185	140	200	110	175	200	95	85	15	5	265	10	0	60	**1,550**
North Down	65	110	180	60	125	220	115	35	10	10	390	10	10	115	**1,455**
Omagh	1,390	140	360	80	90	215	80	50	5	0	180	0	5	45	**2,645**
Strabane	810	90	230	55	40	160	80	55	5	0	75	0	5	30	**1,630**
Northern Ireland	**16,615**	**3,910**	**7,645**	**2,250**	**3,150**	**5,960**	**2,985**	**1,985**	**230**	**120**	**6,845**	**140**	**260**	**1,730**	**53,830**

Sources: UK Business: Activity, Size and Location, 2004, Office for National Statistics; Department of Enterprise, Trade and Investment

7.10

Value Added Tax (VAT) registration and de-registration rates[1] by UK region, 2000 to 2003

Rates

Government Office Region	2000		2001		2002		2003	
	Regis-tration	De-regis-tration	Regis-tration	De-regis-tration	Regis-tration	De-regis-tration	Regis-tration	De-regis-tration
North East	*22*	*20*	*20*	*22*	*21*	*20*	*23*	*20*
North West	*34*	*31*	*33*	*31*	*33*	*33*	*35*	*30*
Yorks & The Humber	*31*	*32*	*34*	*32*	*36*	*33*	*34*	*29*
East Midlands	*36*	*32*	*34*	*32*	*36*	*33*	*37*	*33*
West Midlands	*35*	*31*	*34*	*32*	*34*	*34*	*37*	*34*
East	*43*	*37*	*40*	*39*	*41*	*40*	*42*	*39*
London	*67*	*58*	*59*	*56*	*57*	*60*	*62*	*58*
South East	*46*	*39*	*44*	*40*	*44*	*42*	*47*	*43*
South West	*40*	*37*	*36*	*35*	*37*	*38*	*40*	*37*
England	*42*	*37*	*39*	*37*	*39*	*39*	*42*	*38*
Wales	*27*	*27*	*26*	*26*	*26*	*29*	*29*	*29*
Scotland	*28*	*28*	*28*	*28*	*28*	*27*	*29*	*28*
Northern Ireland	*27*	*29*	*28*	*27*	*27*	*24*	*29*	*30*
United Kingdom	***39***	***35***	***37***	***35***	***37***	***37***	***40***	***36***

Source: Department of Trade and Industry Small Business Service Research and Evaluation Unit

[1] Rates are per 10,000 resident adults aged 16 and over at the middle of each year.

ECONOMY, COMMERCE AND INDUSTRY

7.11 Number of foreign owned companies operating in Northern Ireland by country of ownership, 1999 to 2004

Numbers

Country	1999	2000	2001	2002	2003	2004
Republic of Ireland	139	165	199	232	232	257
United States of America	124	146	161	160	154	169
France	27	36	45	45	47	44
Germany	24	26	41	36	37	41
Netherlands (including Netherlands Antilles)	29	26	36	34	41	43
Channel Islands	4	5	18	18	6	7
Japan	15	14	14	14	12	12
Switzerland	10	7	11	12	12	12
Canada	9	10	13	11	8	10
Denmark	5	12	13	11	13	13
Australia	4	5	7	8	9	9
Sweden	2	3	10	8	8	10
South Korea	8	7	7	8	6	6
Finland	4	5	6	7	9	9
Norway	2	9	5	5	4	4
Belgium	6	3	4	4	3	6
Bermuda	2	0	5	4	8	9
Isle of Man	3	3	2	4	1	1
South Africa	3	3	4	4	3	3
Taiwan	1	1	2	3	3	3
Luxembourg	0	1	1	2	2	3
Cayman Islands	0	0	0	1	1	1
India	0	0	1	1	1	1
Italy	2	0	1	1	2	2
Liechtenstein	0	0	1	1	1	1
Portugal	1	4	2	1	1	3
Spain	0	0	0	1	2	3
Virgin Islands	0	0	1	1	2	2
Austria	1	1	0	0	1	1
Bahamas	1	1	0	0	0	0
Malaysia	1	0	0	0	0	0
Kuwait	0	0	0	0	1	1
Greece	0	0	0	0	1	1
All foreign owned companies	**427**	**493**	**610**	**637**	**631**	**687**

Sources: Inter Departmental Business Register, Office for National Statistics; Department of Enterprise, Trade and Investment

Notes to Economy, Commerce and Industry tables

TABLE 7.1

Under European System of accounts 1995 (ESA95), the term Gross Value Added (GVA) is used to denote estimates that were previously known as Gross Domestic Product (GDP) at basic prices. Under ESA95, the term GDP denotes GVA plus taxes (less subsidies) on products, i.e. at market prices. Regional accounts are currently only published at basic prices, so the figures are now referred to as GVA rather than GDP as in previous publications.

The regional GVA series headlined in this publication have been calculated using a five point moving average. In addition, the method for regional allocation of FISIM has been changed to make it consistent with the regional allocation of the GVA of the Financial Intermediation industry.

The GVA estimates presented here are on a residential basis. The breakdown of the totals by components of income and industry are currently only available on a residence basis.

As with the national accounts, the regional estimates, although calculated as reliably as possible, cannot be regarded as accurate to the last digit shown. The regional GVA estimates are partly based on sample surveys and the quality of the results therefore varies according to sample size. This means that the results for smaller regions are subject to a greater degree of uncertainty than those for larger regions.

TABLE 7.2

Disposable Income is the amount of money that households have available for consumption expenditure or saving. It is equivalent to the excess of their income over the expenditures associated with their income, employment, property ownership and provision for future pension income.

The Headline Gross Disposable Household Income (GDHI) series are presented using a moving average based trend of the unadjusted series for each region. Main data sources for the compilation of the Regional GDHI are Inland Revenue (IR) Pay As You Earn, IR survey of personal incomes, IR Taxes data and various benefit data sets. This is the first publication of regional GDHI since March 2002, and includes revisions to estimates for the period 1995 to 1999.

TABLE 7.3

The NI Index of Services (IOS) is a new experimental quarterly survey of almost 1,500 companies designed to provide the most up-to-date measure of change in the Wholesale and Retail; Business Services and Finance; Transport, Storage and Communication; Hotels and Restaurants and the Other services sectors. The turnover is weighted to reflect the relative share of GVA taken from the NI Annual Business Inquiry and figures are referenced 2002 = 100 in line with the UK Index of Services.

The IOS series has been developed to National Statistics standards but is designated as experimental to allow time to receive user feedback and to monitor performance of the Index. Its experimental status also reflects the fact that a longer time series is required to provide seasonally adjusted results. The IOS is released as an experimental statistic and not a National Statistic, but it is hoped that the IOS data set will eventually become a National Statistic. This method is consistent with the National Statistic protocol on the release of data and mirrors the approach adopted during the launch of the UK Index of Services and the Welsh Index of Distribution.

TABLE 7.4

The NI Index of Production is designed to provide a general measure of changes in the output of the production industries. The Index is a weighted average of individual series. The overall production index is calculated by weighting together 164 class indices that describe the activity of an industry using the Standard Industrial Classification (SIC). Changes in output are not, however, available on a regular basis and proxy indicators have to be used. For most series, the value of sales, deflated to allow for price changes, is used as the indicator. In the remaining cases, changes in the volume of sales / production or the number employed are used.

TABLE 7.5

The NI Productivity Index provides a measure of the number of units of output produced each man hour. The Productivity Index includes seasonally adjusted employee jobs (from the Quarterly Employment Survey, not including self-employed), the Manufacturing Index and average weekly hours (based on hours worked for full-time adult manufacturing workers including overtime from the Annual Survey of Hours and Earnings). An index of man hours is calculated based on the number of employee jobs and average weekly hours. The Index of Manufacturing is divided by the index of man hours to produce the Index of Productivity for Northern Ireland.

The UK Productivity Index provides a measure of the number of units of output produced per actual hour worked. The denominator of this productivity measure is an index based on a combination of seasonally adjusted jobs data from Office for National Statistics short-term surveys (employees plus self employed) and average hours from Labour Force Survey data. The Index of Manufacturing is divided by this index of man hours to produce the Index of Productivity.

These indices reflect changes in productivity only, not absolute levels of productivity.

TABLE 7.6

The Northern Ireland Annual Business Inquiry (NIABI) brings together employment and financial information from a survey of businesses and other establishments to provide a picture of the total value of NI business based activities, their associated costs and incomes and the relative contribution of the major industrial sectors at basic prices. The table contains information on total turnover, which is the total value of sales and work completed by NI based companies, and GVA, which is the total value of business' income once expenditure on external goods and services have been accounted for at basic prices. Other financial information available from the NIABI includes purchases, capital expenditure and employment costs.

TABLE 7.7 AND 7.8

The data in these tables are taken from the Inter-Departmental Business Register (IDBR). The IDBR is based on inputs from three administrative sources: traders registered for Value Added Tax (VAT) purposes with HMRC (Customs); employers operating a Pay As You Earn (PAYE) scheme, registered with the HMRC (Revenue); and incorporated businesses registered at Companies House.

The IDBR covers businesses in all parts of the economy, other than some very small businesses (self-employed and those without employees and low turnover) and some non-profit making organisations. With 2.1 million businesses listed it provides nearly 99 per cent coverage of UK economic activity.

Figures in these tables have been rounded to the nearest 5 and thus may not add to totals.

TABLE 7.9

Figures are rounded to the nearest 5 and thus may not add to totals. Each business is allocated to a Local Government District (LGD) area based on the address at which it is registered for VAT (normally the head office, if the business has a number of work sites). Thus a business with its head office in Belfast is included in the figures for Belfast, even though it may have work sites in other LGDs - for example, banks. Similarly, businesses that have their UK headquarters in Great Britain will be included only in the region where their head office is based. Therefore, many multi-national companies are also excluded from this table.

TABLE 7.10

VAT registrations and de-registrations are the best official guide to the pattern of business start-ups and closures. Coverage includes both companies and self-employed run businesses but excludes those that operate below the VAT threshold.

TABLE 7.11

The market information company Dun & Bradstreet annually supply the Office for National Statistics with information on foreign owned businesses operating in the UK. This information is loaded onto the IDBR and then supplemented by Statistics Branch, Department of Enterprise, Trade and Investment (DETI) with information from two sources: Invest NI's list of client companies and the Investor Responsibility Research Center (IRRC) an independent, non-profit making research firm which produces a quarterly list of publicly traded US companies with subsidiaries, affiliates or branch offices employing more than 10 people in Northern Ireland.

This table is based on these combined sources, year on year figures are not directly comparable as there is a time lag for Statistics and Research Branch, DETI, to become aware of the country of ownership of businesses on the Inter-Departmental Business Register.

Labour Market

- There were 691,600 employee jobs in Northern Ireland at June 2005, 8% more than at June 2000. More than half of the increase in employee jobs during 2000-2005 occurred in part-time work, with female part-time employees accounting for almost two-fifths of the total increase.

- The average (mean) gross weekly wage in Northern Ireland at April 2004 (£431.40) was lower than that of England (£515.50), Scotland (£459.60) and Wales (£441.70).

- In 2004, average gross weekly earnings in Northern Ireland were highest in the electricity, gas and water supply industry, and were higher in the public sector than in the private sector.

- At Spring 2005 there were approximately 38,000 persons unemployed in Northern Ireland, representing 4.9% of the NI labourforce. This compares with an unemployment rate of 5.0% in Spring 2004.

- Over two-fifths of those who are unemployed in Northern Ireland have been out of work for at least one year.

- At Spring 2005, the seasonally adjusted unemployment rate in Northern Ireland (4.9%) was 4.0 percentage points lower than the EU25 average. The harmonised employment rate (based on those aged 15-64) in Northern Ireland for Autumn 2004 was 65.0%, 1.3 percentage points higher than the EU25 average.

Seasonally adjusted labour market structure[1] by gender, 2000 to 2005

Thousands and percentages

	All aged 16 and over[2]	All persons of working age 16-59/64[2]	Economically active: In employment	Economically active: Unemployed	**All economically active**	Economically inactive	Activity rate (%) 16-59/64	Unemployment rate (%)	Employment rate (%) 16-59/64
	A	B	C	D	**E**	F	G	H	I
Males									
March-May 2000	602	515	381	33	**414**	188	*78.2*	*8.0*	*71.8*
March-May 2001	608	520	394	31	**426**	183	*80.1*	*7.3*	*74.1*
March-May 2002	615	525	394	26	**420**	195	*77.9*	*6.1*	*73.0*
March-May 2003	621	530	417	25	**442**	179	*81.4*	*5.7*	*76.6*
March-May 2004	627	534	390	27	**417**	210	*76.8*	*6.5*	*71.7*
March-May 2005	632	538	404	26	**430**	202	*78.5*	*6.0*	*73.7*
Females									
March-May 2000	653	494	298	19	**316**	337	*62.1*	*5.9*	*58.4*
March-May 2001	659	498	311	16	**327**	332	*63.4*	*4.9*	*60.2*
March-May 2002	663	501	322	16	**338**	326	*64.8*	*4.7*	*61.7*
March-May 2003	669	504	327	17	**344**	325	*65.1*	*4.8*	*61.9*
March-May 2004	674	507	323	10	**333**	341	*63.3*	*3.1*	*61.2*
March-May 2005	679	510	333	12	**346**	334	*64.8*	*3.6*	*62.3*
All persons									
March-May 2000	**1,255**	**1,009**	**678**	**52**	**730**	**525**	***70.3***	***7.1***	***65.2***
March-May 2001	**1,267**	**1,018**	**705**	**47**	**752**	**515**	***71.9***	***6.3***	***67.3***
March-May 2002	**1,279**	**1,026**	**716**	**41**	**757**	**521**	***71.5***	***5.5***	***67.5***
March-May 2003	**1,290**	**1,034**	**744**	**42**	**786**	**505**	***73.5***	***5.3***	***69.4***
March-May 2004	**1,301**	**1,041**	**712**	**37**	**750**	**552**	***70.2***	***5.0***	***66.6***
March-May 2005	**1,312**	**1,048**	**738**	**38**	**776**	**536**	***71.8***	***4.9***	***68.2***

Source: Labour Force Survey, Department of Enterprise, Trade and Investment

1 Relationship between columns: A=E+F; E=C+D; H=D/E; G=economically active of working age/total population of working age; I=in employment of working age/total population of working age.

2 A and B are underlying population estimates and are therefore not seasonally adjusted. Estimates have been adjusted to reflect the 2001 Census population data.

Figure 8.1 Working age employment rate by gender during March-May of each year, 2000 to 2005

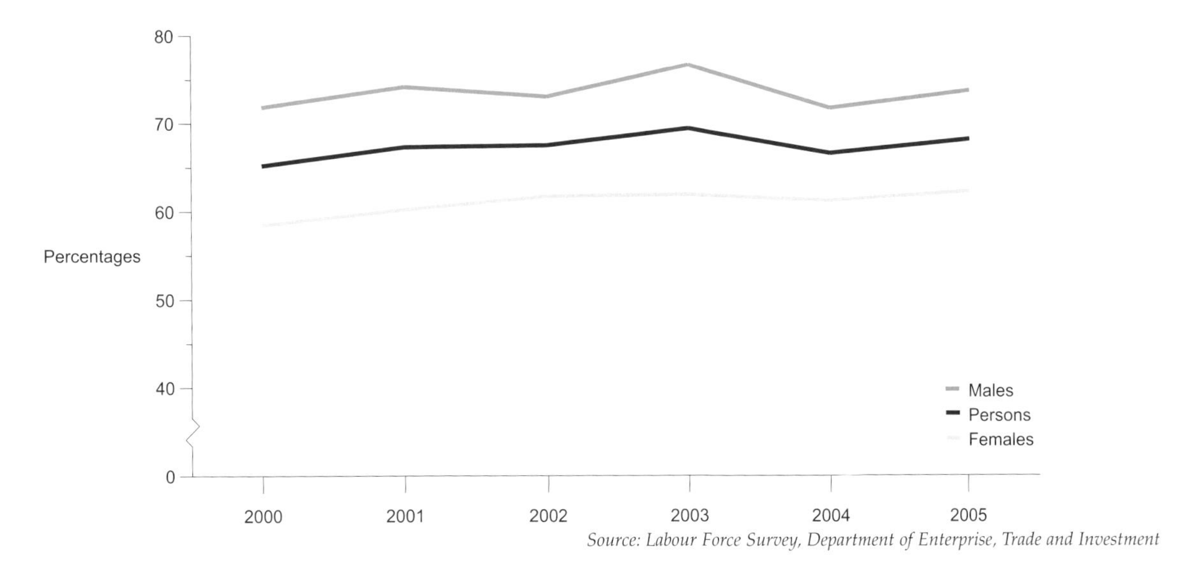

Source: Labour Force Survey, Department of Enterprise, Trade and Investment

8.2 Seasonally adjusted labour market regional summary[1], March-May 2005

Thousands and percentages

Government Office Region	Economically active								
	All aged 16 and over	In employ-ment	Unem-ployed	**All eco-nomically active**	Economically inactive	Activity rate (%) 16-59/64	Claimant count rate (%)[2]	Employee jobs[3]	Unem-ployment rate (%)
	A	B	C	**D**	E	F	G	H	I
United Kingdom	**47,587**	**28,567**	**1,426**	**29,993**	**17,594**	***78.5***	***2.7***	**26,474**	***4.8***
North East	2,032	1,117	76	**1,193**	839	*75.1*	*3.8*	1,008	*6.4*
North West & Merseyside	5,420	3,181	148	**3,329**	2,091	*76.8*	*2.8*	3,020	*4.4*
Yorkshire & the Humber	3,998	2,354	124	**2,478**	1,520	*78.1*	*2.8*	2,183	*5.0*
East Midlands	3,418	2,077	94	**2,171**	1,247	*79.7*	*2.5*	1,754	*4.3*
West Midlands	4,213	2,517	117	**2,634**	1,579	*78.5*	*3.2*	2,320	*4.4*
Eastern	4,364	2,737	105	**2,842**	1,522	*81.9*	*2.0*	2,344	*3.7*
London	5,913	3,515	272	**3,787**	2,127	*74.8*	*3.4*	3,955	*7.2*
South East	6,434	4,077	156	**4,233**	2,201	*81.9*	*1.5*	3,623	*3.7*
South West	4,040	2,487	87	**2,574**	1,466	*82.2*	*1.6*	2,171	*3.4*
England	**39,833**	**24,063**	**1,179**	**25,241**	**14,592**	***78.8***	***2.6***	**22,390**	***4.7***
Wales	2,364	1,314	62	**1,375**	989	*74.7*	*3.0*	1,108	*4.5*
Scotland	4,078	2,443	149	**2,591**	1,487	*79.8*	*3.3*	2,285	*5.7*
Great Britain	**46,275**	**27,819**	**1,389**	**29,208**	**17,067**	***78.7***	***2.6***	**25,783**	***4.8***
Northern Ireland	1,312	738	38	**776**	536	*71.8*	*3.6*	692	*4.9*

Sources: Department of Enterprise, Trade and Investment; Office for National Statistics

1 Relationship between columns: A=D+E; D=B+C; I=C/D, F=economically active of working age/total population of working age. Estimates have been adjusted to reflect the 2001 Census population data.

2 As at June 2005.

3 As at March 2005.

Figure 8.2 Northern Ireland labour market structure, March-May 2005

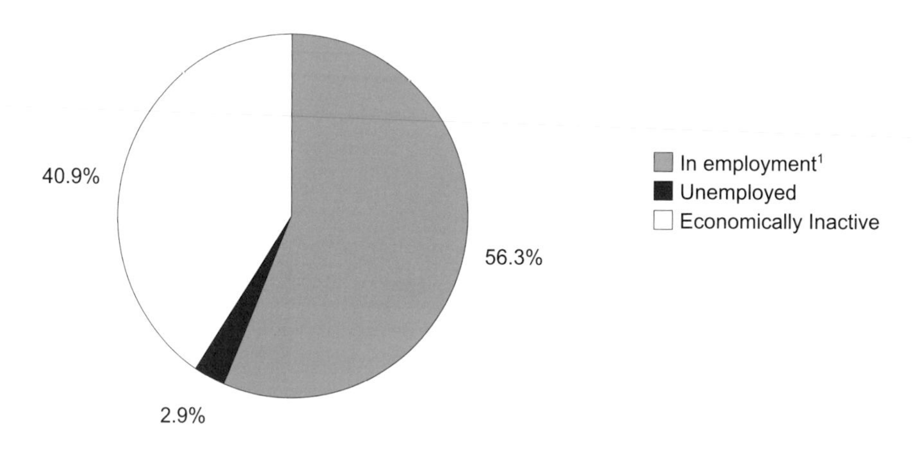

Source: Labour Force Survey, Department of Enterprise, Trade and Investment

1 Includes employees, self employed, Government training, employment schemes and unpaid family workers.

Workforce jobs by gender, 2000 to 2005 (June of each year)

8.3

Numbers

	2000	2001	2002	2003	2004	2005
Males						
Employee jobs	317,300	320,000	324,800	327,500	329,900	334,900
Civil-employment jobs	399,300	407,600	407,100	417,900	420,000	425,100
Workforce jobs	405,800	412,700	411,800	422,700	424,900	429,900
Females						
Employee jobs	323,100	330,100	338,900	345,100	347,900	356,600
Civil-employment jobs	340,700	348,200	357,300	365,500	368,100	376,800
Workforce jobs	343,600	350,400	359,300	367,300	369,900	378,700
All persons						
Employee jobs	**640,400**	**650,000**	**663,600**	**672,600**	**677,700**	**691,600**
Civil-employment jobs	**740,000**	**755,800**	**764,400**	**783,500**	**788,100**	**801,900**
Workforce jobs	**749,400**	**763,100**	**771,100**	**790,100**	**794,900**	**808,600**

Sources: Labour Force Survey, Quarterly Employment Survey, Department of Enterprise, Trade and Investment; Annual Farm Census, Department of Agriculture and Rural Development; Department for Employment and Learning

Figure 8.3 Economic activity rates for 16-59/64 age group by region, March-May 2005

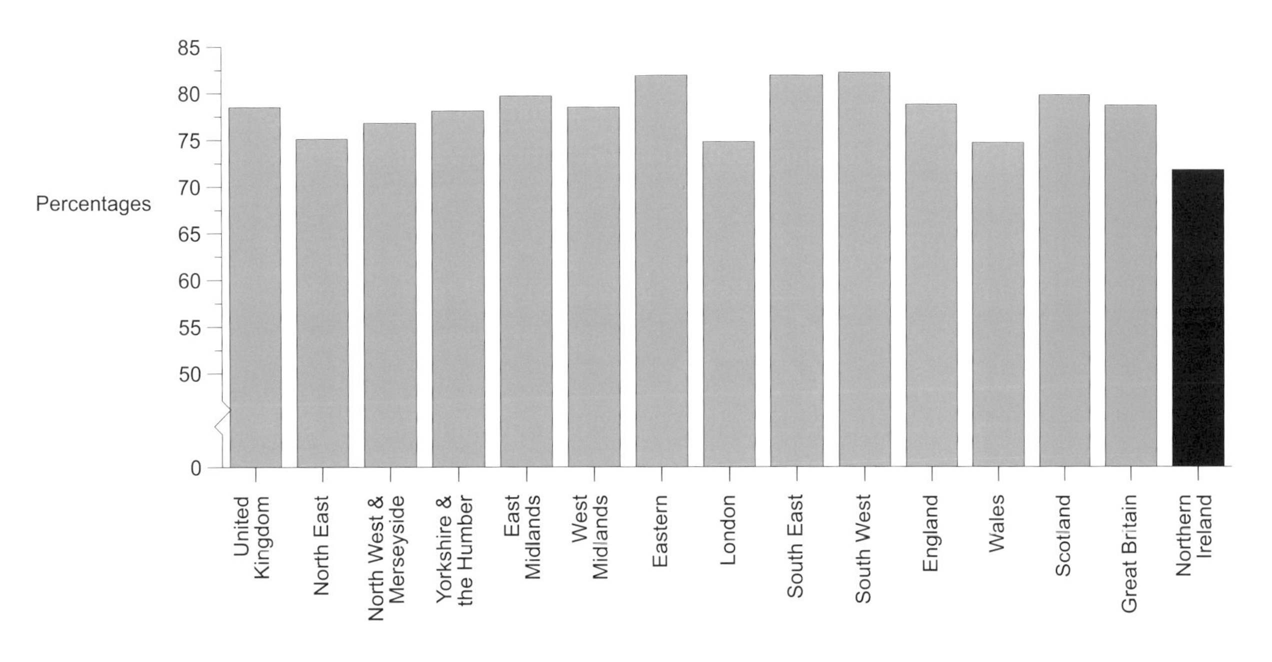

Sources: Labour Force Survey, Department of Enterprise, Trade and Investment; Office for National Statistics

LABOUR MARKET

8.4 Employment by gender and category[1], 2000 to 2005

Thousands

	Employees							
	Full-time	Part-time	**All employment[2]**	Self employed	Government programmes	Employees	Workers with second jobs	Temporary workers
	A	B	**C**	D	E	F	G	H
Males								
March-May 2000	350	25	**377**	82	*	288	19	11
March-May 2001	364	26	**391**	81	11	299	16	14
March-May 2002	364	27	**392**	82	*	304	16	16
March-May 2003	380	32	**415**	89	*	318	13	15
March-May 2004	356	30	**389**	90	*	290	11	14
March-May 2005	373	29	**403**	99	*	297	13	16
Females								
March-May 2000	173	122	**296**	17	*	271	10	23
March-May 2001	191	117	**310**	17	*	286	16	20
March-May 2002	189	132	**321**	17	*	300	11	24
March-May 2003	193	133	**327**	18	*	304	16	21
March-May 2004	203	120	**324**	21	*	298	12	23
March-May 2005	206	126	**333**	20	*	307	11	20
All persons								
March-May 2000	**524**	**148**	**673**	**99**	**10**	**559**	**29**	**34**
March-May 2001	**556**	**143**	**701**	**98**	**15**	**585**	**32**	**34**
March-May 2002	**553**	**159**	**713**	**99**	*	**604**	**27**	**40**
March-May 2003	**573**	**166**	**742**	**106**	**12**	**621**	**29**	**36**
March-May 2004	**558**	**150**	**713**	**110**	**10**	**588**	**23**	**37**
March-May 2005	**578**	**155**	**737**	**119**	**10**	**604**	**24**	**35**

Source: Labour Force Survey, Department of Enterprise, Trade and Investment

[1] Relationship between columns: C=A+B, C=D+E+F.

[2] Includes some who did not state if full or part-time and unpaid family workers.

Northern Ireland employee jobs by Standard Industrial Classification (2003): all persons, 2000 to 2005

8.5

Numbers

Standard Industrial Classification 2003	Section	June 2000 Full-time	June 2000 Part-time	June 2000 All employees	June 2001 Full-time	June 2001 Part-time	June 2001 All employees	June 2002 Full-time	June 2002 Part-time	June 2002 All employees
Agriculture, hunting, forestry and fishing	A/B	3,690	12,040	**15,730**	3,440	11,270	**14,710**	3,280	10,930	**14,210**
Mining and quarrying	C	1,830	70	**1,900**	1,800	70	**1,870**	1,780	60	**1,840**
Manufacturing	D	96,340	7,250	**103,590**	94,700	7,010	**101,710**	90,580	6,860	**97,440**
Electricity, gas and water supply	E	3,470	30	**3,500**	3,030	30	**3,070**	3,020	30	**3,040**
Construction	F	32,010	2,470	**34,470**	33,130	2,680	**35,810**	33,570	2,730	**36,300**
Wholesale and retail trade; repairs	G	59,710	45,730	**105,440**	59,150	47,620	**106,760**	61,450	50,510	**111,950**
Hotels and restaurants	H	14,440	23,260	**37,700**	14,470	24,210	**38,680**	15,240	25,130	**40,370**
Transport, storage and communication	I	21,850	4,410	**26,260**	22,420	4,930	**27,350**	23,480	5,030	**28,510**
Financial intermediation	J	12,020	2,770	**14,790**	12,470	3,160	**15,630**	13,170	3,400	**16,570**
Real estate, renting and business activities	K	33,820	15,220	**49,040**	36,550	15,860	**52,410**	38,060	17,330	**55,380**
Public administration and defence	L	51,380	7,600	**58,980**	51,330	7,980	**59,310**	52,370	8,140	**60,510**
Education	M	36,230	29,690	**65,920**	36,060	29,900	**65,970**	36,200	31,720	**67,920**
Health and social work	N	48,220	46,520	**94,740**	49,710	47,780	**97,490**	50,870	48,810	**99,680**
Other service activities	O	16,190	12,130	**28,330**	16,510	12,740	**29,260**	17,000	12,900	**29,900**
Services	**G-O**	**293,860**	**187,340**	**481,200**	**298,670**	**194,190**	**492,860**	**307,830**	**202,960**	**510,790**
All sections	**A-O**	**431,190**	**209,200**	**640,380**	**434,780**	**215,250**	**650,030**	**440,060**	**223,570**	**663,630**

Standard Industrial Classification 2003	Section	June 2003 Full-time	June 2003 Part-time	June 2003 All employees	June 2004 Full-time	June 2004 Part-time	June 2004 All employees	June 2005 Full-time	June 2005 Part-time	June 2005 All employees
Agriculture, hunting, forestry and fishing	A/B	3,350	11,370	**14,710**	3,350	11,330	**14,680**	3,300	11,350	**14,650**
Mining and quarrying	C	1,840	70	**1,910**	1,900	80	**1,980**	1,930	80	**2,010**
Manufacturing	D	85,470	6,430	**91,890**	82,820	6,200	**89,010**	80,870	5,650	**86,520**
Electricity, gas and water supply	E	2,850	30	**2,880**	2,810	30	**2,840**	2,680	40	**2,720**
Construction	F	33,240	2,690	**35,930**	33,450	2,700	**36,150**	34,750	2,800	**37,550**
Wholesale and retail trade; repairs	G	61,440	51,190	**112,630**	62,700	52,910	**115,610**	63,460	54,830	**118,290**
Hotels and restaurants	H	15,060	25,400	**40,450**	15,460	25,400	**40,860**	16,390	25,090	**41,470**
Transport, storage and communication	I	23,140	5,030	**28,170**	23,330	5,030	**28,360**	23,960	4,800	**28,760**
Financial intermediation	J	13,500	3,580	**17,080**	13,800	3,610	**17,420**	14,030	3,790	**17,820**
Real estate, renting and business activities	K	39,760	18,160	**57,920**	40,920	19,250	**60,180**	44,030	19,960	**63,990**
Public administration and defence	L	54,960	8,530	**63,490**	55,800	8,820	**64,620**	55,370	9,010	**64,380**
Education	M	37,070	32,040	**69,110**	36,470	31,600	**68,070**	38,370	32,960	**71,330**
Health and social work	N	54,330	51,020	**105,340**	55,720	51,910	**107,620**	58,680	52,860	**111,540**
Other service activities	O	17,480	13,590	**31,070**	17,010	13,320	**30,330**	17,250	13,310	**30,570**
Services	**G-O**	**316,730**	**208,540**	**525,270**	**321,210**	**211,850**	**533,060**	**331,530**	**216,610**	**548,140**
All sections	**A-O**	**443,490**	**229,120**	**672,610**	**445,540**	**232,180**	**677,720**	**455,070**	**236,520**	**691,600**

Source: Quarterly Employment Survey, Department of Enterprise, Trade and Investment

8.6 Northern Ireland employee jobs by Standard Industrial Classification (2003): males, 2000 to 2005

Numbers

Standard Industrial Classification 2003	Section	June 2000 Full-time	June 2000 Part-time	June 2000 All Males	June 2001 Full-time	June 2001 Part-time	June 2001 All Males	June 2002 Full-time	June 2002 Part-time	June 2002 All Males
Agriculture, hunting, forestry and fishing	A/B	3,250	10,350	**13,590**	3,030	9,810	**12,840**	2,890	9,490	**12,370**
Mining and quarrying	C	1,670	30	**1,710**	1,640	30	**1,670**	1,610	30	**1,640**
Manufacturing	D	72,090	2,200	**74,290**	71,710	2,240	**73,950**	69,490	2,130	**71,620**
Electricity, gas and water supply	E	3,130	0	**3,130**	2,750	20	**2,770**	2,720	10	**2,730**
Construction	F	29,820	1,270	**31,090**	30,840	1,390	**32,240**	31,190	1,410	**32,600**
Wholesale and retail trade; repairs	G	37,690	11,570	**49,270**	37,300	12,120	**49,420**	38,600	13,360	**51,960**
Hotels and restaurants	H	7,060	8,410	**15,470**	7,200	8,630	**15,830**	7,570	9,130	**16,700**
Transport, storage and communication	I	17,230	2,200	**19,430**	17,600	2,470	**20,080**	18,580	2,560	**21,150**
Financial intermediation	J	4,920	270	**5,190**	5,160	240	**5,400**	5,290	250	**5,550**
Real estate, renting and business activities	K	19,590	3,730	**23,320**	21,390	4,140	**25,530**	22,620	4,780	**27,400**
Public administration and defence	L	31,600	2,440	**34,040**	30,590	2,520	**33,110**	30,720	2,390	**33,110**
Education	M	13,860	3,830	**17,690**	13,650	3,910	**17,560**	13,470	4,200	**17,670**
Health and social work	N	12,120	3,120	**15,230**	12,220	3,230	**15,450**	12,550	3,450	**16,000**
Other service activities	O	9,520	4,350	**13,870**	9,590	4,510	**14,100**	9,790	4,490	**14,280**
Services	**G-O**	**153,580**	**39,930**	**193,510**	**154,720**	**41,780**	**196,500**	**159,190**	**44,620**	**203,810**
All sections	**A-O**	**263,550**	**53,780**	**317,320**	**264,690**	**55,270**	**319,970**	**267,090**	**57,690**	**324,780**

Standard Industrial Classification 2003	Section	June 2003 Full-time	June 2003 Part-time	June 2003 All Males	June 2004 Full-time	June 2004 Part-time	June 2004 All Males	June 2005 Full-time	June 2005 Part-time	June 2005 All Males
Agriculture, hunting, forestry and fishing	A/B	2,950	9,930	**12,880**	2,950	9,910	**12,870**	2,920	9,910	**12,840**
Mining and quarrying	C	1,660	30	**1,700**	1,710	30	**1,740**	1,730	30	**1,770**
Manufacturing	D	66,990	2,100	**69,090**	65,720	2,190	**67,920**	64,650	1,880	**66,540**
Electricity, gas and water supply	E	2,570	10	**2,580**	2,520	10	**2,530**	2,390	10	**2,400**
Construction	F	30,840	1,330	**32,170**	31,030	1,320	**32,350**	32,270	1,350	**33,630**
Wholesale and retail trade; repairs	G	38,620	13,610	**52,220**	39,210	14,060	**53,270**	39,660	14,630	**54,290**
Hotels and restaurants	H	7,600	9,410	**17,010**	7,760	9,350	**17,120**	8,290	9,250	**17,540**
Transport, storage and communication	I	18,430	2,480	**20,910**	18,770	2,490	**21,260**	19,230	2,270	**21,490**
Financial intermediation	J	5,430	260	**5,690**	5,680	270	**5,960**	5,850	320	**6,170**
Real estate, renting and business activities	K	23,590	5,480	**29,070**	24,470	6,010	**30,470**	26,530	6,450	**32,970**
Public administration and defence	L	31,840	2,460	**34,300**	32,290	2,320	**34,610**	32,090	2,310	**34,400**
Education	M	13,620	4,030	**17,640**	13,440	3,970	**17,410**	13,640	3,890	**17,530**
Health and social work	N	13,480	3,930	**17,410**	13,660	4,060	**17,720**	14,540	4,190	**18,730**
Other service activities	O	10,060	4,750	**14,810**	9,810	4,810	**14,620**	9,930	4,720	**14,660**
Services	**G-O**	**162,670**	**46,400**	**209,070**	**165,100**	**47,350**	**212,450**	**169,760**	**48,030**	**217,780**
All sections	**A-O**	**267,680**	**59,800**	**327,480**	**269,040**	**60,820**	**329,860**	**273,730**	**61,220**	**334,950**

Source: Quarterly Employment Survey, Department of Enterprise, Trade and Investment

Northern Ireland employee jobs by Standard Industrial Classification (2003): females, 2000 to 2005

8.7

Numbers

Standard Industrial Classification 2003	Section	June 2000			June 2001			June 2002		
		Full-time	Part-time	**All Females**	Full-time	Part-time	**All Females**	Full-time	Part-time	**All Females**
Agriculture, hunting, forestry and fishing	A/B	440	1,690	**2,130**	410	1,460	**1,870**	400	1,440	**1,840**
Mining and quarrying	C	150	40	**190**	160	40	**200**	170	30	**200**
Manufacturing	D	24,240	5,060	**29,300**	22,990	4,770	**27,750**	21,090	4,740	**25,830**
Electricity, gas and water supply	E	340	30	**360**	280	20	**300**	290	20	**310**
Construction	F	2,190	1,200	**3,390**	2,290	1,290	**3,570**	2,380	1,320	**3,700**
Wholesale and retail trade; repairs	G	22,020	34,160	**56,170**	21,850	35,490	**57,340**	22,840	37,150	**60,000**
Hotels and restaurants	H	7,380	14,850	**22,230**	7,270	15,580	**22,850**	7,670	15,990	**23,670**
Transport, storage and communication	I	4,620	2,210	**6,830**	4,820	2,460	**7,270**	4,890	2,470	**7,360**
Financial intermediation	J	7,100	2,500	**9,610**	7,310	2,920	**10,230**	7,880	3,150	**11,030**
Real estate, renting and business activities	K	14,230	11,490	**25,720**	15,150	11,720	**26,870**	15,440	12,550	**27,980**
Public administration and defence	L	19,780	5,160	**24,940**	20,740	5,460	**26,200**	21,650	5,750	**27,390**
Education	M	22,370	25,860	**48,230**	22,410	26,000	**48,410**	22,730	27,520	**50,250**
Health and social work	N	36,110	43,400	**79,510**	37,490	44,550	**82,040**	38,320	45,350	**83,680**
Other service activities	O	6,680	7,780	**14,460**	6,920	8,240	**15,160**	7,210	8,410	**15,620**
Services	**G-O**	**140,280**	**147,410**	**287,690**	**143,950**	**152,410**	**296,360**	**148,640**	**158,340**	**306,980**
All sections	**A-O**	**167,640**	**155,420**	**323,060**	**170,080**	**159,980**	**330,060**	**172,970**	**165,880**	**338,850**

Standard Industrial Classification 2003	Section	June 2003			June 2004			June 2005		
		Full-time	Part-time	**All Females**	Full-time	Part-time	**All Females**	Full-time	Part-time	**All Females**
Agriculture, hunting, forestry and fishing	A/B	400	1,440	**1,830**	400	1,410	**1,810**	380	1,430	**1,810**
Mining and quarrying	C	180	40	**210**	190	50	**230**	200	50	**250**
Manufacturing	D	18,480	4,330	**22,810**	17,090	4,010	**21,100**	16,220	3,770	**19,980**
Electricity, gas and water supply	E	290	10	**300**	290	20	**310**	290	30	**320**
Construction	F	2,400	1,370	**3,770**	2,410	1,380	**3,790**	2,480	1,450	**3,930**
Wholesale and retail trade; repairs	G	22,820	37,590	**60,410**	23,490	38,850	**62,330**	23,800	40,200	**64,000**
Hotels and restaurants	H	7,460	15,990	**23,450**	7,690	16,050	**23,740**	8,100	15,830	**23,930**
Transport, storage and communication	I	4,710	2,540	**7,260**	4,560	2,540	**7,100**	4,740	2,530	**7,270**
Financial intermediation	J	8,070	3,320	**11,390**	8,120	3,340	**11,460**	8,180	3,470	**11,650**
Real estate, renting and business activities	K	16,170	12,680	**28,850**	16,460	13,250	**29,710**	17,500	13,520	**31,020**
Public administration and defence	L	23,110	6,080	**29,190**	23,510	6,500	**30,000**	23,280	6,700	**29,970**
Education	M	23,450	28,020	**51,470**	23,030	27,630	**50,670**	24,730	29,070	**53,800**
Health and social work	N	40,840	47,090	**87,930**	42,060	47,850	**89,900**	44,140	48,660	**92,800**
Other service activities	O	7,430	8,840	**16,260**	7,200	8,500	**15,710**	7,320	8,590	**15,910**
Services	**G-O**	**154,070**	**162,140**	**316,210**	**156,110**	**164,500**	**320,620**	**161,770**	**168,580**	**330,350**
All sections	**A-O**	**175,810**	**169,330**	**345,130**	**176,500**	**171,370**	**347,860**	**181,350**	**175,300**	**356,650**

Source: Quarterly Employment Survey, Department of Enterprise, Trade and Investment

8.8 Employee jobs, June 2005

Numbers

Standard Industrial Classification (2003)	Class	Males Full-time	Males Part-time	**All males**	Females Full-time	Females Part-time	**All females**	**All persons**
Agriculture, hunting and related activities	01	2,490	9,890	**12,380**	320	1,380	**1,700**	**14,080**
Forestry, logging and related activities	02	310	10	**320**	50	40	**80**	**400**
Fishing, operation of fish hatcheries	05	120	20	**140**	20	10	**30**	**170**
Mining of coal and lignite: extraction of peat	10	220	10	**230**	50	0	**50**	**290**
Extraction of crude petroleum and natural gas: service activities incidental to oil and gas extraction excluding surveying	11	10	0	**10**	0	0	**0**	**10**
Mining of uranium and thorium ores	12	0	0	**0**	0	0	**0**	**0**
Mining of metal ores	13	0	0	**0**	0	0	**0**	**0**
Other mining and quarrying	14	1,510	20	**1,530**	150	40	**190**	**1,720**
Manufacture of food products, beverages and tobacco	15/16	11,870	870	**12,740**	4,730	1,440	**6,170**	**18,910**
Manufacture of textiles	17	2,140	30	**2,170**	1,110	240	**1,350**	**3,520**
Manufacture of wearing apparel	18	350	20	**370**	820	150	**980**	**1,350**
Manufacture of leather and leather products	19	20	0	**30**	30	10	**40**	**70**
Manufacture of wood and wood products	20	2,990	110	**3,100**	320	110	**430**	**3,530**
Manufacture of pulp, paper and paper products	21	1,360	10	**1,370**	330	60	**390**	**1,750**
Publishing, printing and production of recorded media	22	2,440	120	**2,570**	1,390	430	**1,820**	**4,390**
Manufacture of coke, refined petroleum products and nuclear fuels	23	60	0	**60**	10	0	**10**	**60**
Manufacture of chemicals and chemical products	24	2,070	30	**2,090**	990	70	**1,060**	**3,150**
Manufacture of rubber and plastic products	25	5,940	110	**6,050**	1,050	200	**1,250**	**7,300**
Manufacture of other non-metallic mineral products	26	4,760	150	**4,910**	710	160	**870**	**5,780**
Manufacture of basic metals	27	440	20	**460**	30	10	**40**	**500**
Manufacture of fabricated metal products except machinery	28	5,880	150	**6,030**	680	230	**910**	**6,940**
Manufacture of machinery and equipment not elsewhere classified	29	5,770	90	**5,860**	670	200	**870**	**6,730**
Manufacture of office machinery and equipment	30	1,770	10	**1,780**	370	40	**410**	**2,190**
Manufacture of electrical machinery and apparatus not elsewhere classified	31	2,840	10	**2,850**	490	70	**560**	**3,410**
Manufacture of radio, television and communication equipment	32	1,220	10	**1,230**	790	40	**830**	**2,060**
Manufacture of medical, precision and optical instruments, watches and clocks	33	870	10	**880**	470	60	**530**	**1,410**
Manufacture of motor vehicles, trailers and semi-trailers	34	3,070	10	**3,070**	150	20	**180**	**3,250**
Manufacture of other transport equipment	35	5,680	10	**5,690**	450	50	**500**	**6,190**
Manufacture of furniture; manufacture not elsewhere classified	36	2,670	110	**2,780**	520	170	**680**	**3,460**
Recycling	37	440	20	**460**	110	20	**120**	**580**

Table 8.8 Employee jobs, June 2005 (continued)

Numbers

Standard Industrial Classification (2003)	Class	Males			Females			
		Full-time	Part-time	**All males**	Full-time	Part-time	**All females**	**All persons**
Electricity, gas, steam and hot water supply	40	1,480	10	**1,490**	290	30	**320**	**1,810**
Collection, purification and distribution of water	41	910	0	**910**	0	0	**0**	**920**
Construction	45	32,270	1,350	**33,630**	2,480	1,450	**3,930**	**37,550**
Sale, maintenance and repair of motor vehicles; retail of automotive fuel	50	8,420	1,530	**9,950**	2,260	2,430	**4,700**	**14,650**
Wholesale trade and commission trade	51	16,090	1,060	**17,150**	4,660	1,750	**6,410**	**23,560**
Retail trade	52	15,150	12,040	**27,190**	16,870	36,010	**52,890**	**80,070**
Hotels and restaurants	55	8,290	9,250	**17,540**	8,100	15,830	**23,930**	**41,470**
Land transport, transport via pipelines	60	10,230	1,080	**11,310**	1,080	960	**2,040**	**13,350**
Water transport	61	380	10	**390**	180	30	**210**	**600**
Air transport	62	220	10	**230**	350	110	**450**	**680**
Supporting and auxiliary transport activities; travel agents	63	2,560	380	**2,940**	1,580	560	**2,140**	**5,080**
Post and telecommunications	64	5,830	790	**6,620**	1,560	870	**2,430**	**9,050**
Financial intermediation except insurance and pension funding	65	3,990	200	**4,190**	5,650	2,590	**8,240**	**12,430**
Insurance and pension funding, except compulsory social security	66	830	20	**850**	1,010	290	**1,300**	**2,150**
Activities auxiliary to financial intermediation	67	1,020	100	**1,120**	1,520	590	**2,110**	**3,230**
Real estate activities	70	1,680	310	**1,990**	1,350	710	**2,060**	**4,050**
Renting of equipment and machinery without operator	71	1,110	240	**1,350**	310	380	**690**	**2,040**
Computer and related activities	72	4,370	130	**4,490**	1,590	270	**1,870**	**6,360**
Research and development	73	990	20	**1,010**	520	100	**620**	**1,630**
Other business activities	74	18,380	5,760	**24,130**	13,730	12,050	**25,780**	**49,910**
Public administration and defence; compulsory social security	75	32,090	2,310	**34,400**	23,280	6,700	**29,970**	**64,380**
Education	80	13,640	3,890	**17,530**	24,730	29,070	**53,800**	**71,330**
Health and social work	85	14,540	4,190	**18,730**	44,140	48,660	**92,800**	**111,540**
Sewage and refuse disposal, sanitation and similar activities	90	2,110	70	**2,190**	200	110	**300**	**2,490**
Activities of membership organisation not elsewhere classified	91	2,330	1,570	**3,900**	1,670	2,790	**4,460**	**8,350**
Recreational, cultural and sporting activities	92	4,870	2,890	**7,760**	3,430	4,150	**7,580**	**15,350**
Other service activities	93	620	200	**810**	2,020	1,540	**3,570**	**4,380**
All Classes		**273,730**	**61,220**	**334,950**	**181,350**	**175,300**	**356,650**	**691,600**

Source: Quarterly Employment Survey, Department of Enterprise, Trade and Investment

8.9 Northern Ireland Annual Survey of Hours and Earnings – average (mean) gross weekly earnings by Standard Industrial Classification (SIC 92 & 03), 2001 to 2004

£s

SIC (92 & 03)	2001			2002			2003			2004		
	Male	Female	**All persons**	Male	Female	**All persons**	Male	Female	**All persons**	Male	Female	**All persons**
A. Agriculture, hunting and forestry	227.23	236.22	**288.74**	254.30	204.75	**245.12**	289.12	198.52	**278.51**	249.84	233.76	**246.99**
B. Fishing	.	.	**.**	.	.	**.**	.	.	**.**	.	.	**.**
C. Mining and quarrying	362.26	*	**361.20**	402.03	*	**395.68**	354.18	*	**349.81**	389.11	*	**387.07**
D. Manufacturing	384.50	272.15	**357.47**	383.64	297.31	**365.22**	401.07	304.76	**380.96**	405.64	308.55	**386.29**
E. Electricity, gas and water supply	497.98	*	**484.10**	600.11	*	**580.95**	622.72	*	**607.80**	626.21	*	**607.72**
F. Construction	351.49	296.73	**346.89**	370.99	280.91	**362.48**	386.94	303.24	**379.74**	405.32	313.26	**398.03**
G. Wholesale and retail trade	353.90	235.76	**313.12**	369.01	240.21	**319.78**	386.26	266.85	**341.52**	406.57	313.03	**372.51**
H. Hotels and restaurants	276.13	201.14	**237.42**	283.41	214.90	**251.29**	320.81	213.72	**269.32**	289.96	252.20	**275.64**
I. Transport, storage and communication	390.86	314.97	**375.70**	412.16	322.98	**396.09**	407.85	315.63	**392.55**	448.10	426.89	**444.78**
J. Financial intermediation	622.68	335.99	**475.92**	631.82	368.62	**486.98**	680.27	397.70	**531.75**	687.82	402.86	**515.59**
K. Real estate, renting and business activities	461.21	271.08	**372.93**	474.46	305.26	**403.51**	469.65	314.91	**401.14**	474.06	323.89	**409.52**
L. Public administration and defence; compulsory social security	497.75	320.96	**433.86**	521.81	326.44	**450.06**	549.91	347.36	**471.79**	574.32	373.97	**511.39**
M. Education	483.31	429.18	**448.96**	522.21	475.79	**492.42**	542.74	490.19	**509.53**	536.35	491.68	**507.81**
N. Health and social work	508.20	361.84	**395.74**	528.43	375.32	**410.74**	558.86	382.27	**420.86**	547.53	393.73	**435.17**
O. Other community, social and personal service activities	403.29	305.49	**365.12**	390.03	307.06	**357.68**	387.94	335.46	**369.59**	531.67	337.56	**466.34**
P. Private households with employed persons	.	*	*	.	*	*	.	*	*	.	*	*
Q. Extra-territorial organisations and bodies	.	.	**.**	.	.	**.**	.	.	**.**	.	.	**.**
G-Q All service industries	**445.30**	**332.60**	**391.97**	**462.94**	**349.79**	**408.95**	**477.63**	**363.36**	**422.71**	**496.25**	**390.57**	**445.77**
C-E Index of Production industries	**389.53**	**272.89**	**362.79**	**392.23**	**298.60**	**373.00**	**408.48**	**306.68**	**387.90**	**412.89**	**312.03**	**393.48**
A-Q All industries	**418.94**	**323.55**	**381.49**	**431.95**	**342.10**	**396.84**	**447.68**	**355.92**	**411.50**	**464.19**	**381.88**	**431.36**

Source: Northern Ireland Annual Survey of Hours and Earnings, Department of Enterprise, Trade and Investment

8.10 Northern Ireland Annual Survey of Hours and Earnings – average (mean) gross weekly earnings by Standard Occupational Classification (SOC 2000), 2002 to 2004

£s

SOC 2000	2002 Male	2002 Female	2002 **All persons**	2003 Male	2003 Female	2003 **All persons**	2004 Male	2004 Female	2004 **All persons**
1 Managers and Senior Officials	633.82	405.85	**569.67**	649.36	443.77	**592.34**	656.50	456.95	**597.94**
2 Professional Occupations	627.15	533.59	**582.21**	635.59	552.23	**597.50**	651.99	557.81	**606.35**
3 Associate Professional and Technical Occupations	519.62	423.09	**479.10**	552.76	440.10	**502.51**	551.98	464.23	**513.49**
4 Administrative and Secretarial Occupations	306.09	266.64	**274.99**	304.43	279.15	**284.34**	329.34	288.88	**297.94**
5 Skilled Trade Occupations	361.57	239.92	**353.60**	369.39	244.46	**363.82**	373.89	247.81	**368.12**
6 Personal Service Occupations	270.17	238.89	**248.30**	268.08	241.32	**248.72**	290.32	251.38	**260.88**
7 Sales and Customer Service Occupations	270.96	209.46	**231.62**	275.85	208.99	**235.92**	265.58	224.04	**241.87**
8 Process, Plant and Machine Operatives	326.75	266.71	**318.29**	329.17	265.43	**318.58**	336.47	270.08	**327.89**
9 Elementary Occupations	272.36	216.33	**255.24**	275.44	224.72	**260.93**	286.42	246.32	**276.74**
All Occupations	**431.95**	**342.10**	**396.84**	**447.68**	**355.92**	**411.50**	**464.19**	**381.88**	**431.36**
Skill Level 1	272.36	216.33	**255.24**	275.44	224.72	**260.93**	286.42	246.32	**276.74**
Skill Level 2	313.09	251.52	**281.44**	313.94	259.68	**285.10**	323.18	269.16	**294.81**
Skill Level 3	432.40	399.86	**423.36**	450.36	424.02	**442.87**	464.68	448.09	**459.70**
Skill Level 4	643.27	504.70	**589.30**	656.47	524.38	**607.30**	662.93	532.48	**611.10**

Source: Northern Ireland Annual Survey of Hours and Earnings, Department of Enterprise, Trade and Investment

8.11 Comparison of public and private sector average (mean) gross weekly earnings of full-time employees, 1999 to 2004

£s

Year and sector	Males	Females	**All Persons**
1999			
Public	439.01	348.19	**395.17**
Private	348.44	247.44	**315.07**
2000			
Public	472.22	364.45	**419.82**
Private	370.31	254.65	**333.85**
2001			
Public	486.96	378.44	**431.03**
Private	390.83	272.65	**352.83**
2002			
Public	510.25	402.21	**454.68**
Private	400.33	287.72	**364.18**
2003			
Public	520.04	412.54	**463.15**
Private	405.71	301.21	**371.11**
2004			
Public	540.02	431.34	**481.92**
Private	415.95	318.19	**384.54**

Source: Northern Ireland Annual Survey of Hours and Earnings, Department of Enterprise, Trade and Investment

8.12 Average (mean) gross weekly earnings by region for full-time employees, April 2004

£s

Government Office Region	Males	Females	**All Persons**
North East	473.7	379.6[1]	**436.2**
North West & Merseyside	519.5	390.8	**469.5**
Yorkshire & the Humber	497.0	384.9	**455.3**
East Midlands	489.0	374.2[1]	**448.4**
West Midlands	505.2	384.9	**461.7**
South West	509.1	384.6	**462.7**
Eastern	558.9	409.8	**506.1**
London	765.4	548.2	**680.1**
South East	591.2	441.1	**535.5**
England	**568.7**	**426.7**	**515.5**
Wales	480.4	377.4[1]	**441.7**
Scotland	506.6	396.4	**459.6**
Great Britain	**559.4**	**421.3**	**507.0**
Northern Ireland	464.2	381.9	**431.4**

Sources: Northern Ireland Annual Survey of Hours and Earnings, Department of Enterprise, Trade and Investment; Great Britain Annual Survey of Hours and Earnings, Office for National Statistics

[1] Regions where average earnings are lower than in Northern Ireland.

Figure 8.4 Average (mean) gross weekly earnings by region for full-time employees, April 2004

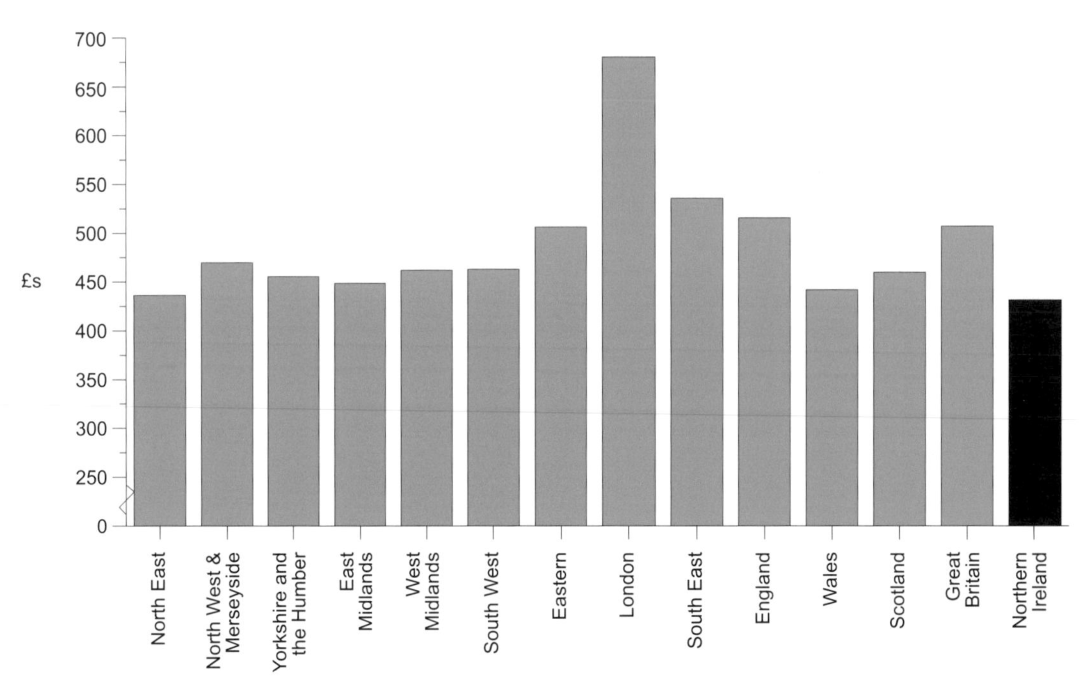

Sources: Northern Ireland Annual Survey of Hours and Earnings, Department of Enterprise, Trade and Investment; Great Britain Annual Survey of Hours and Earnings, Office for National Statistics

Average (mean) gross hourly earnings by full-time and part-time status, 1999 to 2004

8.13

£s

Year and full/ part-time status	Males	Females	All Persons
1999			
Part-time	6.62	5.95	**6.07**
Full-time	9.41	8.00	**8.89**
2000			
Part-time	6.13	6.37	**6.33**
Full-time	9.76	8.30	**9.24**
2001			
Part-time	6.62	6.61	**6.61**
Full-time	10.18	8.62	**9.60**
2002			
Part-time	7.13	6.91	**6.94**
Full-time	10.50	9.18	**10.02**
2003			
Part-time	7.54	7.43	**7.45**
Full-time	10.99	9.55	**10.45**
2004			
Part-time	8.17	7.93	**7.97**
Full-time	11.30	10.18	**10.88**

Source: Northern Ireland Annual Survey of Hours and Earnings, Department of Enterprise, Trade and Investment

Self-employment jobs by gender and sector, 1999 to 2004

8.14

Numbers

Gender and sector	1999	2000	2001	2002	2003	2004
Males						
Agriculture, forestry and fishing	21,500	19,700	19,300	19,900	18,800	17,900
Production and construction	26,900	28,100	30,500	31,600	35,300	34,500
Services	28,700	34,100	37,900	30,800	36,400	37,700
All males	**77,100**	**82,000**	**87,600**	**82,300**	**90,500**	**90,200**
Females						
Agriculture, forestry and fishing	*	*	*	*	*	*
Production and construction	*	*	*	*	*	*
Services	15,900	15,300	15,200	15,600	16,400	17,900
All females	**18,600**	**17,600**	**18,200**	**18,400**	**20,400**	**20,200**
All persons						
Agriculture, forestry and fishing	**23,100**	**21,000**	**20,700**	**21,500**	**20,200**	**19,000**
Production and construction	**28,100**	**29,200**	**32,000**	**32,800**	**37,800**	**35,800**
Services	**44,600**	**49,400**	**53,100**	**46,400**	**52,800**	**55,600**
All persons	**95,700**	**99,600**	**105,800**	**100,800**	**110,800**	**110,300**

Sources: Labour Force Survey, Department of Enterprise, Trade and Investment; Farm Census, Department of Agriculture and Rural Development

8.15 Unemployment by age group, 2000 to 2005

Thousands and percentages

	Age group							
	18-24		25-49		50 and over		16 and over	
	Number	%	Number	%	Number	%	Number	%
All persons								
March-May 2000	11	*10.4*	30	*6.6*	*	*	50	*6.9*
March-May 2001	11	*10.1*	26	*5.6*	*	*	46	*6.2*
March-May 2002	12	*11.1*	22	*4.6*	*	*	41	*5.4*
March-May 2003	12	*9.9*	20	*4.2*	*	*	41	5.2
March-May 2004	10	*9.2*	17	*3.7*	*	*	35	*4.7*
March-May 2005	14	*12.5*	16	*3.4*	*	*	36	*4.6*

Source: Labour Force Survey, Department of Enterprise, Trade and Investment

8.16 Unemployment by duration, 2000 to 2005

Thousands and percentages

	Duration of unemployment					
	Up to 6 months	6-12 months	Over 12 months	Over 24 months	Total unemployed[1]	Long term unemployed as percentage of total[2]
All persons						
March-May 2000	24	*	20	14	50	*39.8*
March-May 2001	19	*	20	13	46	*43.0*
March-May 2002	21	*	15	10	41	*37.8*
March-May 2003	17	*	17	11	41	*42.5*
March-May 2004	12	*	16	12	35	*45.7*
March-May 2005	14	*	15	9	36	*43.5*

Source: Labour Force Survey, Department of Enterprise, Trade and Investment

[1] Includes some who did not state duration of unemployment.

[2] Unemployed for 1 year or more.

Claimant count trends – seasonally adjusted claimant count[1], 1994 to 2005

8.17

Numbers and rates

Year	Males	Females	**All persons**	Males	Females	**All persons**
1994	75,083	21,650	**96,733**	*16.6*	*6.8*	***12.6***
1995	68,550	19,275	**87,825**	*15.1*	*5.9*	***11.2***
1996	64,883	18,875	**83,758**	*14.1*	*5.7*	***10.6***
1997	49,908	13,500	**63,408**	*10.9*	*4.0*	***8.0***
1998	44,833	12,608	**57,442**	*10.0*	*3.7*	***7.3***
1999	39,317	11,425	**50,742**	*8.7*	*3.3*	***6.3***
2000	32,008	10,058	**42,067**	*7.2*	*2.8*	***5.3***
2001	29,958	9,517	**39,475**	*6.6*	*2.7*	***4.9***
2002	27,817	8,617	**36,433**	*6.1*	*2.3*	***4.4***
2003	26,408	8,192	**34,600**	*5.8*	*2.2*	***4.2***
2004	23,475	7,367	**30,842**	*5.1*	*1.9*	***3.6***
January 2005	22,000	7,000	**29,000**	*4.7*	*1.8*	***3.4***
February 2005	22,100	7,000	**29,100**	*4.8*	*1.8*	***3.4***
March 2005	22,100	7,000	**29,100**	*4.8*	*1.8*	***3.4***
April 2005	22,000	7,000	**29,000**	*4.7*	*1.8*	***3.4***
May 2005	22,000	6,900	**28,900**	*4.7*	*1.8*	***3.4***
June 2005	21,800	6,800	**28,600**	*4.7*	*1.8*	***3.4***
July 2005	21,300	6,700	**28,000**	*4.6*	*1.8*	***3.3***

Source: Department of Enterprise, Trade and Investment

[1] 1994-2004 counts are annual averages.

Long-term[1] and youth[2] claimant count trends[3] by gender, 1994 to 2005

8.18

Numbers and percentages

	Long-term claimants						Youth claimants					
				% of all claimants						% of all claimants		
Year	Males	Females	**Persons**	Males	Females	**Persons**	Males	Females	**Persons**	Males	Females	**Persons**
1994[4]	45,943	8,744	**54,688**	*60.2*	*38.7*	***55.3***	17,682	8,052	**25,734**	*23.2*	*35.7*	***26.0***
1995[5]	40,910	7,575	**48,480**	*60.3*	*39.2*	***55.6***	14,925	6,790	**21,715**	*22.0*	*35.2*	***24.9***
1996	37,615	6,845	**44,465**	*58.1*	*36.1*	***53.1***	14,275	6,615	**20,890**	*22.0*	*34.9*	***25.0***
1997	27,430	4,470	**31,900**	*55.3*	*33.4*	***50.6***	11,245	5,150	**16,395**	*22.7*	*38.4*	***26.0***
1998	21,835	3,555	**25,390**	*49.0*	*28.4*	***44.5***	10,080	4,690	**14,765**	*22.6*	*37.5*	***25.9***
1999	17,425	2,760	**20,185**	*44.8*	*24.4*	***40.2***	8,335	4,070	**12,410**	*21.4*	*36.0*	***24.7***
2000	11,230	2,005	**13,235**	*35.4*	*20.1*	***31.7***	7,550	3,740	**11,290**	*23.8*	*37.4*	***27.1***
2001	10,230	1,925	**12,155**	*34.4*	*20.3*	***31.0***	7,280	3,645	**10,920**	*24.5*	*38.5*	***27.9***
2002	7,700	1,575	**9,275**	*27.9*	*18.4*	***25.6***	7,480	3,385	**10,865**	*27.1*	*39.5*	***30.0***
2003	6,325	1,300	**7,625**	*24.1*	*16.0*	***22.2***	7,235	3,205	**10,435**	*27.6*	*39.4*	***30.4***
2004	6,435	1,300	**7,730**	*27.6*	*17.7*	***25.3***	6,495	2,840	**9,335**	*27.9*	*38.8*	***30.5***
Jan-05	5,730	1,215	**6,945**	*25.4*	*18.3*	***23.8***	6,585	2,580	**9,165**	*29.2*	*38.8*	***31.4***
Feb-05	5,590	1,150	**6,740**	*24.8*	*17.4*	***23.1***	6,685	2,600	**9,285**	*29.6*	*39.3*	***31.8***
Mar-05	5,415	1,105	**6,520**	*24.3*	*17.1*	***22.7***	6,580	2,575	**9,160**	*29.6*	*39.8*	***31.9***
Apr-05	5,270	1,070	**6,345**	*24.1*	*16.8*	***22.5***	6,360	2,450	**8,815**	*29.1*	*38.4*	***31.2***
May-05	5,130	1,060	**6,190**	*23.9*	*17.0*	***22.4***	6,230	2,365	**8,595**	*29.1*	*37.9*	***31.1***
Jun-05	4,975	1,080	**6,055**	*23.5*	*16.2*	***21.7***	6,385	2,745	**9,130**	*30.1*	*41.3*	***32.8***
Jul-05	4,905	1,075	**5,980**	*22.9*	*13.8*	***20.5***	6,530	3,340	**9,870**	*30.5*	*42.8*	***33.8***

Source: Department of Enterprise, Trade and Investment

[1] Long-term refers to those claiming benefit for 1 year or more.

[2] Youth unemployment refers to those claimants under 25 years old.

[3] Data from 1994 to 2004 are annual averages.

[4] Data for 1994 show computerised and clerical claims.

[5] Data from 1995 onwards show computerised claims only.

8.19 Claimant count by Local Government District: number, rate and percentage change, July 2005

Numbers, rates and percentages

Local Government District	All unemployed			% of Working Age			Change over month		Change over year	
	Males	Females	**All persons**	Males	Females	**All persons**	Number	%	Number	%
Antrim	371	162	**533**	*2.2*	*1.1*	***1.7***	-6	*-1.1*	-17	*-3.1*
Ards	824	277	**1,101**	*3.5*	*1.2*	***2.4***	54	*5.2*	-40	*-3.5*
Armagh	461	185	**646**	*2.6*	*1.2*	***1.9***	-9	*-1.4*	-206	*-24.2*
Ballymena	537	249	**786**	*2.9*	*1.4*	***2.2***	76	*10.7*	46	*6.2*
Ballymoney	248	97	**345**	*2.8*	*1.2*	***2.0***	29	*9.2*	-22	*-6.0*
Banbridge	263	132	**395**	*1.9*	*1.0*	***1.5***	49	*14.2*	-40	*-9.2*
Belfast	5,644	1,498	**7,142**	*6.8*	*1.8*	***4.3***	237	*3.4*	-430	*-5.7*
Carrickfergus	423	149	**572**	*3.5*	*1.3*	***2.4***	-1	*-0.2*	-143	*-20.0*
Castlereagh	446	153	**599**	*2.2*	*0.8*	***1.5***	62	*11.5*	-88	*-12.8*
Coleraine	808	305	**1,113**	*4.7*	*1.9*	***3.3***	-109	*-8.9*	-17	*-1.5*
Cookstown	248	173	**421**	*2.3*	*1.8*	***2.1***	71	*20.3*	77	*22.4*
Craigavon	744	312	**1,056**	*2.9*	*1.3*	***2.1***	104	*10.9*	-70	*-6.2*
Derry	2,590	784	**3,374**	*7.7*	*2.4*	***5.1***	118	*3.6*	-187	*-5.3*
Down	764	266	**1,030**	*3.7*	*1.4*	***2.6***	54	*5.5*	-37	*-3.5*
Dungannon	351	226	**577**	*2.3*	*1.6*	***2.0***	45	*8.5*	25	*4.5*
Fermanagh	685	319	**1,004**	*3.6*	*1.9*	***2.8***	42	*4.4*	-295	*-22.7*
Larne	296	118	**414**	*3.0*	*1.3*	***2.2***	-23	*-5.3*	-122	*-22.8*
Limavady	425	250	**675**	*3.7*	*2.6*	***3.2***	26	*4.0*	15	*2.3*
Lisburn	1,080	372	**1,452**	*3.1*	*1.1*	***2.2***	78	*5.7*	12	*0.8*
Magherafelt	238	163	**401**	*1.8*	*1.4*	***1.6***	59	*17.3*	-1	*-0.2*
Moyle	201	86	**287**	*3.9*	*1.8*	***2.9***	-2	*-0.7*	-31	*-9.7*
Newry & Mourne	1,078	430	**1,508**	*3.8*	*1.6*	***2.8***	107	*7.6*	-137	*-8.3*
Newtownabbey	822	245	**1,067**	*3.3*	*1.0*	***2.2***	53	*5.2*	64	*6.4*
North Down	716	249	**965**	*2.9*	*1.1*	***2.0***	81	*9.2*	-63	*-6.1*
Omagh	581	354	**935**	*3.6*	*2.5*	***3.1***	126	*15.6*	9	*1.0*
Strabane	819	344	**1,163**	*6.6*	*3.1*	***4.9***	62	*5.6*	-49	*-4.0*
Northern Ireland	**21,663**	**7,898**	**29,561**	***4.0***	***1.6***	***2.8***	**1,383**	***4.9***	**-1,747**	***-5.6***

Source: Department of Enterprise, Trade and Investment

Figure 8.5 Northern Ireland claimant count rates by Local Goverment District, July 2005

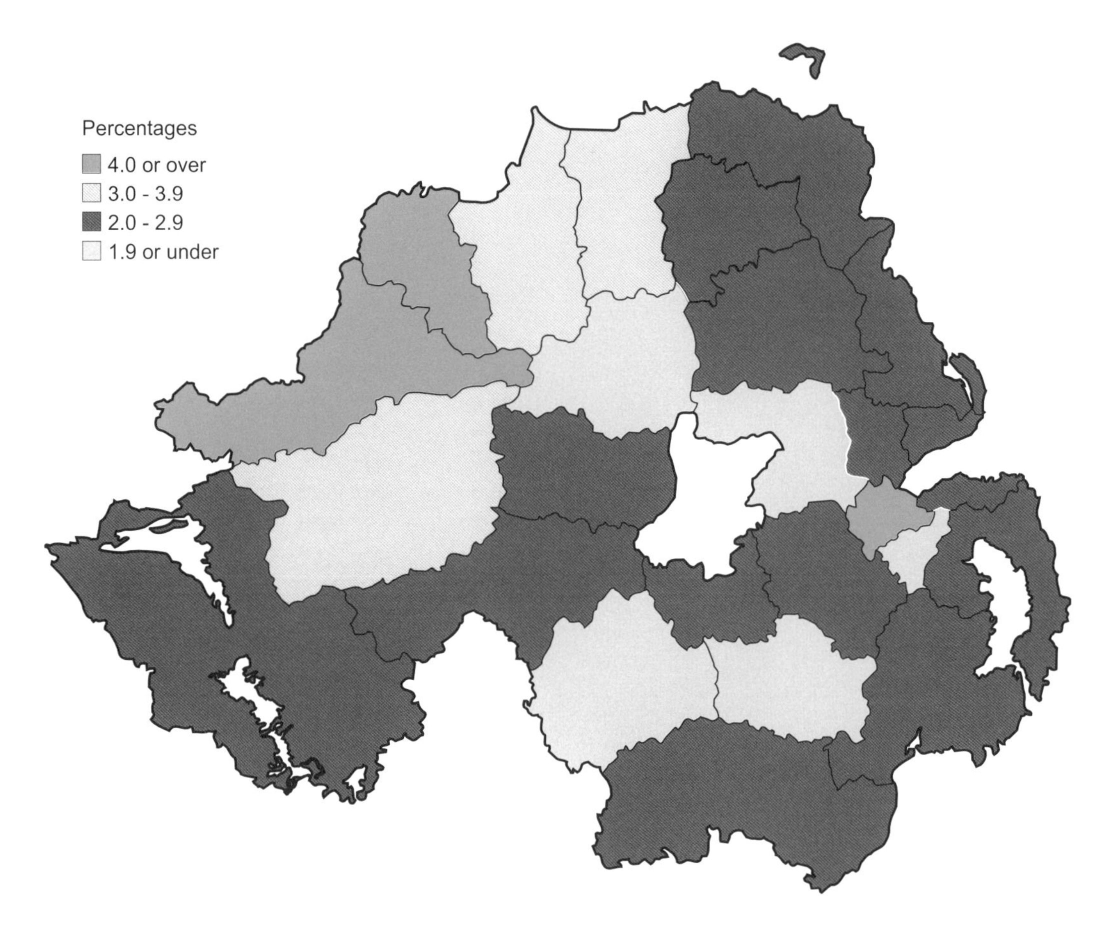

Source: Department of Enterprise, Trade and Investment

8.20 International comparisons of unemployment and employment, 2004 to 2005

Percentages and rates

International Area	Latest period	ILO Employment rate Unadjusted[1]	Change on year	Latest month	Unmployment rate[2]	Change on year
As per Eurostat						
Austria	Oct-Dec 2004	*68.1*	*-0.9*	Apr 2005	*4.6*	*0.1*
Belgium	Oct-Dec 2004	*60.6*	*0.2*	Apr 2005	*8.0*	*0.3*
Cyprus	Oct-Dec 2004	*68.8*	.	Apr 2005	*4.8*	*0.0*
Czech Republic	Oct-Dec 2004	*64.5*	*0.1*	Apr 2005	*8.2*	*-0.2*
Denmark	Oct-Dec 2004	*75.6*	*0.6*	Apr 2005	*4.9*	*-0.6*
Estonia	Oct-Dec 2004	*63.4*	*-0.3*	Apr 2005	*7.9*	*-1.8*
Finland	Oct-Dec 2004	*67.1*	*0.6*	Apr 2005	*8.6*	*-0.4*
France	Oct-Dec 2004	*62.9*	*0.0*	Apr 2005	*9.8*	*0.2*
Germany	Jul-Sep 2004	*65.8*	*0.5*	Apr 2005	*10.0*	*0.5*
Greece	Oct-Dec 2004	*59.6*	*0.8*	Dec 2004	*10.2*	*0.4*
Hungary	Oct-Dec 2004	*57.0*	*-0.5*	Apr 2005	*6.3*	*0.5*
Ireland	Oct-Dec 2004	*66.7*	*1.0*	Apr 2005	*4.2*	*-0.4*
Italy	Oct-Dec 2004	*58.0*	*1.7*	Dec 2004	*8.0*	*-0.2*
Latvia	Oct-Dec 2004	*62.2*	*0.8*	Apr 2005	*9.2*	*-0.6*
Lithuania	Oct-Dec 2004	*61.4*	*0.7*	Apr 2005	*8.5*	*-2.8*
Luxembourg	Oct-Dec 2004	*61.6*	*-1.1*	Apr 2005	*4.6*	*0.4*
Malta	Oct-Dec 2004	*54.0*	*0.3*	Apr 2005	*6.9*	*-0.6*
Netherlands	Oct-Dec 2004	*73.1*	*-0.2*	Apr 2005	*5.0*	*0.4*
Poland	Oct-Dec 2004	*52.4*	*1.0*	Apr 2005	*17.9*	*-1.1*
Portugal	Oct-Dec 2004	*67.8*	*-0.1*	Apr 2005	*7.2*	*0.7*
Slovak Republic	Oct-Dec 2004	*57.5*	*-0.3*	Apr 2005	*15.6*	*-3.1*
Slovenia	Oct-Dec 2004	*64.9*	*1.6*	Apr 2005	*5.8*	*-0.3*
Spain	Oct-Dec 2004	*61.5*	*1.3*	Apr 2005	*10.0*	*-1.2*
Sweden	Oct-Dec 2004	*71.5*	*-0.5*	Mar 2005	*6.3*	*0.0*
Northern Ireland[3]	Sep-Nov 2004	*65.0*	*0.7*	Mar-May 2005	*4.9*	*-0.1*
United Kingdom[3]	Oct-Dec 2004	*71.8*	*-0.2*	Feb 2005	*4.5*	*-0.2*
EU 25[4]	**Jul-Sep 2004**	***63.7***	***0.4***	**Apr 2005**	***8.9***	***-0.1***
EU 15[5]	**Jul-Sep 2004**	***65.2***	***0.4***	**Apr 2005**	***8.1***	***0.0***
As per Statistical Offices						
Northern Ireland	Mar-May 2005	*68.2*	*1.6*	Mar-May 2005	*4.9*	*-0.1*
United Kingdom	Mar-May 2005	*74.7*	*0.0*	Mar-May 2005	*4.8*	*-0.1*
Canada	Jan-Mar 2005	*71.1*	*0.2*	May 2005	*6.8*	*-0.3*
Japan	Jan-Mar 2005	*68.2*	*0.3*	Apr 2005	*4.4*	*-0.3*
United States	Jan-Mar 2005	*71.2*	*0.1*	Apr 2005	*5.2*	*-0.4*

Sources: United Kingdom Labour Force Survey, Office for National Statistics; Eurostat

1 Employment rates for the United Kingdom are for those aged 16 to 59/64, for EU countries 15 to 59/64, for the US 16 to 64 and for Japan and Canada 15 to 64. All employment rates are not seasonally adjusted except the Northern Ireland and United Kingdom rates as published by statistical offices.

2 Eurostat compiles 'harmonised' unemployment rates for most countries (but not NI and UK) by extrapolating from the most recent Labour Force Survey (LFS) data using monthly registered unemployment data. For further information see the Monthly Eurostat news release.

3 A NI employment rate comparable to the Eurostat figures has been produced from the Summer 2004 LFS dataset. It is based on the population aged 15-64 and differs from the working age rates (16-64 for men and 16-59 for women), which take account of both the school-leaving and state pension age. The UK employment rate as published by Eurostat will differ from the working age rate (16-59/64) published by ONS for the same reason.

4 EU25: EU15 + Cyprus, Czech Republic, Estonia, Hungary, Latvia, Lithuania, Malta, Poland, Slovak Republic and Slovenia.

5 EU15: Austria, Belgium, Denmark, Finland, France, Germany, Greece, Ireland, Italy, Luxembourg, the Netherlands, Portugal, Spain, Sweden and the United Kingdom.

Employment and training measures, 2002 to 2005

8.21

Numbers

Measures undertaken	June 2002	Sept 2002	Dec 2002	March 2003	June 2003	Sept 2003	Dec 2003	March 2004	June 2004	Sept 2004	Dec 2004	March 2005
Future Managers Training	350	250	450	500	250	250	400	400	150	250	350	400
Adults in Enterprise Ulster (trainees)[1]	300	100	<50	.	.	.	.	.	.	.	.	.
Adults in Enterprise Ulster (employees)[1]	150	150	<50	.	.	.	.	.	.	.	.	.
Employment Support (for the disabled)	850	850	850	850	850	850	850	850	850	850	850	850
Training for Work (Pilot)[2]	150	300	400	500	450	700	800	850	700	750	700	650
Jobskills[3] - adults	<50	<50	<50	<50	.	.	.	.	.	.	.	.
Jobskills[3] - young persons	11,000	13,750	13,550	12,650	11,550	14,400	14,950	12,650	12,100	10,850	14,950	13,200
New Deal												
18 - 24 year olds	2,950	3,100	3,050	3,400	3,300	3,250	3,000	3,250	2,900	2,750	2,550	2,850
25+ year olds	4,600	4,200	3,650	3,200	2,650	2,700	2,650	2,750	2,800	2,800	2,900	2,850
Worktrack	900	850	900	1,050	950	950	850	950	1,000	900	1,250	1,250

Source: Department for Employment and Learning

1 Enterprise Ulster's mainstream programme ceased in January 2003 (figures below 50 in December 2002) however the organisation continues to deliver other government-funded training programmes.

2 The Training for Work Programme is being piloted by Enterprise Ulster. Figures for number of participants are available from January 2002.

3 With the introduction of New Deal arrangements from 6th April 1998, which provides for adults, Jobskills now concentrates largely on meeting the training needs of unemployed 16 and 17 year olds for whom the Government guarantees a training place. The residual number of adults on Jobskills has fallen below 50, therefore numbers are not shown.

Note: The data presented in this table are not National Statistics.

8.22 Reasons[1] for economic inactivity (those who want work) by gender, 2000 to 2005

Thousands

	Does not want job	Wants Job[2]	Wants job but not seeking in last 4 weeks: Available	Not Available	**Total**	Long-term sick	Family & home care	Other[3]	**Total aged 16 or over**[2]	Total persons working age 16-59/64
	A	B	C	D	**E**	F	G	H	**I**	J
Males										
March-May 2000	168	24	*	16	**22**	11	*	*	**191**	115
March-May 2001	162	24	*	18	**21**	12	*	*	**186**	106
March-May 2002	175	23	*	16	**22**	11	*	9	**198**	118
March-May 2003	163	19	*	13	**17**	10	*	*	**182**	101
March-May 2004	194	19	*	12	**17**	*	*	9	**213**	127
March-May 2005	191	14	*	8	**12**	*	*	*	**206**	120
Females										
March-May 2000	301	40	11	27	**38**	9	22	*	**340**	190
March-May 2001	298	36	*	27	**34**	8	18	8	**334**	185
March-May 2002	293	35	10	24	**33**	*	21	*	**327**	178
March-May 2003	290	36	*	27	**35**	8	21	*	**326**	176
March-May 2004	309	31	*	23	**29**	*	14	9	**341**	186
March-May 2005	309	25	*	21	**24**	*	13	*	**334**	180
All persons										
March-May 2000	**468**	**63**	**16**	**44**	**60**	**20**	**25**	**15**	**531**	**305**
March-May 2001	**461**	**59**	**10**	**45**	**55**	**21**	**19**	**15**	**520**	**291**
March-May 2002	**467**	**58**	**15**	**40**	**55**	**18**	**23**	**14**	**525**	**296**
March-May 2003	**453**	**54**	**11**	**40**	**51**	**18**	**23**	**11**	**508**	**277**
March-May 2004	**503**	**50**	**11**	**35**	**46**	**14**	**14**	**18**	**554**	**312**
March-May 2005	**500**	**40**	*	**29**	**36**	**13**	**13**	**10**	**539**	**299**

Source: Labour Force Survey, Department of Enterprise, Trade and Investment

1 Relationship between columns: E=C+D or F+G+H; I=A+B.

2 Includes a small number of people who wanted a job, were seeking but unavailable.

3 Includes discouraged workers, students, temporary sick or injured, waiting for reply to job application, not yet looking and not looking.

Reasons[1] for economic inactivity (those who do not want work) by gender, 2000 to 2005

8.23

Thousands

	Total persons working age (16-19/64)	Wants job	Does not want job				Of which	
			Total	Long-term sick	Family and home	Other[2]	Retired	Student
	A	B	**C**	D	E	F	G	H
Males								
March-May 2000	**115**	22	**93**	40	*	48	10	33
March-May 2001	**106**	23	**83**	38	*	39	*	26
March-May 2002	**118**	23	**95**	39	*	51	9	38
March-May 2003	**101**	18	**83**	36	*	44	9	29
March-May 2004	**127**	18	**108**	48	*	55	10	39
March-May 2005	**120**	14	**105**	45	*	55	10	40
Females								
March-May 2000	**190**	38	**152**	33	69	50	*	41
March-May 2001	**185**	34	**151**	32	67	51	*	40
March-May 2002	**178**	34	**144**	35	62	47	*	40
March-May 2003	**176**	34	**142**	35	56	51	*	37
March-May 2004	**186**	31	**155**	42	64	49	*	37
March-May 2005	**180**	24	**156**	40	68	48	*	39
All Persons								
March-May 2000	**305**	**60**	**245**	**73**	**74**	**99**	**12**	**75**
March-May 2001	**291**	**58**	**233**	**71**	**73**	**90**	**11**	**67**
March-May 2002	**296**	**57**	**239**	**74**	**67**	**98**	**10**	**78**
March-May 2003	**277**	**52**	**226**	**71**	**60**	**95**	**14**	**66**
March-May 2004	**312**	**49**	**263**	**90**	**70**	**103**	**14**	**76**
March-May 2005	**299**	**38**	**261**	**84**	**74**	**103**	**14**	**79**

Source: Labour Force Survey, Department of Enterprise, Trade and Investment

1 Relationship between columns: A=B+C; C=D+E+F.

2 Includes students, retired persons, temporary sick or injured, those waiting for reply to job application and those who do not want/need job.

Notes to Labour Market tables

TABLES 8.1, 8.2, 8.4, 8.15, 8.16, 8.20, 8.22 AND 8.23

In Employment

Employment can be discussed in terms of the number of people in employment or the number of jobs. These are two quite separate concepts since some people in employment will have more than one job. People are classed as employed by the Labour Force Survey (LFS), if they have done at least one hour of work in the reference week.

Employees

The division between employees and self-employed in the LFS is based on survey respondents' own assessment of their employment status. Note that there are revisions to the component employee and self-employment series back to Spring 1992. These arise from improvements to the LFS editing procedures, based on the SOC 2000 Occupational Classification, which allows data edits to be removed which previously re-classified some self-employed as employees.

Unpaid Family Workers

The separate identification of this group in the LFS is in accordance with international recommendations. It comprises those doing unpaid work for a business they own or for a business that a relative owns.

Working Age

Working age is taken as ages 16 to 59 for females and 16 to 64 for males.

Employment rate (working age)

The number of working age in employment as a percentage of the total population of working age.

Unemployment

The International Labour Organisation (ILO) measure of unemployment refers to people without a job who were available to start work in the two weeks following their LFS interview and had either looked for work in the four weeks prior to interview or were waiting to start a job they had already obtained. This definition of unemployment is in accordance with that adopted by the 14th International Conference of Labour Statisticians and promulgated by the ILO in 1987.

To reflect the fact that the LFS measure of unemployment following ILO guildelines is the official NI measure, the term 'Unemployment' is used in labelling tables in place of 'ILO Unemployment' from January 2003.

Duration of Unemployment

Duration of unemployment is defined as the shorter of the following two periods: (a) duration of active search for work; and (b) length of time since employment. The short-term unemployed are those people who have been unemployed for under 1 year while the long-term unemployed are defined as those who have unemployed for 1 year or more.

Unemployment Rate

The percentage of economically active people who are unemployed on the ILO measure.

Economically Active

People aged 16 and over who are either in employment or unemployed.

Economic Activity Rate (working age)

The number of people who are in employment or unemployed as a percentage of the total population of working age.

Economically Inactive

People who are neither in employment nor unemployed on the ILO measure. This group includes, for example, all those who were looking after a home or retired. Although no estimates appear in this publication, for other LFS analyses, this group would also include all people aged under 16.

Full-time/Part-time

The classification of employees, self-employed, those on Government work-related training programmes and unpaid family workers in their main job as full-time or part-time is on the basis of self-assessment. People on Government supported training and employment programmes who are at college in the survey reference week are classified, by convention, as part-time.

Temporary Employees

These are defined as those employees who say that their main job is non-permanent in one of the following ways: fixed period contract; agency temping; casual work; seasonal work; other temporary work.

Sampling

The LFS is a sample survey, and as such, estimates obtained from it are subject to sampling variability. If a series of samples were drawn each would give a different result.

Publication Threshold

It is the nature of a sampling variability that the smaller the group whose size is being estimated, the (proportionately) less precise that estimate is. LFS estimates of under 8,000 are not published in this report as they are likely to be unreliable.

Regrossing of LFS estimates

The full regrossing of all LFS estimates in line with the 2001 Census of Population is now complete and have been calculated for all periods back to Spring 1992. These regrossed estimates replace both the previous 1991 Census based estimates and the interim 2001 Census adjusted estimates which were available for key headline aggregates. All estimates in this report are based on the full regrossed Census 2001 basis.

Claimant count

Claimant count rates are calculated by expressing the numbers of unemployed claimants as a percentage of the estimated total workforce (sum of employee jobs, unemployed, self-employment jobs, armed forces and participants on work-related Government training programmes) at mid 2004 for 2005 figures.

TABLES 8.5 TO 8.8

Estimates of the number of employee jobs are obtained from the Quarterly Employment Survey (QES). The QES covers all public sector bodies, all private sector firms with 25 or more employees and a sample of the remainder. The sample size has been chosen in order that estimates of total employee jobs should be accurate to within +/- 1% of the Census of Employment total. The survey collects information on the numbers of persons in full-time and part-time employment.

It should be noted that the survey counts the number of jobs rather than the number of persons with jobs. For example, a person holding both a full-time job and a part-time job, or someone with two part-time jobs, will be counted twice.

The quarterly survey covers all Industrial Sections apart from Agriculture. Overall employment (i.e. employee and self-employment) estimates for the agricultural sector are provided, on an annual basis, from the Department of Agriculture and Rural Development's (DARD) Farm Census. The Farm Census defines self-employment agriculture workers as including full-time farmers and partners on all agricultural businesses. Agriculture employees include all workers on agricultural businessess other than (a) part-time farmers and partners and (b) farmers'spouses. They include full-time, part-time and casual workers, both paid and unpaid.

SIC 03 = Standard Industrial Classification 2003.

TABLES 8.9 TO 8.13

The Annual Survey of Hours and Earnings (ASHE) provides a wide range of information on earnings and hours worked. Historically, this information was gained through the New Earnings Survey (NES). To improve coverage and hence make the survey more representative, supplementary information was collected from the 2004 ASHE survey on businesses not registered for VAT and for people who changed or started new jobs between sample selection and the survey reference period. The improvements in sample coverage have caused a discontinuity between 2003 and previous data when no supplementary data was collected.

There are two sets of results for the 2004 ASHE; the headline results that include the supplementary information and the results that exclude this information. Tables 8.9 to 8.13 display the results that include the supplementary information.

1) Earnings are a measure of the money people receive in return for work done. It includes salaries and bonuses but does not include non-monetary perks such as benefits in kind. This differs from income, which is the amount of money received from all sources. Income includes interest from building society and bank accounts, dividends from shares, benefit receipts, trust funds, etc.

2) Unless otherwise stated, average earnings figures relate to:

   - Gross pay (including basic pay, incentive pay, overtime pay, commissions, shift pay and bonuses).
   - Before statutory deductions (PAYE, National Insurance etc.).
   - Full-time employees (those working more than 30 hours each week excluding overtime and main meal breaks - 25 hours for teachers and academics) on adult rates.

   Average Earnings figures exclude those whose pay has been affected by absence.

3) Industrial classifications according to Standard Industrial Classification 1992 (SIC 92).

4) Occupational classifications according to Standard Occupational Classification (SOC).

TABLE 8.10

Skill levels are approximated by the length of time deemed necessary for a person to become fully competent in the performance of the tasks associated with a job. This, in turn, is a function of the time taken to gain necessary formal qualifications or the required amount of work-based training.

Apart from formal training and qualifications, some tasks require varying types of experience, possibly in other tasks, for competence to be acquired. Within the broad structure of the SOC classification (major groups and sub-major groups) reference can be made to four skill levels.

Skill Level 1

The first skill level equates with the competence associated with a general education, usually acquired by the time a person completes his/her compulsory education and signalled via a set of satisfactory school-leaving examination grades.

Competent performance of jobs classified at this level will also involve knowledge of appropriate health and safety regulations and may require short periods of work-related training.

This skill level includes SOC 2000 sub-major groups 91 and 92, and examples of occupations at this level include cleaners and catering assistants.

Skill Level 2

The second skill level covers a large group of occupations, all of which require the knowledge provided via a good general education as for occupations at the first skill level, but which typically have a longer period of work-related training or work experience.

This skill level includes SOC 2000 sub-major groups 41, 42, 61, 62, 71, 72, 81 and 82. Occupations classified at this level include machine operators, driving, retailing, and clerical and secretarial occupations.

Skill Level 3

The third skill level applies to occupations that normally require a body of knowledge associated with a period of post-compulsory education but not to degree level.

A number of technical occupations fall into this category, as do a variety of trades occupations and proprietors of small businesses. In the latter case, educational qualifications at sub-degree level or a lengthy period of vocational training may not be a necessary prerequisite for competent performance of tasks, but a significant period of work experience is typical.

This skill level includes SOC 2000 sub-major groups 12, 31, 32, 33, 34, 35, 51, 52, 53 and 54.

Skill Level 4

The fourth skill level relates to what are termed 'professional' occupations and managerial positions in corporate enterprises or national/local government.

Occupations at this skill level normally require a degree or equivalent period of relevant work experince.

This skill level includes SOC 2000 sub-major groups 11, 21, 22, 23 and 24.

TABLE 8.14

The estimates include second self-employment jobs.

TABLES 8.17 AND 8.18

Claimant Count Unemployment figures are derived from records of claimants held at Social Security Offices (SSOs).

The term 'claimants' in the claimant count is used to include those who claim Jobseekers' Allowance and national insurance credits. The figures include the severely disabled unemployed, but exclude students seeking vacation work and the temporarily stopped.

The NI claimant count rate is calculated by expressing the numbers of unemployed claimants as a percentage of the estimated total workforce (sum of employee jobs, unemployed, self-employment jobs, armed forces and participants on work-related Government training programmes) at mid 2004 for 2004 and 2005 figures and at the corresponding mid-year for earlier years.

The seasonally adjusted series takes account of past discontinuities to be consistent with the current coverage. The seasonally adjusted unemployment series relates only to claimants aged 18 and over. Seasonally adjusted totals are subject to an annual update to take account of the latest assessment of trends.

Annual average figures for 1994 to 2004 have been calculated using the four quarters January, April, July and October. The percentages relating to long-term and youth unemployment are calculated by expressing the numbers of long-term or youth unemployed as a percentage of total claimant unemployment.

TABLE 8.19

Local Government District claimant count rates are calculated by expressing the numbers of unemployed claimants as a percentage of the resident working age population (females 16-59, males 16-64) at mid-2003 for 2005 data.

TABLE 8.21

Employment and Training Measures refer to schemes run and/or financed by the Department for Employment and Learning (DEL). Figures have been rounded to the nearest 50. Further details on individual schemes are published by DETI or can be obtained from DEL.

Transport, Travel and Tourism

- Over the ten year period from 1994 to 2004, the NI licensed vehicle stock increased by 48% compared with 37% in Wales, 29% in Scotland and 27% in England.

- The pass rates for the 'L' driving test in Northern Ireland has been consistently above those in Great Britain for both males and females over the period 2000-01 to 2004-05.

- During the year 2004, there were just over 5,600 injury collisions on Northern Ireland's roads. This was the lowest number recorded in the ten years since 1994. These collisions resulted in more than 9,500 casualties (deaths and injuries).

- As a proportion of the number of registered vehicles, Northern Ireland had much higher levels of injury road traffic collisions rates than England, Scotland and Wales throughout the period 1994 to 2002. However, in 2003 and 2004 NI rates fell to similiar or lower levels than those in England.

- Collisions in non built-up areas accounted for less than half of all people injured on the roads during 2004, but for over 80% of road deaths.

- Whilst the Citybus fleet has become generally younger over the period 1994-95 to 2004-05, the average age of the Ulsterbus fleet has been generally increasing.

- **There were almost 7 million rail passenger journeys undertaken in 2004-05. These generated passenger receipts of approximately £17.2 million.**

- **The number of terminal passengers using Belfast City Airport in 2004 was 63% greater than in 1999.**

- **Between 2003 and 2004, the number of visitors to Northern Ireland from overseas increased by 11%, whilst the number of visitors from other parts of the United Kingdom increased by 2%. There was a 6% increase in the number of visitors from the Republic of Ireland during 2004. £325 million of tourism revenue was generated in 2004.**

9.1 Vehicles currently licensed by taxation group, 1994 to 2004

Numbers

Taxation group	1994	1995	1996[1]	1997	1998	1999	2000	2001[2]	2002[2]	2003[2]	2004[2]
Cycles	8,775	9,142	10,026	10,932	11,663	13,087	14,116	15,205	17,598	23,820	24,533
Motor-hackneys	3,078	2,092	2,090	2,144	2,175	2,204	2,266	2,315	2,322	2,353	2,378
Agricultural tractors and engines	7,317	9,074	5,911	6,378	5,906	5,505	5,048	4,901	5,731	7,503	8,674
Goods vehicles	20,714	16,338	17,401	18,172	18,312	17,075	17,864	19,415	20,244	22,100	23,062
Private cars	514,760	521,610	540,083	575,923	584,706	608,316	615,180	644,968	666,731	711,913	737,198
Other	41,307	53,306	63,775	70,020	72,669	74,458	76,256	80,501	81,851	85,053	87,416
All vehicles	**595,951**	**611,562**	**639,286**	**683,569**	**695,431**	**720,645**	**730,730**	**767,305**	**794,477**	**852,742**	**883,261**
Current driving licences[3,4]	1,005,000	1,041,000	1,077,000	1,167,930	1,185,651	1,199,052	1,225,163	1,266,854	985,329	1,037,781	1,174,128

Source: Driver and Vehicle Licensing Northern Ireland

1 In 1996 vehicle classes were revised to take account of changes to taxation classes during 1995. The 1996 figures relate to revised categories as given at the end of this chapter and are not directly comparable with previous years' figures.

2 Figures for 2001 onwards are based on revised taxation classes.

3 Figures reflect current licences at 31 March.

4 Figures for 2002 to 2004 reflect current valid licences. Figures for 1994 to 2001 reflect all records held.

Note: The data presented in this table are not National Statistics.

9.2 Motor vehicles registered for the first time by taxation group, 1994 to 2004

Numbers

Taxation group	1994	1995	1996[1]	1997	1998	1999	2000	2001[2]	2002[2]	2003[2]	2004[2]
Cycles	1,943	2,362	2,803	3,376	4,307	5,310	6,010	5,591	5,596	6,804	4,601
Motor-hackneys	1,143	622	724	714	486	568	565	451	439	609	467
Agricultural tractors and engines	1,558	1,619	1,292	1,364	971	987	1,313	301	1	9	2
Goods vehicles	9,576	10,292	10,724	11,989	13,679	14,751	16,122	17,808	15,676	15,551	15,077
Private cars	70,765	73,718	77,817	83,968	91,141	89,078	84,977	88,592	83,402	87,506	85,190
Exempt from duty	6,423	8,333	10,520	10,885	10,718	11,083	10,809	12,126	12,515	11,907	12,881

Source: Driver and Vehicle Licensing Northern Ireland

1 In 1996 vehicle classes were revised to take account of changes to taxation classes during 1995. The 1996 figures relate to revised categories as given at the end of this chapter and are not directly comparable with previous years' figures.

2 Figures for 2001 onwards are based on revised taxation classes.

Note: The data presented in this table are not National Statistics.

Figure 9.1 Index of vehicles licensed in Northern Ireland, 1994 to 2004

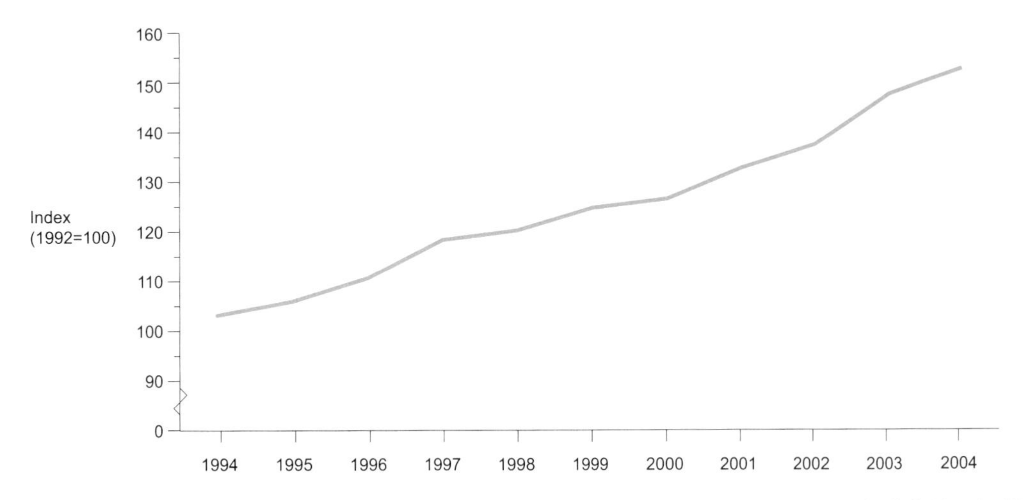

Source: Driver and Vehicle Licensing Northern Ireland

9.3 UK comparisons of licensed vehicle stock, 1994 to 2004

Thousands and indices (1992=100)

	England[r]		Scotland[r]		Wales[r]		Northern Ireland	
Year	Number	Index	Number	Index	Number	Index	Number	Index
1994	21,639	99.6	1,900	100.0	1,177	95.8	596	103.1
1995	21,730	100.0	1,910	100.5	1,175	95.6	612	105.9
1996	22,477	103.5	1,966	103.5	1,264	102.8	639	110.6
1997	23,177	106.4	2,023	106.5	1,301	105.9	684	118.3
1998	23,657	108.9	2,073	109.1	1,334	108.5	695	120.2
1999	24,236	111.6	2,131	112.2	1,376	112.0	721	124.7
2000	24,856	114.4	2,188	115.2	1,380	112.3	731	126.5
2001	25,532	117.5	2,262	119.1	1,433	116.6	767	132.7
2002	26,168	120.5	2,330	122.6	1,497	121.8	794	137.4
2003	26,653	122.7	2,383	125.4	1,547	125.9	853	147.6
2004	27,393	126.1	2,448	128.8	1,617	131.6	883	152.8

Sources: Driver and Vehicle Licensing Northern Ireland; Department for Transport

Note: The data presented in this table are not National Statistics.

9.4 'L' driving tests[1] conducted, passed and pass rates by gender, NI/GB comparison, 2000-01 to 2004-05

Numbers and percentages

	2000-01		2001-02		2002-03		2003-04		2004-05	
'L' driving tests	NI	GB	NI	GB	NI	GB	NI	GB	NI	GB
Tests conducted										
Male	18,602	516,778	20,433	575,787	19,135	643,880	21,070	656,771	18,823	807,898
Female	18,747	576,438	20,741	631,695	20,625	705,412	24,425	742,243	21,498	867,924
All persons	**37,349**	**1,093,216**	**41,174**	**1,207,482**	**39,760**	**1,349,292**	**45,495**	**1,399,014**	**40,321**	**1,675,822**
Tests passed										
Male	10,475	248,148	10,021	271,502	9,827	299,551	11,015	303,744	9,986	368,003
Female	9,062	232,070	9,557	252,277	8,788	283,218	10,276	294,440	9,222	341,345
All persons	**19,537**	**480,218**	**19,578**	**523,779**	**18,615**	**582,769**	**21,291**	**598,184**	**19,208**	**709,348**
Percentage passed										
Male	*56*	*48*	*49*	*47*	*51*	*47*	*52*	*46*	*53*	*46*
Female	*48*	*40*	*46*	*40*	*43*	*40*	*42*	*40*	*43*	*39*
All persons	***52***	***44***	***48***	***43***	***47***	***43***	***47***	***43***	***48***	***42***

Sources: Driver and Vehicle Testing Agency; Driving Standards Agency

[1] Includes motorcycle tests.

Note: The data presented in this table are not National Statistics.

Figure 9.2 Injury road traffic collisions and casualties, 1994 to 2004

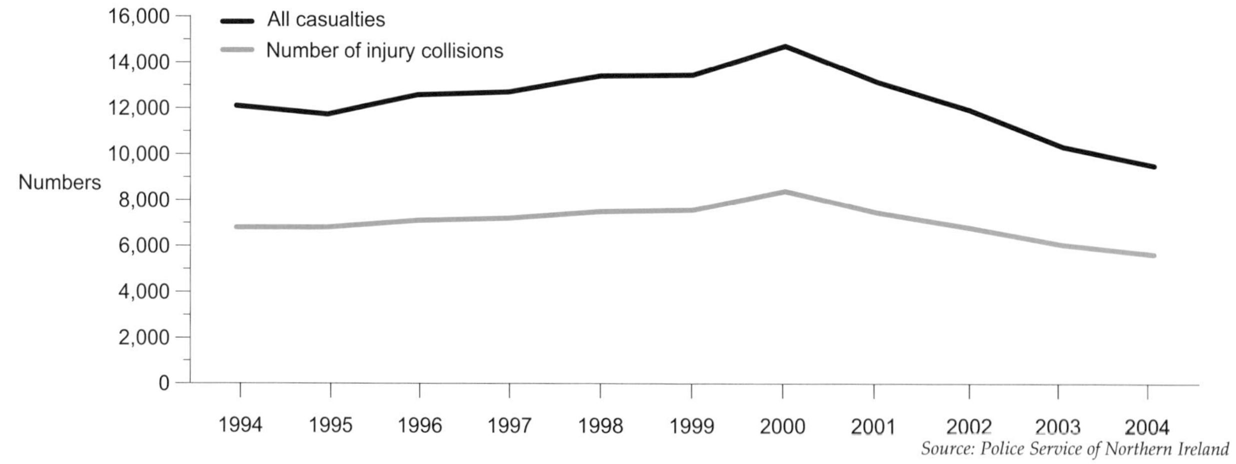

Source: Police Service of Northern Ireland

9.5 Injury road traffic collisions and casualties, 1994 to 2004

Numbers

Injury collisions and casualties	1994	1995	1996	1997	1998	1999	2000	2001	2002	2003	2004
Number of injury collisions	6,783	6,792	7,093	7,192	7,487	7,562	8,388	7,447	6,784	6,049	5,633
Casualties											
Killed	157	144	142	144	160	141	171	148	150	150	147
Seriously injured	1,648	1,532	1,599	1,548	1,538	1,509	1,786	1,682	1,526	1,288	1,183
Slightly injured	10,289	10,049	10,834	11,006	11,704	11,799	12,763	11,312	10,238	8,887	8,177
All casualties	**12,094**	**11,725**	**12,575**	**12,698**	**13,402**	**13,449**	**14,720**	**13,142**	**11,914**	**10,325**	**9,507**
Child casualties[1]	1,749	1,719	1,869	1,706	1,899	1,746	1,836	1,579	1,493	1,229	1,102

Source: Police Service of Northern Ireland

[1] Figures for child casualties refer to casualties aged under 16.

9.6 Injury road traffic collision rates by UK region, 1994 to 2004

Rates per 10,000 vehicles

Year	Northern Ireland	England	Scotland	Wales
1994	*114*	*96*	*88*	*90*
1995	*111*	*94*	*87*	*87*
1996	*111*	*93*	*82*	*81*
1997	*105*	*92*	*82*	*79*
1998	*108*	*90*	*80*	*75*
1999	*105*	*87*	*72*	*72*
2000	*115*	*84*	*69*	*69*
2001	*97*	*80*	*65*	*66*
2002	*85*	*76*	*61*	*65*
2003	*71*	*71*	*58*	*63*
2004	*64*	*67*	*57*	*59*

Sources: Police Service of Northern Ireland; Department for Transport

9.7 Injury road traffic collision casualty rates by UK region, 1994 to 2004

Rates per 100,000 population

Year	Northern Ireland	England	Scotland	Wales
1994	*736*	*576*	*443*	*523*
1995	*711*	*565*	*435*	*518*
1996	*757*	*585*	*426*	*514*
1997	*760*	*597*	*445*	*512*
1998	*799*	*590*	*442*	*501*
1999	*801*	*581*	*411*	*495*
2000	*875*	*580*	*404*	*485*
2001	*778*	*566*	*392*	*473*
2002	*702*	*542*	*381*	*490*
2003	*606*	*517*	*369*	*487*
2004	*556*	*499*[1]	*364*[1]	*466*[1]

Sources: Police Service of Northern Ireland; Department for Transport

[1] As GB population figures for 2004 are not yet available, rates have been calculated using the mid year population estimates for 2003.

9.8 Vehicles involved in injury road traffic collisions by type of vehicle, 1994 to 2004

Numbers

Type of vehicle	1994	1995	1996	1997	1998	1999	2000	2001	2002	2003	2004
Motor cars[1]	10,293	10,232	10,694	11,030	11,467	11,617	13,010	11,519	10,500	9,213	8,631
Motor cycles	265	268	243	298	334	362	508	469	504	485	516
Pedal cycles	324	391	375	349	333	280	271	215	176	197	162
Vans and lorries	1,213	1,184	1,242	1,167	1,239	1,371	1,460	1,343	1,219	1,047	1,034
Omnibuses[2]	224	213	259	246	253	278	308	275	250	239	155
Others[3]	249	225	213	238	225	241	254	230	217	200	181
All vehicles	**12,568**	**12,513**	**13,026**	**13,328**	**13,851**	**14,149**	**15,811**	**14,051**	**12,866**	**11,381**	**10,679**

Source: Police Service of Northern Ireland

[1] Figures include motor cars and cars used as taxis.

[2] 'Omnibuses' are passenger carrying vehicles with seating for 8 or more passengers e.g. minibuses, buses and coaches.

[3] 'Others' includes, for example, tractors, hackney type taxis, motor caravans and horse-drawn vehicles.

9.9 Injury road traffic collisions by responsibility, 1994 to 2004

Numbers

Primarily attributable to	1994	1995	1996	1997	1998	1999	2000	2001	2002	2003	2004
Drivers of vehicles[1]	5,198	5,131	5,382	5,629	5,880	6,039	6,750	6,000	5,513	4,934	4,596
Motorcyclists	102	97	86	110	120	125	213	204	211	207	222
Pedal cyclists	184	227	237	203	184	173	159	122	96	99	91
Pedestrians	939	914	907	880	856	770	777	638	589	493	426
Passengers	22	40	41	50	38	24	32	25	27	22	16
Road conditions	131	163	188	97	183	212	229	228	176	137	155
Vehicle defects	71	80	104	88	78	73	93	96	72	67	58
Other causes	136	140	148	135	148	146	135	141	125	117	93
All collisions	**6,783**	**6,792**	**7,093**	**7,192**	**7,487**	**7,562**	**8,388**	**7,454**[2]	**6,809**[2]	**6,076**[2]	**5,657**[2]

Source: Police Service of Northern Ireland

[1] Excludes collisions attributable to motorcyclists or pedal cyclists.

[2] From 2001 onwards, dual or multiple responsibility collisions involving drivers of vehicles, motorcyclists and pedal cyclists have been accounted for. Therefore, totals may not equal the actual number of collisions (as quoted in Table 9.5).

Injury road traffic collision casualties by location, 1994 to 2004

9.10

Numbers

Area and killed/injured	1994	1995	1996	1997	1998	1999	2000	2001	2002	2003	2004
Built-up areas[1]											
Killed	41	44	40	44	38	32	50	37	39	43	29
Injured	6,704	6,740	7,205	7,293	7,670	7,529	8,575	7,438	6,640	5,882	5,099
Non built-up areas											
Killed	116	100	102	100	122	109	121	111	111	107	118
Injured	5,233	4,841	5,228	5,261	5,572	5,779	5,974	5,556	5,124	4,293	4,261
All areas											
Killed	**157**	**144**	**142**	**144**	**160**	**141**	**171**	**148**	**150**	**150**	**147**
Injured	**11,937**	**11,581**	**12,433**	**12,554**	**13,242**	**13,308**	**14,549**	**12,994**	**11,764**	**10,175**	**9,360**

Source: Police Service of Northern Ireland

[1] Those roads which have a speed limit of 40 miles per hour or less.

Public road passenger transport, 1994-95 to 2004-05

9.11

Units as indicated

	1994 -95	1995 -96	1996 -97	1997 -98	1998 -99	1999 -00	2000 -01	2001 -02	2002 -03	2003 -04	2004 -05
Citybus											
Passenger journeys (millions)	27.0	25.4	24.3	23.1	21.9	21.3	20.3	20.2	19.9	19.5	19.9
Bus miles (000s)	7,500	7,500	7,300	7,100	6,900	7,000	6,800	6,700	6,900	7,100	6,700
Bus kilometres (000s)	12,075	12,075	11,753	11,431	11,109	11,270	11,000	10,800	11,100	11,400	10,800
Local (Stage) passenger receipts (£000)	17,300	17,100	16,900	16,500	16,700	17,100	17,100	17,900	18,500	19,600	21,300
Staff employed (numbers)	727	741	727	654	658	673	644	647	672	661	701
Number of buses (numbers)	284	282	270	266	265	278	260	267	257	244	256
Average age of buses (years)	8.8	9.8	8.0	8.5	9.5	8.3	8.2	8.5	9.3	6.9	7.0
Ulsterbus											
Passenger journeys (millions)	54.5	55.4	53.9	51.6	49.4	48.2	46.8	44.8	46.0	45.9	45.2
Bus miles (000s)	37,400	38,800	38,000	36,500	35,400	35,500	34,500	34,700	35,200	35,300	35,800
Bus kilometres (000s)	60,214	62,468	61,180	58,765	56,994	57,155	55,700	56,000	56,700	56,800	57,600
Local (Stage) passenger receipts (£000)	48,000	49,600	50,800	51,900	52,900	54,300	55,000	57,200	60,900	64,800	68,400
Staff employed (numbers)	2,250	2,231	2,183	2,107	2,127	2,175	2,155	2,206	2,239	2,276	2,309
Number of buses (numbers)	1,293	1,224	1,221	1,181	1,171	1,186	1,167	1,206	1,195	1,240	1,220
Average age of buses (years)	7.9	8.5	9.9	10.3	11.3	11.1	12.0	11.9	12.8	11.6	12.6

Source: Translink

Note: The data presented in this table are not National Statistics.

9.12 Rail transport, 1994-95 to 2004-05

Units as indicated

	1994 -95	1995 -96	1996 -97	1997 -98	1998 -99	1999 -00	2000 -01	2001 -02	2002 -03	2003 -04	2004 -05
Passenger journeys (millions)	6.1	6.4	6.2	6.4	5.8	5.9	5.9	6.2	6.3	6.9	6.9
Route miles of track	209	209	211	211	211	211	211	211	211	211	211
Passenger receipts (£000s)	8,676	9,772	9,959	12,511	12,786	13,366	14,126	14,987	15,394	16,759	17,194
Staff employed (number)	820	784	726	669	671	694	720	734	772	788	811
Power units											
Number	41	41	36	36	36	36	34	35	33	33	40
Average age (years)	18.0	19.0	16.8	17.8	18.8	19.8	20.0	21.0	22.0	23.0	21.0
Carriages and trailers											
Number	82	82	96	96	96	105	105	105	105	104	108
Average age (years)	19.0	20.0	16.1	17.1	18.1	18.9	20.0	21.0	22.0	23.0	22.0

Source: Translink

Note: The data presented in this table are not National Statistics.

9.13 Terminal passengers by UK airports, 1999 and 2004

Thousands and percentages

Airport	1999 Terminal passengers	1999 Percentage of passengers at all UK airports	2004 Terminal passengers	2004 Percentage of passengers at all UK airports	Percentage change 1999-2004
Heathrow	61,975	*36.8*	67,109	*31.1*	*8.3*
Gatwick	30,408	*18.1*	31,391	*14.6*	*3.2*
Manchester	17,418	*10.3*	20,969	*9.7*	*20.4*
Stansted	9,409	*5.6*	20,907	*9.7*	*122.2*
Birmingham	6,935	*4.1*	8,797	*4.1*	*26.8*
Glasgow	6,755	*4.0*	8,557	*4.0*	*26.7*
Edinburgh	5,084	*3.0*	7,992	*3.7*	*57.2*
Luton	5,246	*3.1*	7,520	*3.5*	*43.3*
Newcastle	2,930	*1.7*	4,708	*2.2*	*60.7*
Bristol	1,966	*1.2*	4,603	*2.1*	*134.1*
Belfast International	**3,012**	***1.8***	**4,403**	***2.0***	***46.2***
East Midlands	2,217	*1.3*	4,375	*2.0*	*97.3*
Liverpool	1,301	*0.8*	3,352	*1.6*	*157.6*
Aberdeen	2,432	*1.4*	2,634	*1.2*	*8.3*
Leeds Bradford	1,450	*0.9*	2,368	*1.1*	*63.3*
Belfast City	**1,282**	***0.8***	**2,091**	***1.0***	***63.1***
Cardiff Wales	1,297	*0.8*	1,873	*0.9*	*44.4*
London City	1,384	*0.8*	1,675	*0.8*	*21.0*
Southampton	749	*0.4*	1,531	*0.7*	*104.4*
Teesside	725	*0.4*	787	*0.4*	*8.6*
Other airports	4,388	*2.6*	8,039	*3.7*	*83.2*
All	**168,363**	***100.0***	**215,681**	***100.0***	***28.1***

Source: Civil Aviation Authority

Note: The data presented in this table are not National Statistics.

Figure 9.3 Number of terminal passengers by NI airports, 1999 and 2004

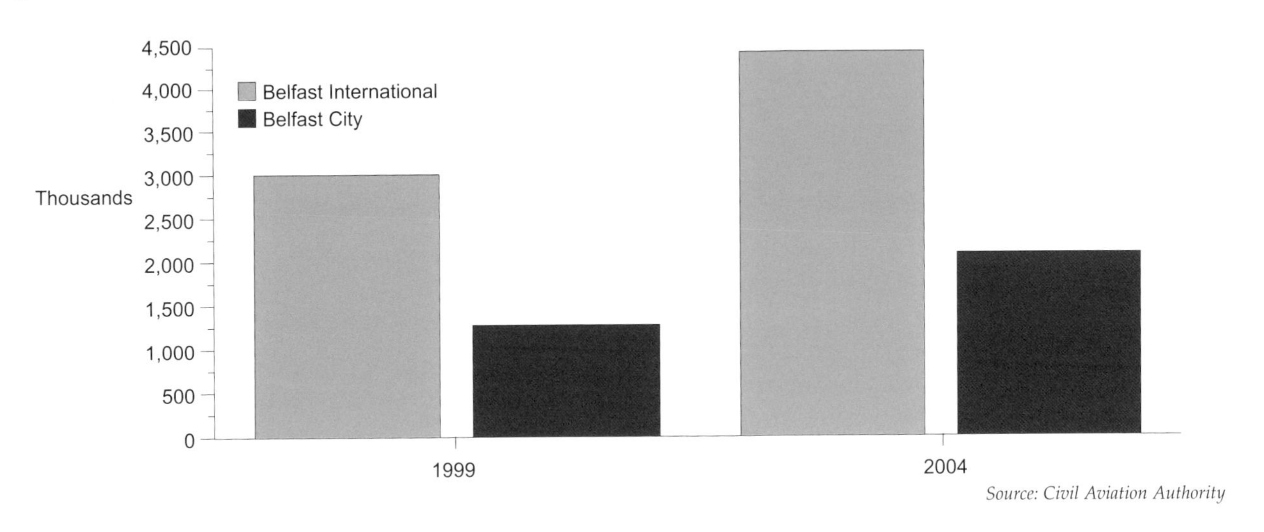

Source: Civil Aviation Authority

9.14

Tourism in Northern Ireland: visitors, revenue and purpose of visit[1], 1994 to 2004

Units as indicated

Visitors, revenue and purpose of visit	1994	1995	1996	1997	1998	1999	2000	2001	2002	2003[r]	2004
Staying visitors											
From Great Britain (000s)	708	810	825	799	838	1,002	950	1,053	1,160	1,379	1,408
From Republic of Ireland (000s)	390	470	370	345	360	384	380	365	330	340	360
From overseas (000s)	196	277	241	271	279	269	341	258	252	294	325
All staying visitors (000s)	**1,294**	**1,557**	**1,436**	**1,415**	**1,477**	**1,655**	**1,672**	**1,676**	**1,741**	**2,013**	**2,093**
All revenue (£ millions)	**183**	**214**	**206**	**208**	**217**	**265**	**265**	**282**	**274**	**297**	**325**
Purpose of visit											
Visiting friends or relatives (000s)	522	564	590	577	617	684	743	773	817	874	872
%	*40*	*36*	*41*	*41*	*42*	*41*	*44*	*46*	*47*	*43*	*42*
Holiday (000s)	275	461	297	263	277	305	306	274	285	365	405
%	*21*	*30*	*21*	*19*	*19*	*18*	*18*	*16*	*16*	*18*	*19*
Business (000s)	388	402	409	419	434	501	464	501	518	618	631
%	*30*	*26*	*28*	*29*	*29*	*30*	*28*	*30*	*30*	*31*	*30*
Other (000s)	109	130	140	156	149	165	159	128	121	156	185
%	*9*	*8*	*10*	*11*	*10*	*10*	*10*	*8*	*7*	*8*	*9*
All visits (000s)	**1,294**	**1,557**	**1,436**	**1,415**	**1,477**	**1,655**	**1,672**	**1,676**	**1,741**	**2,013**	**2,093**

Source: Northern Ireland Tourist Board

[1] Data from 2003 onwards cannot be compared to previous years due to changes in methodologies to reflect comparable changes to Northern Ireland Tourist Board (NITB) and Fáilte Ireland surveys.

Note: The data presented in this table are not National Statistics.

Notes to Transport, Travel and Tourism tables

TABLES 9.1 AND 9.2

Vehicle Licensing

The following notes provide some details on the figures included in the tables from 1994 to 1995:

- Cycles: Motorcycles, scooters and mopeds.
- Motor hackneys: Includes only vehicles taxed in the relevant category, no tramcars are identified.
- Agricultural tractors and engines: Includes only vehicles with the relevant body type, used on a public road.
- Goods vehicles: Includes general and farmer's goods.
- Private cars: Includes all vehicles taxed as private light goods except cars classified by horsepower.
- Exempt from duty: Includes crown vehicles.
- All vehicles: The total number of vehicles counted in the census irrespective of vehicle type or taxation class.

In 1996 vehicle classes were revised as a result of changes to taxation classes during July and November 1995. Categories from 1996 to 2000 are defined as follows:

- Cycles: Motorcycles, scooters and mopeds.
- Buses, hackneys: Includes only vehicles taxed in the relevant category, no tramcars are identified.
- Agricultural tractors, machines and mowing machines: Includes only vehicles with the relevant body type, used on the public road.
- Goods vehicles: Includes general and farmer's goods.
- Private light goods: Includes all vehicles taxed as private light goods including private cars and vans.
- Exempt from duty: Includes crown vehicles.
- All vehicles: The total number of vehicles counted in the census irrespective of vehicle type or taxation class.

In 2001 vehicle classes were revised as a result of changes to taxation classes. Categories from 2001 onwards are defined as follows:

- Cycles: Motorcycles, scooters and mopeds.
- Motor hackneys: Buses and PRV Bus.
- Agricultural tractors: Machines and mowing machines. Includes only vehicles with the relevant body type, used on a public road.
- Goods vehicles: Includes general and farmer's goods, HGV CT, RPV HGV, RPV trailer HGV, RPV HGV CT.
- Private light goods: Includes all vehicles taxed as private light goods, light goods vehicles, petrol cars, diesel cars and alternative fuel vehicles.
- Exempt from duty: Includes crown vehicles.
- All vehicles: The total number of vehicles counted in the census irrespective of vehicle type or taxation class. In 2003 new tax class 36 (Euro 4 Light) was introduced into the Private Light Goods taxation group.

TABLES 9.5 AND 9.10

Road traffic collision fatalities are defined as deaths that occur within 30 days from injuries received in a collision.

TABLE 9.14

A staying visitor is defined as any non-resident of Northern Ireland who spends at least one night in the region on holiday, on business, or visiting friends or relatives. The same person visiting Northern Ireland on two separate occasions is counted as two visitors.

10

Agriculture, Forestry and Fishing

- Between 2003 and 2004, Total Income From Farming (TIFF) - the return to farmers and all members of their families working on farms - increased by 7% to £173 million from a (revised) 2003 figure of £162 million.

- Gross value added from agriculture increased in 2004 by 6% to £516 million. Net value added (gross value added less consumption of fixed capital) also rose by 6% to £318 million.

- Agricultural labour and total factor productivity have both increased over the period 1999 to 2004.

- The number of sheep on farms has decreased by 23% between 1999 and 2004. Poultry numbers have been steadily increasing since 2001 and rose by almost 11% between 2003 and 2004.

- Over the period 1999 to 2004, average earnings per week for full time paid male agricultural workers increased by almost a third (31%), whilst average weekly hours increased by almost 2%.

- In 2004, there were 2% fewer farmers (including partners) than in 2003, with the number of full time farmers decreasing by 5%. The total labour force, comprising farmers and other workers also decreased by 2% over the same period.

- In 2003, the external sales of Northern Ireland's food and drinks processing sector were worth an estimated £1.3 billion. Approximately two thirds of these external sales were accounted for by three sub-sectors: milk and milk products; beef and sheepmeat; and poultrymeat.

- The amount of forested land has increased steadily between 1993-94 and 2003-04, with privately owned forests accounting for most of this increase.

- In 2003-04, there were 86,000 hectares of forested land in Northern Ireland. State forests represented almost three quarters of this total, the remainder was privately owned. Timber production from state forests was valued at approximately £5.4 million.

- Between 2003 and 2004 the amount of fish landed in Northern Ireland fell by a quarter to 13,700 tonnes. This was the largest annual fall in the tonnage of fish landed in Northern Ireland over the period 2000 to 2004. The full period has seen the volume of fish fall from 23,600 tonnes in 2000 to 13,700 in 2004.

- In 2004, the agricultural industry accounted for 2.2% of NI gross value added (GVA), compared with 0.8% of UK GVA. Similarly, employment in agriculture accounted for 4.5% of all employment in Northern Ireland, compared with 1.4% of all employment in the United Kingdom.

Aggregate Agricultural Account: estimated output, input, value added and income of agriculture, 1999 to 2004

10.1

£ millions

Item	1999	2000	2001	2002	2003[r]	2004[p]
Output[1]						
Livestock and livestock products[2]						
Finished cattle and calves[3]	325.0	332.6	333.7	361.7	371.9	404.2
Finished sheep and lambs[4]	68.6	66.5	65.4	59.0	57.5	64.6
Finished pigs[5]	59.4	52.3	62.5	58.0	69.5	65.8
Poultry[6]	98.3	97.6	106.5	115.8	121.7	136.3
Eggs[7]	20.6	24.5	22.4	26.5	37.0	21.0
Milk	301.5	302.6	351.5	292.8	331.2	347.4
Minor products[8]	7.7	8.5	8.3	8.1	8.4	8.4
Total livestock and livestock products	**881.1**	**884.6**	**950.3**	**922.0**	**997.2**	**1,047.6**
Field crops						
Potatoes	33.0	17.3	21.2	21.5	22.2	21.3
Cereals[9]	25.3	25.6	23.7	20.7	26.5	28.0
Of which:						
- Barley[9]	20.9	19.8	19.2	14.3	18.2	18.0
- Wheat[9]	2.7	4.1	3.1	5.2	6.7	8.4
- Oats[9]	1.6	1.7	1.4	1.3	1.6	1.6
Other crops[9,10]	8.2	8.0	9.2	6.9	7.8	6.6
Total field crops	**66.4**	**50.8**	**54.1**	**49.1**	**56.4**	**55.9**
Horticultural products						
Fruit	5.4	5.4	6.9	4.1	5.8	7.7
Vegetables	10.1	14.6	15.6	15.1	16.1	16.2
Mushrooms	30.0	27.6	28.8	27.1	25.1	23.5
Ornamental and hardy nursery stock	12.3	12.6	12.6	13.1	13.8	14.2
Total horticultural products	**57.8**	**60.3**	**63.9**	**59.4**	**60.8**	**61.6**
Capital formation (breeding livestock)	36.2	39.2	58.1	46.6	59.5	48.8
Agricultural contract work[11]	29.0	32.9	36.6	37.3	40.8	41.9
Milk quota leasing	9.3	1.4	0.8	3.7	4.3	9.0
Inseparable non-agricultural activities[12]	11.7	12.9	13.6	18.5	21.6	22.1
A. Gross output	**1,091.7**	**1,081.7**	**1,177.4**	**1,136.3**	**1,240.5**	**1,286.8**
of which: subsidies (less taxes) on products	194.9	194.8	194.2	210.9	205.3	240.5
Input (also known as 'intermediate consumption')						
Expenditure						
Feedstuffs[13]	261.0	249.0	273.6	286.7	335.1	345.4
Seeds[14]	9.5	7.0	7.6	8.8	10.0	10.0
Marketing expenses[15]	35.3	33.1	30.7	34.0	34.1	33.8
Fertilisers and lime	60.2	56.3	56.7	58.9	55.7	50.7
Total machinery expenses (excl. depreciation)	73.3	73.8	76.4	79.1	85.3	90.5
Farm maintenance	27.2	28.2	30.4	26.6	31.8	30.7
Veterinary expenses and medicines	27.7	27.2	28.4	31.5	32.2	32.3
Miscellaneous expenses	108.2	104.1	111.4	111.3	120.7	124.4
Agricultural contract work	29.0	32.9	36.6	37.3	40.8	41.9
Milk quota leasing	8.5	2.8	1.8	6.0	5.9	11.5
B. Gross input	**639.8**	**614.4**	**653.7**	**680.2**	**751.6**	**771.0**
C. Gross value added (A-B)	**451.6**	**467.4**	**523.7**	**456.0**	**488.9**	**515.8**

10.1 Aggregate Agricultural Account: estimated output, input, value added and income of agriculture, 1999 to 2004 (continued)

£ millions

Item	1999	2000	2001	2002	2003[r]	2004[p]
Consumption of fixed capital						
Livestock	42.8	37.9	56.4	48.9	44.6	54.5
Plant, machinery and vehicles	79.7	77.6	78.7	80.2	78.7	79.3
Buildings and works	95.4	94.1	93.5	93.9	94.1	90.7
D. Total consumption of fixed capital	**217.8**	**209.7**	**228.5**	**223.0**	**217.4**	**224.5**
Other subsidies (not paid on products)[16]	5.1	6.0	33.2	32.6	33.1	32.5
Other taxes (not levied on products)[17]	5.4	5.3	5.1	5.3	5.7	6.0
E. Other subsidies (less taxes)	**-0.3**	**0.8**	**28.2**	**27.3**	**27.4**	**26.5**
F. Net value added at factor cost (C-D+E)	**233.7**	**258.5**	**323.4**	**260.4**	**298.9**	**317.7**
G. Paid labour	44.7	48.2	48.0	48.6	52.2	52.9
H. Interest	44.0	46.0	40.4	34.8	34.5	41.5
I. Net rent[18]	49.4	46.6	49.4	51.3	50.6	50.2
J. Total income from farming[19] (F-G-H-I)	**95.2**	**117.5**	**185.6**	**125.6**	**161.6**	**173.1**

Source: Department of Agriculture and Rural Development

1 Output represents the estimated value of home-produced sales, including the value of inter-farm transfers and on-farm use. It includes the value of subsidies on products, the sale value of store animals imported from the Republic of Ireland and Great Britain and finished in Northern Ireland and the value of produce used in farm households. Stock change estimates are included within the individual output and input items.

2 Includes finished, breeding and store animals exported to the Republic of Ireland and shipped to Great Britain. The value of imported animals has been deducted.

3 Includes Suckler Cow Premium, Hill Livestock Compensatory Allowance, Beef Special Premium, Beef Deseasonalisation Premium, Extensification Supplement, Agrimoney Compensation, Slaughter Premium, Flagged Suckler Herd Payments, BSE related supplements, receipts from the Over Thirty Months Scheme and Calf Processing Aid Scheme and Foot and Mouth (non-capital) compensation payments. The Less Favoured Area (LFA) Compensatory Allowance, introduced in 2001, is included in 'other subsidies'.

4 Includes Sheep Annual Premium, Rural World (LFA) Supplement, Hill Livestock Compensatory Allowance, Agrimoney Compensation and Foot and Mouth (non-capital) compensation payments. The LFA Compensatory Allowance, introduced in 2001, is included in 'other subsidies'.

5 Includes Pig Welfare Slaughter Scheme and Foot and Mouth (non-capital) compensation and Pig Industry Restructuring Scheme (Ongoers) payments.

6 Includes shipments and exports of breeding and non-breeding birds, and eggs for hatching.

7 Includes eggs for processing and duck eggs.

8 Includes horses, wool, deer and minor livestock products.

9 Includes Arable Area Payments but excludes set-aside payments, which are included in 'other subsidies'.

10 Hay, straw, flax, linseed, oilseed rape, mixed corn, protein crops, lawn turf and associated Arable Area Payments.

11 Receipts to both farmer contractors and specialist contractors.

12 Receipts from non-agricultural activities which use farm resources.

13 Includes home-fed cereals, proteins and stockfeed potatoes.

14 Includes home-saved seed.

15 Hired transport charges, auction fees, slaughter charges and inter farm expenses.

16 Includes LFA Compensatory Allowance, set-aside payments and payments for the non-capital element of the Environmentally Sensitive Area scheme, Newcastle disease compensation and other minor grants and subsidies.

17 Farm rates and vehicle road tax.

18 Conacre payments to non-producing landowners.

19 This estimate should be regarded only as an indicator of trend. The income estimate, being a residual, is subject to cumulative errors in the estimation of input and output items.

Figure 10.1 Total income from farming, 1994 to 2004

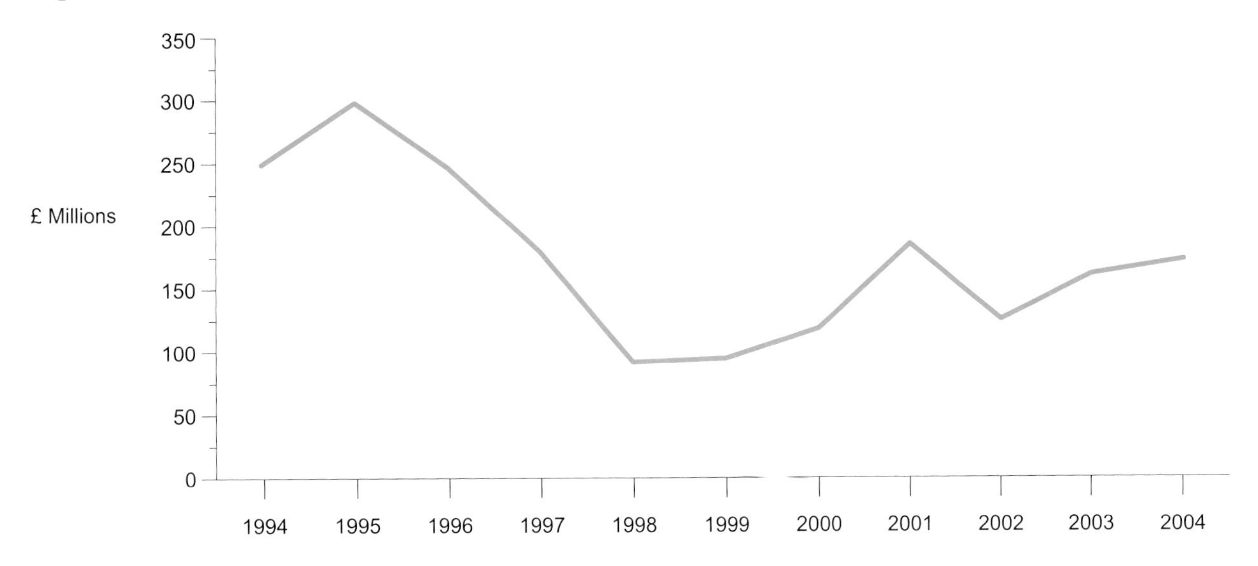

Source: Department of Agriculture and Rural Development

10.2 Summary agricultural income indicators at current prices and in real terms[1], 1999 to 2004

Indices: 2000 = 100

Indicator	1999	2000	2001	2002	2003	2004[P]
Index at current prices						
Net value added	90.4	100.0	125.1	100.7	115.6	122.9
Total income from farming	81.4	100.0	157.9	106.9	137.5	147.2
Index in real terms						
Net value added	93.1	100.0	122.9	97.3	108.6	112.1
Total income from farming	83.8	100.0	155.0	103.3	129.1	134.3

Source: Department of Agriculture and Rural Development

[1] Deflated by the retail prices index.

10.3 Agricultural output and input volume and productivity indices, 1999 to 2004

Indices: 2000 = 100

Indicator	1999	2000	2001	2002	2003	2004[P]
Gross output at constant 2000 prices[1]	102.3	100.0	105.4	105.5	108.7	110.2
Gross input at constant 2000 prices[1]	107.2	100.0	100.7	103.4	106.3	104.8
Gross value added at constant 2000 prices[1]	95.8	100.0	111.6	108.3	111.9	117.3
Net value added at constant 2000 prices[1]	88.5	100.0	121.2	115.1	124.2	132.0
Total factor productivity[2]	95.6	100.0	104.7	104.0	108.0	111.8
Labour productivity[3]	85.4	100.0	124.7	122.5	133.4	146.6

Source: Department of Agriculture and Rural Development

[1] Calculated by applying 2000 output and input prices to the volume of each item of output and input in every year. The resulting series, therefore, represent volume changes.

[2] Calculated as the ratio of output at constant prices to all inputs (including labour and capital) at constant prices.

[3] Calculated as the ratio of net value added at constant prices to total labour input (in Annual Work Units).

10.4 Indices of producer prices[1] of agricultural output, 1999 to 2004

Indices: 2000 = 100

Item	Weights[2]	1999	2000	2001	2002	2003	2004[P]
Finished steers and heifers[3]	222	99	100	100	101	105	111
Culled cows and bulls[3]	32	107	100	105	105	102	92
Store cattle exported	3	91	100	105	104	112	117
Finished sheep and lambs	48	93	100	129	118	125	121
Finished clean pigs	63	85	100	111	103	110	115
Culled sows and boars	1	77	100	101	80	72	84
Milk	361	103	100	102	88	100	101
Eggs for consumption	29	86	100	87	102	141	87
Broilers	81	102	100	104	103	101	105
Ware potatoes (maincrop)	19	173	100	136	136	141	145
Seed potatoes	3	252	100	131	237	190	179
Barley	16	109	100	102	99	113	117
Wheat	3	105	100	107	96	117	118
Mushrooms	33	96	100	93	99	97	97
Apples	6	92	100	101	108	238	142
Total products index[2]	**920**	**101**	**100**	**104**	**98**	**107**	**107**

Source: Department of Agriculture and Rural Development

1 The indices relate to prices from which marketing expenses have not been deducted. Animals slaughtered under Foot and Mouth Disease control measures are not included.

2 The total products index is calculated by taking into account the significance of each item in the base period (2000). This is shown in the column of weights. Since only the main items of output are included, the total of their weights does not add to 1,000. Also, since the price index does not cover items such as production grants, compensation payments and gross fixed capital formation, it should not be regarded as a 'deflator' to be used in estimating the volume of output.

3 Includes cattle slaughtered under the Over Thirty Months Scheme.

Figure 10.2 Index of producer prices of agricultural output, 1994 to 2004[P]

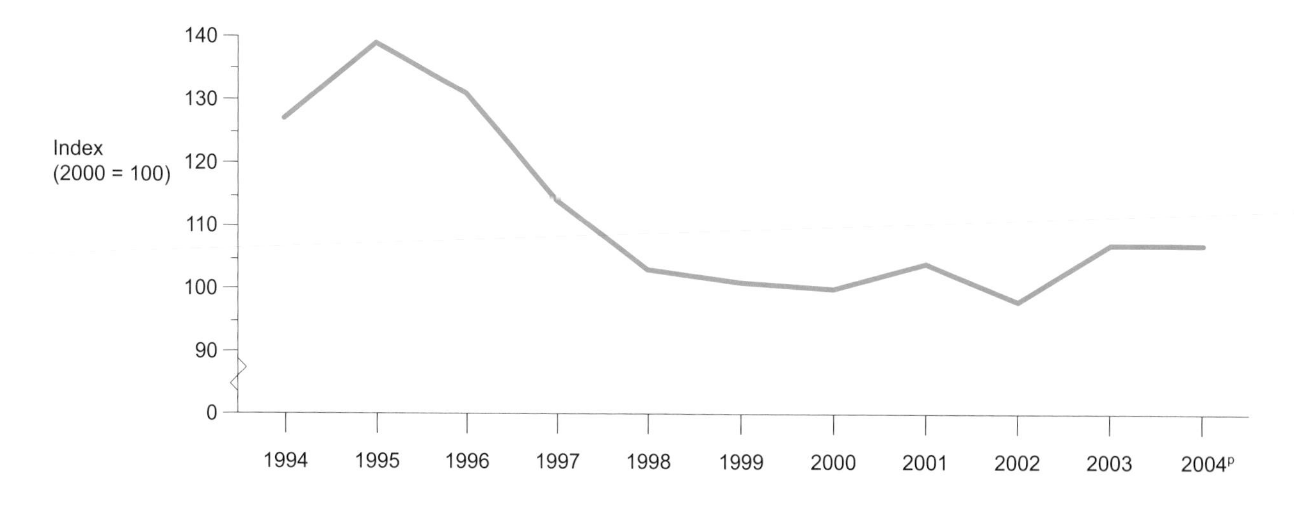

Source: Department of Agriculture and Rural Development

Areas of crops, grass, rough grazing and other land, 1999 to 2004

Thousand hectares

	1999	2000	2001	2002	2003	2004
Oats	2.8	2.9	2.4	2.4	2.5	2.5
Wheat	3.3	5.0	4.1	7.2	7.3	8.6
Barley						
- Winter	5.1	5.2	2.8	3.9	4.1	4.5
- Spring	30.6	27.4	30.0	24.5	23.6	22.5
Mixed corn	0.2	0.2	0.2	0.1	0.2	0.2
Potatoes	7.5	6.8	6.7	6.7	6.0	5.7
Arable crop silage	2.4	2.2	2.3	1.9	2.3	2.8
Other field crops	1.3	1.1	2.4	2.7	3.6	4.0
All agricultural crops	**53.2**	**50.8**	**50.9**	**49.5**	**49.8**	**50.7**
Fruit	1.7	1.6	1.5	1.5	1.6	1.5
Vegetables	1.5	1.5	1.5	1.5	1.5	1.4
Other horticultural crops	0.1	0.1	0.1	0.1	0.2	0.2
All horticultural crops	**3.3**	**3.3**	**3.1**	**3.2**	**3.3**	**3.1**
Grass						
Under 5 years old	140.9	141.6	140.2	136.4	138.0	141.8
5 years old and over	697.2	687.9	699.9	707.3	710.3	696.7
All grass	**838.1**	**829.4**	**840.1**	**843.7**	**848.2**	**838.5**
All crops and grass	**894.6**	**883.5**	**894.1**	**896.3**	**901.3**	**892.3**
Rough grazing[1]	158.7	156.5	154.1	151.6	152.9	151.2
Woods and plantations	8.2	8.6	8.2	7.9	8.4	8.2
Other land[2]	11.5	11.8	11.8	11.3	11.2	11.0
Total area of agricultural holdings	**1,073.0**	**1,060.5**	**1,068.2**	**1,067.2**	**1,073.7**	**1,062.8**

Source: Department of Agriculture and Rural Development

[1] Excludes common rough grazing (35,500 hectares in 2003 and 29,400 hectares in 2004).

[2] Includes set aside.

10.6 Livestock numbers, 1999 to 2004

Thousands

	1999	2000	2001	2002	2003	2004
Cattle						
Dairy cows						
In milk	267.1	265.7	275.4	276.2	268.7	265.9
In calf	19.3	18.6	19.6	21.7	21.5	22.4
All dairy cows	**286.4**	**284.4**	**295.0**	**297.9**	**290.1**	**288.3**
Beef cows						
In milk	274.2	262.2	260.2	255.5	239.9	240.5
In calf	58.0	55.8	51.6	51.5	55.5	55.7
All beef cows	**332.2**	**318.0**	**311.8**	**307.0**	**295.4**	**296.2**
All cows	**618.6**	**602.3**	**606.8**	**604.9**	**585.6**	**584.5**
Heifers						
Dairy heifers in calf	60.0	60.9	60.7	58.5	60.0	62.5
Beef heifers in calf	34.6	31.5	33.1	33.0	33.3	34.3
All heifers in calf	**94.6**	**92.4**	**93.7**	**91.5**	**93.3**	**96.7**
Bulls for service	16.9	16.3	16.7	16.5	16.6	17.0
Other cattle						
Over 2 years	105.7	106.8	110.3	111.4	114.8	115.4
1-2 years	402.1	387.8	380.3	387.8	403.5	397.3
Under 1 year	480.7	470.9	471.3	472.4	471.5	466.7
All other cattle	**988.5**	**965.5**	**961.9**	**971.6**	**989.8**	**979.4**
All cattle	**1,718.6**	**1,676.5**	**1,679.1**	**1,684.5**	**1,685.3**	**1,677.6**
Sheep						
Breeding ewes	1,404.9	1,332.6	1,232.3	1,128.6	1,105.6	1,100.5
Other sheep	1,504.0	1,408.0	1,293.3	1,195.5	1,135.5	1,124.9
All sheep	**2,908.9**	**2,740.6**	**2,525.6**	**2,324.2**	**2,241.1**	**2,225.4**
Pigs						
Sows and gilts	47.1	41.8	40.6	39.3	42.9	37.8
Other pigs	443.1	371.7	345.0	348.4	390.8	386.2
All pigs	**490.2**	**413.5**	**385.6**	**387.7**	**433.7**	**424.1**
Poultry						
Laying birds	2,140.1	2,300.0	2,142.6	2,099.4	2,203.2	2,266.1
Growing pullets	781.3	798.3	735.1	534.1	552.9	509.8
Breeding flock	2,266.1	2,196.3	2,145.2	2,506.2	2,518.2	2,284.8
Table fowl	9,342.0	9,655.4	8,863.6	11,273.3	12,811.4	15,006.9
All ordinary fowl	**14,529.5**	**14,950.0**	**13,886.5**	**16,413.0**	**18,085.8**	**20,067.6**
Other poultry	518.4	425.9	461.0	448.8	439.6	441.7
All poultry	**15,047.9**	**15,375.9**	**14,347.5**	**16,861.8**	**18,525.4**	**20,509.2**
Horses and ponies	9.9	9.5	10.1	10.1	9.9	9.2
Goats	3.5	3.4	3.4	3.3	2.9	2.7

Source: Department of Agriculture and Rural Development

Earnings and hours of agricultural workers, 1999 to 2004

10.7

Units as indicated

	1999	2000	2001	2002	2003	2004[P]
Full-time paid male workers						
Average weekly hours	40.65	41.46	42.43	42.85	41.92	41.30
Average earnings (£ per hour)[1]	4.67	5.17	5.27	5.33	5.56	6.00
Average earnings (£ per week)[1]	189.84	214.35	223.61	228.39	233.08	247.80
Volume of paid labour (million hours)[2]	**9.53**	**9.19**	**9.07**	**8.94**	**9.16**	**8.62**
Value of paid labour (£ million)[2]	**44.7**	**48.2**	**47.9**	**48.5**	**52.2**	**52.9**

Source: Department of Agriculture and Rural Development

[1] Gross wage before deduction of tax and national insurance, and including the value of perks.

[2] Excludes labour used on capital projects.

Number of persons working on farms, 1999 to 2004

10.8

Numbers

Agricultural labour force[1]	1999	2000	2001	2002	2003	2004
Farmers and partners						
Full time	21,536	20,534	20,169	19,706	19,265	18,329
Part time	16,073	15,386	15,786	14,826	14,728	14,934
All farmers and partners	**37,609**	**35,920**	**35,955**	**34,532**	**33,993**	**33,263**
Spouses of farmers	7,034	7,034	6,520	6,201	6,428	6,396
Other workers						
Full time	3,030	3,005	2,797	2,720	2,794	2,741
Part time	2,793	3,062	2,782	2,773	2,848	2,785
Casual/seasonal	8,785	8,802	8,308	8,047	8,423	8,147
All other workers	**14,608**	**14,869**	**13,887**	**13,540**	**14,065**	**13,673**
Total agricultural labour force	**59,251**	**57,823**	**56,362**	**54,273**	**54,486**	**53,332**

Source: Department of Agriculture and Rural Development

[1] Full-time work is defined as involving 30 hours per week or more and casual work as covering less than 20 weeks per year.

10.9 Estimated full-time equivalent employment in the food and drinks processing and input supply sectors, 1998 to 2003[1]

Numbers

Subsector	1998	1999	2000	2001	2002	2003[P]
Food and drinks processing[2]						
Animal by-products	251	277	264	270	264	265
Bakeries	3,326	3,324	3,331	3,416	3,521	3,520
Beef and sheepmeat	2,247	2,501	2,803	2,770	2,813	2,810
Drinks	1,843	1,820	1,763	1,780	1,630	1,660
Eggs	242	221	192	205	201	215
Fish	1,119	948	992	996	1,000	1,000
Fruit and vegetables	1,303	1,369	1,433	1,499	1,538	1,615
Milk and milk products	2,589	2,458	2,383	2,227	2,313	2,310
Pigmeat	2,360	1,990	1,510	1,454	1,485	1,515
Poultrymeat	4,113	3,915	4,205	4,160	4,178	4,385
All processing sector	**19,393**	**18,822**	**18,875**	**18,774**	**18,942**	**19,295**
Manufacture and supply of agricultural inputs[3]						
Animal feed	820	790	820	800	810	800
Fertilisers and lime	520	490	500	500	500	330
Other requisites (incl. medicines)	820	820	830	830	830	830
Farm machinery (incl. servicing)	920	900	880	870	870	870
Services[4]	1,530	1,520	1,500	1,400	1,380	1,350
All supply sector	**4,610**	**4,520**	**4,530**	**4,400**	**4,390**	**4,180**
All ancillary employment	**24,003**	**23,342**	**23,405**	**23,174**	**23,332**	**23,475**

Source: Department of Agriculture and Rural Development

1 Figures for 2003 have been estimated by adjusting the 2002 baseline, largely on the basis of information available within the Department of Agriculture and Rural Development (DARD).

2 For a description of how the data for the processing sector have been estimated, see the publication 'Size and Performance of the Northern Ireland Food and Drinks Processing Sector', DARD.

3 Estimated from trade directory information and other (mainly DARD) sources.

4 Includes contractors, veterinary surgeons, workers in auction marts, employees of farming and marketing associations and artificial insemination workers.

10.10 External sales of the food and drinks processing sector[1], 1998 to 2003

£ millions

Subsector	1998	1999	2000	2001	2002	2003
Animal by-products	20	19	20	19	20	20
Bakeries	30	36	36	37	47	45
Beef and sheepmeat	225	222	250	277	291	290
Drinks	51	51	95	106	152	150
Eggs	23	23	26	26	26	25
Fish	66	59	61	61	63	60
Fruit and vegetables	70	69	75	67	80	80
Milk and milk products	352	344	336	345	348	345
Pigmeat	125	112	78	77	82	80
Poultrymeat	182	182	195	212	233	230
All processing sector	**1,143**	**1,118**	**1,170**	**1,227**	**1,342**	**1,325**

Source: Department of Agriculture and Rural Development

1 The term 'external sales' refers to sales to Great Britain, Republic of Ireland, foreign countries and into intervention.

10.11

Forestry area, production and employment, 1993-94 to 2003-04

Units as indicated

Forestry	1993-94	1994-95	1995-96	1996-97	1997-98	1998-99	1999-00	2000-01	2001-02	2002-03	2003-04
Forested area (thousand hectares)											
State	61	61	61	61	61	61	61	61	61	61	62
Private	17	18	19	20	20	21	22	22	23	24	24
All forested areas	**78**	**79**	**80**	**81**	**81**	**82**	**83**	**83**	**84**	**85**	**86**
Annual planting area (hectares)											
State[1]	816	826	774	643	725	734	756	999	912	799	1,069
Private[2]	928	624	836	679	617	697	725	783	677	523	414
All planted areas	**1,744**	**1,450**	**1,610**	**1,322**	**1,342**	**1,431**	**1,481**	**1,782**	**1,589**	**1,322**	**1,483**
Timber production from state forests											
Volume (thousand m^3)[3]	222	222	223	230	229	260	300	359	421	417	423
Value (£ thousands)[4]	3,340	5,900	5,000	5,990	5,710	5,100	4,110	4,006	4,641	5,915	5,394
Employees (number)											
State Forest Service	469	446	460	401	391	366	367	360	350	332	323

Source: Department of Agriculture and Rural Development

1 Area includes replanting.

2 Area of planting grant applications approved and planted during the year.

3 Volume of timber sold.

4 Value of timber sold.

10.12

Liveweight and estimated value of all landed fish, 2000 to 2004

Tonnes and £ thousands

Type of fish	2000 Tonnes	2000 £	2001 Tonnes	2001 £	2002 Tonnes	2002 £	2003 Tonnes	2003 £	2004 Tonnes	2004 £
Pelagic										
Herring	4,589	458	7,576	1,682	3,905	491	2,746	275	1,782	175
Other	5,132	1,044	2,500	388	2,418	779	3,109	893	1,419	427
Demersal										
Cod	913	1,453	790	1,250	1,136	1,816	435	742	576	1,106
Haddock	1,148	1,365	1,223	1,365	662	712	228	222	456	495
Hake	471	982	266	640	279	725	267	704	345	804
Whiting	630	380	483	278	317	198	134	75	93	49
Other	2,879	2,180	3,350	3,129	4,260	3,770	5,333	4,370	2,810	2,368
Shellfish										
Nephrops	5,191	8,193	4,831	8,539	4,779	7,722	4,375	6,647	4,729	7,272
Other	2,690	1,797	2,178	1,701	2,385	1,985	1,567	1,707	1,460	1,481
Weight and value of all fish landed in Northern Ireland	**23,643**	**17,852**	**23,197**	**18,973**	**20,141**	**18,198**	**18,194**	**15,635**	**13,670**	**14,177**
Of which, landed by NI boats	19,247	16,612	18,455	17,579	17,153	15,511	16,647	14,907	13,528	14,038
Weight and value of all fish landed by NI boats outside Northern Ireland	**12,225**	**4,261**	**13,509**	**8,002**	**18,745**	**9,225**	**13,583**	**6,934**	**21,817**	**10,910**

Source: Department of Agriculture and Rural Development

10.13 Agriculture: UK comparisons, 2004

Units as indicated

	Northern Ireland	Scotland	Wales	England	United Kingdom
Share of gross value added (GVA) (%)	*2.2*	*1.3*[1]	*1.1*[1]	*0.7*[1]	*0.8*
Numbers employed in agriculture, forestry & fishing (thousands)	33	38	32	284	387
Share of employment (%)	*4.5*	*1.6*	*2.4*	*1.2*	*1.4*
Number of farms (thousands)	28	51	36	193	307
Average farm size (hectares)	38.5	109.6[1]	41.0	53.0	56.5[1]

Sources: Labour Force Survey, Department of Enterprise, Trade and Investment; Agricultural Census, Department of Agriculture and Rural Development

[1] Figures are for 2003.

Figure 10.3 Agriculture: UK comparisons, 2004

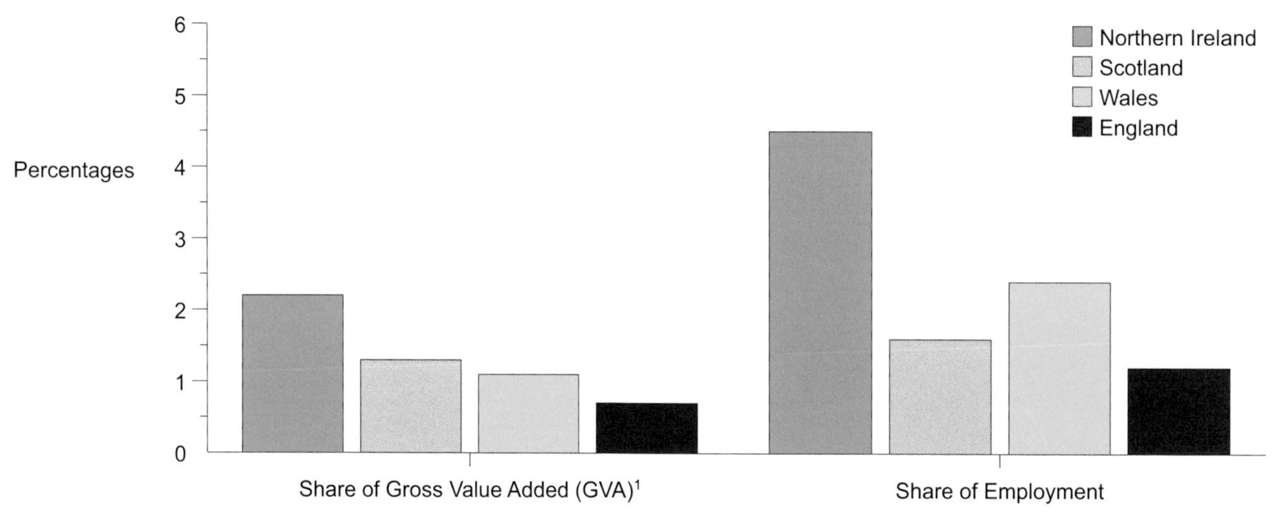

Sources: Labour Force Survey, Department of Enterprise, Trade and Investment; Agricultural Census, Deparment of Agriculture and Rural Development

[1] The Northern Ireland GVA figure is for 2004, whereas figures for Scotland, Wales and England refer to 2003.

Notes to Agriculture, Forestry and Fishing tables

TABLES 10.1 TO 10.3

Aggregate Agricultural Account

Estimates of agriculture's output, input, value added and income are obtained from the Aggregate Agricultural Account (AAA). Major revisions to the AAA were made in 1998. These changes were necessary to bring the AAA into line with the new United Nations System of National Accounts 1993, the subsequent European System of Accounts 1995 and the revised European Union (EU) Manual on the Economic Accounts for Agriculture 1997, introduced throughout the United Kingdom in 1998.

The main features of the AAA are as follows:

(i) The AAA is conducted on a 'sector' basis. This means that agricultural activity includes 'inseparable non-agricultural activities', such as pony trekking, which are carried out on-farm and for which the inputs cannot be separated from farming inputs.

(ii) The AAA is calculated on an accruals basis, i.e 'as due' rather than 'as paid'. This means that subsidies such as the Suckler Cow Premium and Arable Area Payments are counted in the year in which they are due rather than in the year when they are paid.

(iii) Rent paid on 'conacre' (short-term lettings) to non-farming persons is included as an expense.

(iv) Capital formation in, and depreciation of, breeding livestock is included.

(v) Direct inter-farm sales and on-farm use of finished products such as cereals are included as both outputs and inputs thereby, in most cases, leaving gross and net product and total income from farming unchanged.

Because of these changes, the statistics in Tables 10.1 to 10.3 are not comparable with those published in pre-1999 editions of the Annual Abstract. (For a more detailed description of the changes, see the Appendix to the Statistical Review of Northern Ireland Agriculture 2004, obtainable from the Department of Agriculture and Rural Development.)

The main indicator of the return to all of the factors of production, i.e. land, labour, capital and 'enterprise', is net value added (at factor cost). This is defined as gross output less expenditure on material and service inputs purchased from outside the sector (and less consumption of fixed capital, or depreciation, plus subsidies not paid on products). Hence:

Gross output - gross input (or 'intermediate consumption') = **gross value added**

Gross value added - consumption of fixed capital
+ subsidies not paid on products
= **net value added** (at factor cost)

The income of farm families is given by **total income from farming (TIFF)**. This includes returns to farmers, their spouses and family workers for their labour and 'enterprise' and on their own capital invested. It therefore represents the income of all those with an entrepreneurial involvement in farming. TIFF conforms to national and international accounting practice and forms the basis of a Eurostat indicator used for income comparisons across the EU. The derivation of TIFF is:

Net value added (at factor cost)

less paid labour
(or 'compensation of employees')
interest
net rent
= TIFF

Series showing net value added (the broadest income measure) and TIFF are presented in Table 10.2 in current prices and as indices in 'real' terms, i.e. deflated by the retail prices index. Table 10.3 gives the main aggregates at constant (2000) prices, thereby representing volume changes.

TABLES 10.5, 10.6 AND 10.8

These tables are based on the results of the June Agricultural Census which covers all active farm businesses.

TABLE 10.8

Agricultural manpower statistics (as used in aggregate labour statistics produced by the Department of Enterprise, Trade and Investment) refer to the count of employees and self-employed workers in agriculture. The self-employed count includes farmers and partners who work full-time on their farms; the employee count includes all other workers except part-time farmers and partners and farmers' spouses.

Energy and Environment

- Sales of electricity increased by almost a quarter in volume terms between 1994-95 and 2004-05.

- There were 62 exceedences of the standards for ozone at the Derry monitoring site during 2004, compared with 18 exceedences at the Belfast Centre site and 17 at the Lough Navar site. The standard for carbon monoxide has not been exceeded throughout the period 1999 to 2004.

- In 2003 and 2004, no exceedences of the standard for sulphur dioxide were recorded at any of the urban monitoring sites.

- In 2004, lower levels of exceedence of the standards for particulate matter at urban monitoring sites were recorded at the Belfast Centre and Derry sites than the previous year. There were no exceedences at the Lough Navar site in 2004.

- In 2002-04, the chemical quality of around 58% of the 4,900 kilometres of Northern Ireland's river water measured was found to be "very good" or "good". This compares with 56% of the river water monitored in 1997-99. Conversely, in 2002-04, 7% of the river water tested was found to be "poor" or "bad" compared with 4% in 1997-99.

- **In 2004, two of the identified bathing waters in Northern Ireland failed to comply with the European Community Bathing Water Directive coliform standards. This compares with 2003 when none of the 16 identified bathing waters failed to comply.**

- **In 2004-05, £306,000 was awarded in historic churches grants, a decrease of almost half on the previous year. Local authority grants more than doubled during the same period.**

- **There were two conservation area designations in 2004-05, the first since 2000-01. Sixty-six properties were listed in 2004-05, the highest annual number of listings since 1995-96.**

11.1 Electricity generation, distribution and sales, 1994-95 to 2004-05

Units as indicated

	1994-95	1995-96	1996-97	1997-98	1998-99	1999-00	2000-01	2001-02	2002-03	2003-04	2004-05
All sales (in Gwh)[1]	6,529	6,723	6,890	6,996	7,291	7,441	7,615	7,654	7,867	7,979	8,067
All consumers (at March year end - number)	643,650	654,650	664,950	673,150	681,800	687,450	697,450	710,550	724,200	742,030	757,610
Current sent out half hour maximum demand (MW)[2]	1,365	1,389	1,423	1,431	1,459	1,454	1,464	1,446	1,526	1,523	1,559

Source: Northern Ireland Electricity

[1] Gigawatt hours (= millions of kilowatt hours).

[2] Megawatt.

Note: The data presented in this table are not National Statistics.

11.2 Direct deliveries of petroleum products for consumption in Northern Ireland, 1999 to 2004

Tonnes

	1999	2000	2001	2002	2003	2004
Gases; Propane and butane	**29,550**	**29,550**	**29,500**	**30,000**	**18,500**	**1,526**
Motor spirit[1]						
Premium 4 star (leaded premium)[2]	34,598	.	.	.	.	.
Lead replacement petrol (LRP)[3]	.	17,713	..	..	..	496
Unleaded super	5,581	3,312	..	..	..	6,590
Unleaded premium	299,497	271,080	..	..	..	0
Ultra Low Sulpur Petrol (ULSP)[4]	.	.	.	..	..	351,605
All motor spirit	**339,676**	**292,105**	**395,000**[r]	**384,000**[r]	**371,970**[r]	**358,690**
Burning oil						
Aviation spirit and wide-cut gasoline	2,661	4,121	3,151	1,118	1,490	1,635
Aviation turbine fuel	71,879	70,718	73,354	70,989	71,101	79,337
Burning oil - premium	0	0	77	0	0	32,660
Burning oil - standard	705,915	604,270	696,003	646,333	806,484	1,046,940
All burning oil	**780,455**	**679,109**	**772,585**	**718,440**	**879,075**	**1,160,572**
Fuel oil						
Derv	211,943	149,829	224,000[r]	257,000[r]	292,000[r]	356,619
Gas/diesel oil	408,556	368,125	449,701	456,225	473,611	505,994
Fuel oil	258,551	144,935	152,631	135,108	153,212	137,428
All fuel oil	**879,050**	**662,889**	**826,332**[r]	**848,333**[r]	**918,823**[r]	**1,000,041**
Non-energy						
Industrial spirits	0	0	0	0	0	0
White spirit	0	0	0	0	0	0
Lubricating oil	7,721	5,429	3,300	3,461	3,565	636
Bitumen	111,488	72,504	82,961	111,261	107,815	90,659
Petroleum waxes	0	0	0	3	0	19
Miscellaneous	345	185	27	0	0	6,912
All non-energy	**119,554**	**78,118**	**86,288**	**114,725**	**111,380**	**98,226**
All petroleum products	**2,148,285**	**1,741,771**	**2,109,705**[r]	**2,095,498**[r]	**2,299,748**[r]	**2,619,055**

Source: Department of Trade and Industry

[1] Splits for individual motor spirit categories are unavailable for years 2001 to 2003.

[2] Leaded petrol removed from UK forecourts from 1 January 2000.

[3] LRP came onto the market from 1 January 2000.

[4] ULSP came onto the market from 1 January 2002.

11.3 Shipments of coal and other solid fuels into Northern Ireland, 1994 to 2004

Thousand tonnes

Use	1994	1995	1996	1997	1998	1999	2000	2001	2002	2003	2004
Domestic	1,211	932	919	997	732	795	617	589	442	357	480
Industrial	190	206	246	132	57	91	189	133	236	242	194
Electricity	1,225	1,660	1,525	1,293	1,375	1,318	1,542	1,620	1,224	1,091	1,125
All shipments	**2,626**	**2,798**	**2,690**	**2,422**	**2,164**	**2,204**	**2,348**	**2,343**	**1,901**	**1,690**	**1,799**

Source: Department of Enterprise, Trade and Investment

11.4 Ozone, nitrogen dioxide and carbon monoxide exceedences, 1999 to 2004

Numbers

	Ozone[1]		Nitrogen dioxide[2]			Carbon monoxide[3]	
Site	Exceedences (8 hour)	Days	Exceedences (1 hour)	Days	Annual mean	Exceedences (8 hour)	Days
1999							
Belfast Centre	54	7	0	0	18	0	0
Lough Navar	31	6	.	.	.	.	.
Derry	39	4	0	0	8	0	0
2000							
Belfast Centre	9	2	0	0	16	0	0
Lough Navar	36	7	.	.	.	.	.
Derry	65	11	0	0	8	0	0
2001							
Belfast Centre	9	2	3	1	17	0	0
Lough Navar	53	9	.	.	.	.	.
Derry	8	2	0	0	8	0	0
2002							
Belfast Centre	0	0	2	1	16	0	0
Lough Navar	3	1	.	.	.	.	.
Derry	100	19	0	0	8	0	0
2003							
Belfast Centre	33	9	0	0	17	0	0
Lough Navar	30	6	.	.	.	.	.
Derry	137	16	0	0	9	0	0
2004							
Belfast Centre	18	5	0	0	15	0	0
Lough Navar	17	3	.	.	.	.	.
Derry	62	10	0	0	8	0	0

Source: National Environmental Technology Centre

[1] The standard for ozone is 100µg/m^3 (50ppb) measured as a running 8 hour mean. This is not to be exceeded more than 10 days per year.

[2] The standards for nitrogen dioxide are 200µg/m^3 (105ppb) measured as a 1 hour mean and 40µg/m^3 (21ppb) measured as an annual mean. Not to be exceeded more than 18 times per year

[3] The standard for carbon monoxide is 11.6mg/m^3 (10ppm) measured as a running 8 hour mean.

Note: The data presented in this table are not National Statistics.

Figure 11.1 Ozone exceedences, 1999 to 2004

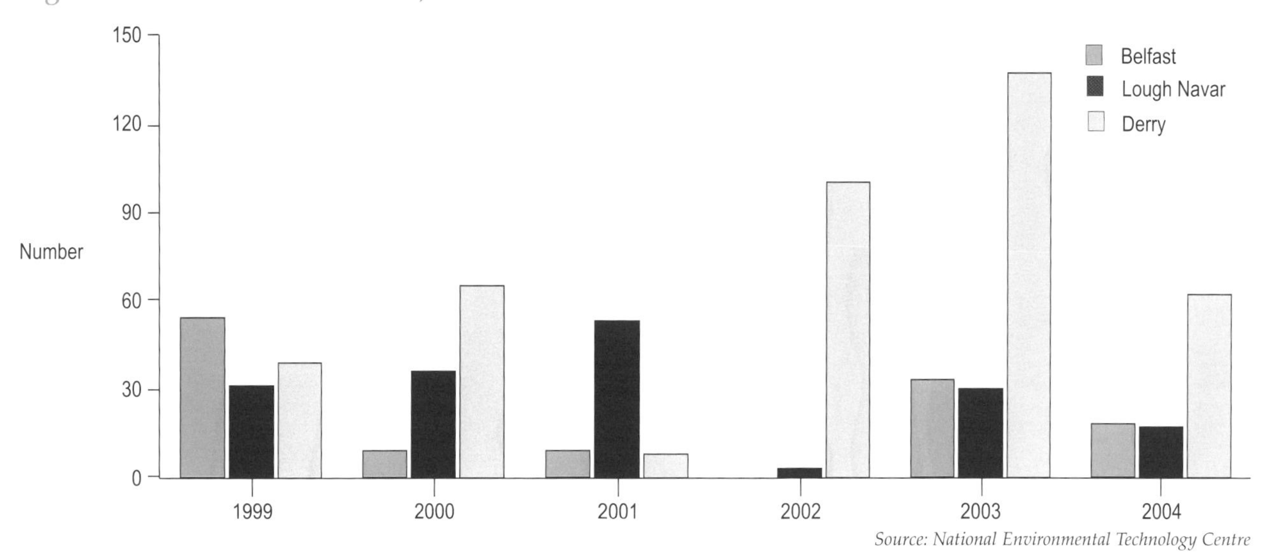

Source: National Environmental Technology Centre

Sulphur dioxide and particulate matter (PM_{10}) exceedences, 1999 to 2004

11.5

Numbers

Site	Sulphur dioxide[1] Exceed-ences (15 mins)	Days	Exceed-ences (1 hour)	Days	Exceed-ences (24 hour)	Particulate matter[2] (PM_{10}) Exceed-ences (24 hour)	Annual mean
1999							
Belfast Centre	5	1	0	0	0	15	26
Belfast East	98	15	5	3	5	.	.
Lough Navar	.	.	.	.	.	0	12
Derry	0	0	0	0	0	11	26
2000							
Belfast Centre	16	5	0	0	0	8	25
Belfast East	38	7	2	1	0	.	.
Lough Navar	.	.	.	.	.	0	12
Derry	19	6	1	1	0	6	20
2001							
Belfast Centre	2	2	0	0	0	15	25
Belfast East	139	14	13	4	5	.	.
Lough Navar	.	.	.	.	.	0	13
Derry	0	0	0	0	0	15	23
2002							
Belfast Centre	2	1	0	0	0	8	23
Belfast East	5	1	0	0	0	.	.
Lough Navar	.	.	.	.	.	2	15
Derry	0	0	0	0	0	9	22
2003							
Belfast Centre	0	0	0	0	0	26	23
Belfast East	0	0	0	0	0	.	.
Lough Navar	.	.	.	.	.	1	14
Derry	0	0	0	0	0	20	23
2004							
Belfast Centre	0	0	0	0	0	10	21
Belfast East	0	0	0	0	0	.	.
Lough Navar	.	.	.	.	.	0	10
Derry	0	0	0	0	0	3	20

Source: National Environmental Technology Centre

1 The standards for sulphur dioxide are 266μg/m³ (100ppb) measured as a 15 minute mean, (not to be exceeded more than 35 times a year), 350μg/m³ (132ppb) measured as a 1 hour mean (not to be exceeded more than 24 times a year) and 125μg/m³ (47 ppb) measured as a 24 hour mean, (not to be exceeded more than 3 times a year).

2 The standards for particulate matter (PM_{10}) are 50μg/m³ measured as a 24 hour mean (not to be exceeded more than 35 times a year) and 40μg/m³ measured as an annual mean. PM concentrations converted to gravimetric equivalent.

Note: The data presented in this table are not National Statistics.

11.6 Chemical quality of river waters, 1997-99 to 2002-04

Kilometres and percentages

Chemical quality	1997-99	1998-00	1999-01	2000-02	2001-03	2002-04
Very good						
km	197.4	166.8	216.0	251.0	411.0	581.0
%	*8.1*	*6.9*	*9.0*	*6.1*	*9.5*	*11.8*
Good						
km	1,167.9	1,246.5	1,187.0	2,033.0	2,079.0	2,265.0
%	*48.2*	*51.9*	*49.4*	*49.3*	*48.1*	*46.1*
Fairly good						
km	684.6	634.4	589.0	1,215.0	1,054.0	1,347.0
%	*28.2*	*26.4*	*24.5*	*29.4*	*24.4*	*27.4*
Fair						
km	272.4	252.2	303.0	506.0	474.0	385.0
%	*11.2*	*10.5*	*12.6*	*12.3*	*11.0*	*7.8*
Poor						
km	97.4	102.8	107.0	121.0	298.0	283.0
%	*4.0*	*4.3*	*4.5*	*2.9*	*6.9*	*5.8*
Bad						
km	6.4	0.0	0.0	0.0	6.0	54.0
%	*0.3*	*0.0*	*0.0*	*0.0*	*0.1*	*1.1*
Length of all rivers classified						
km	**2,426.1**	**2,402.6**	**2,402.0**	**4,126.0**	**4,322.0**	**4,915.0**
%	***100***	***100***	***100***	***100***	***100***	***100***

Source: Environment and Heritage Service, Department of the Environment

Note: The data presented in this table are not National Statistics.

Figure 11.2 Chemical quality of river waters, 2002-04

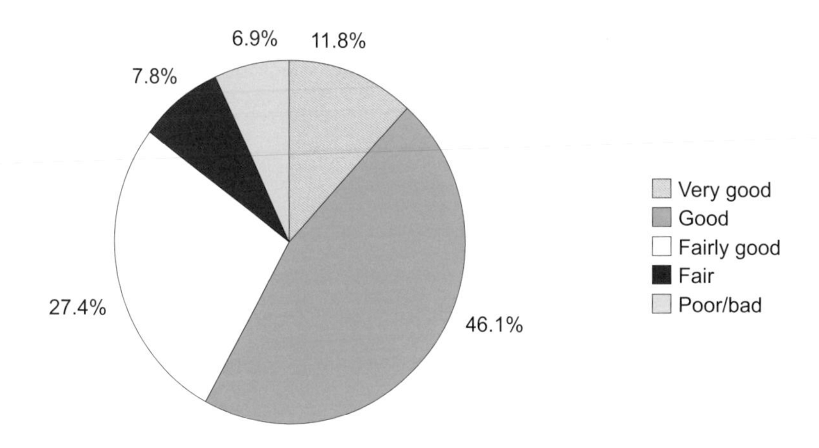

Source: Environment and Heritage Service, Department of the Environment

Radioactivity concentrations in fish from the Irish Sea by type of fish and isotope, 1994 to 2004

11.7

Becquerels per kilogram (wet)

Type of fish and isotope	1994	1995	1996	1997	1998	1999	2000	2001	2002	2003	2004
Whiting[1]											
K40	127.0	114.0	122.0	123.0	111.0	116.9	113.7	120.7	118.2	104.7	113.2
Cs134	-	-	-	<0.1	<0.1	-	-	-	-	-	<0.5
Cs137	6.8	5.2	4.1	4.1	4.5	4.9	3.4	3.5	2.5	2.6	1.8
All beta	-	-	-	-	-	-	-	-	-	-	-
Nephrops[1,2]											
K40	113.0	108.0	101.0	111.0	107.0	109.9	106.7	106.3	104.2	98.3	106.1
Cs134	-	-	-	<0.1	-	-	-	-	-	-	<0.1
Cs137	2.2	1.9	1.3	1.5	1.2	1.2	1.3	1.2	1.0	0.8	0.8
All beta	-	-	-	-	-	-	-	-	-	-	-
Winkles[3]											
K40	55.0	74.0	48.0	44.0	50.0	48.3	49.1	42.1	44.5	38.9	40.8
Cs134	-	-	-	<0.1	<0.1	-	-	-	-	-	<0.1
Cs137	0.6	0.6	0.5	0.5	0.4	0.4	0.4	0.3	0.3	<0.2	0.4
All beta	-	-	-	-	-	-	-	-	-	-	-

Source: Environment and Heritage Service, Department of the Environment

1 Sample taken at Portavogie and Kilkeel each year.

2 Analysis for 2000 based on samples of Norway Lobster taken at Portavogie and Kilkeel.

3 Sample taken on Ards Peninsula.

Note: The data presented in this table are not National Statistics.

Radioactivity concentrations in seaweed from Northern Ireland shoreline by type of seaweed and isotope, 1994 to 2004

11.8

Becquerels per kilogram (wet)

Type of seaweed and isotope	1994	1995	1996	1997	1998	1999	2000	2001	2002	2003	2004
Fucus Vesiculosus[1]											
K40	216	196	230	217	162	181	186	170	168	189	176
Cs134	-	-	-	-	-	-	-	-	-	-	<0.2
Cs137	1.7	1.2	0.9	0.9	0.7	1.0	0.8	0.9	0.6	0.6	0.6
All beta	-	-	-	-	-	-	-	-	-	-	-
Rhodymenia Palmata[2]											
K40	486	488	408	-	104	308	230	310	96	228	277
Cs134	-	-	-	-	-	-	-	-	-	-	<0.2
Cs137	3.5	2.5	1.5	1.7	0.9	1.0	1.0	1.0	0.5	0.8	1.0
All beta	-	-	-	-	-	-	-	-	-	-	-

Source: Environment and Heritage Service, Department of the Environment

1 Sample taken at Ardglass each year.

2 Sample taken at Portaferry each year.

Note: The data presented in this table are not National Statistics.

11.9 Percentage of identified bathing waters that complied with the European Community Bathing Water Directive coliform standards[1], 1999 to 2004

Percentages

	1999	2000	2001	2002	2003	2004
Complying with coliform standards	*100*	*100*	*81*	*94*	*100*	*88*

Source: Environment and Heritage Service, Department of the Environment

[1] At least 95 per cent of samples must have counts not exceeding the mandatory limit values for total coliforms.

Note: The data presented in this table are not National Statistics.

11.10 Gamma dose rates in air, 1994 to 2004

Microrays per hour

Type of reading	1994	1995	1996	1997	1998	1999	2000	2001	2002	2003	2004
Maximum reading[1]											
Over sand	0.108	0.100	0.116	0.114	0.120	0.116	0.117	0.119	0.124	0.127	0.128
Over mud	0.103	0.097	0.096	0.091	0.104	0.100	0.097	0.105	0.102	0.106	0.104
Minimum reading											
Over sand	0.050	0.053	0.052	0.054	0.054	0.051	0.054	0.054	0.057	0.055	0.061
Over mud	0.077	0.073	0.072	0.065	0.067	0.063	0.066	0.061	0.066	0.084	0.061
Average reading											
Over sand	0.069	0.068	0.067	0.067	0.070	0.068	0.072	0.073	0.079	0.095	0.075
Over mud	0.088	0.083	0.081	0.076	0.081	0.081	0.083	0.087	0.088	0.094	0.089

Source: Environment and Heritage Service, Department of the Environment

[1] Obtained in areas which have granite sub-layers. In these locations readings up to 0.28 micrograys per hour can be readily obtained inland from the coastline.

Note: The data presented in this table are not National Statistics.

11.11 Environmental grants by type and amount, 1994-95 to 2004-05

Units as indicated

Type of grant and amount	1994-95	1995-96	1996-97	1997-98	1998-99	1999-00	2000-01	2001-02	2002-03	2003-04	2004-05
Historic buildings grants (£)	1,141,970	1,214,031	1,406,310	1,363,746	1,173,000	1,254,000	2,177,327	1,616,281	1,523,835	1,062,000	969,000
Local authority grants (£)	130,000	130,000	100,000	372,723	539,188	273,320	666,065	149,995	3,750	55,000	114,000
Conservation area grants (£)	450,000	527,567	650,678	605,811	656,565	362,995	44,315	15,565	0	1,713,000	2,068,000
National Trust grants (£)	376,038	401,501	429,394	400,460	444,391	292,437	418,371	51,220	90,920	435,000	913,000
Historic churches grants (£)	322,025	498,437	294,145	214,329	157,000	676,000	712,475	357,800	825,175	603,000	306,000
European Community Structural Funds (£)	606,130	699,991	668,518	756,443	423,337	288,773	238,433	0	0	0	3,427,000
Environmental Protection Grants (£'000)	..	..	..	..	..	..	..	..	..	10,843	12,488
Total Heritage Lottery Fund Award (£'000)	.	4,523	9,841	5,330	19,501	14,354	10,787	8,273	11,664	6,174	15,371

Sources: Environment and Heritage Service, Department of the Environment; Heritage Lottery Fund

Note: The data presented in this table are not National Statistics.

11.12 Listing/Scheduling statistics, 1994-95 to 2004-05

Numbers

Listings	1994-95	1995-96	1996-97	1997-98	1998-99	1999-00	2000-01	2001-02	2002-03	2003-04	2004-05
Listing statistics											
Properties listed	131	70	14	28	2	16	14	52	38	35	66
Properties de-listed	10	27	0	33	28	3	39	42	57	53	38
Archaelological Sites											
State Care Monuments	0	0	0	0	0	0	0	0	0	0	0
Scheduled Monuments	46	47	60	70	70	70	50	40	60	65	65

Source: Environment and Heritage Service, Department of the Environment

Note: The data presented in this table are not National Statistics.

11.13 Designation of conservation areas, 1994-95 to 2004-05

Numbers

Designation	1994-95	1995-96	1996-97	1997-98	1998-99	1999-00	2000-01	2001-02	2002-03	2003-04	2004-05
Conservation areas											
Designations	3	2	4	0	1	0	5	0	0	0	2
Variations / Extensions	0	0	0	1	0	0	1	0	0	1	0
Cancellations	0	0	0	0	0	0	1	0	0	0	0

Source: Planning Service, Department of the Environment

Note: The data presented in this table are not National Statistics.

Notes to Energy and Environment tables

TABLE 11.3

Figures are inclusive of all types and sources of coal shipped (bulk cargo and containerised) to Northern Ireland including cross channel and foreign imports. Excess coal not required for domestic use is sold for industrial or other purposes.

TABLES 11.4 AND 11.5

Standards for air pollution are concentrations over a given time period that are considered to be acceptable in the light of what is known about the effects of each pollutant on health and the environment. They can also be used as a benchmark to see if air pollution is getting better or worse.

An exceedence of a standard is a period of time (which is defined in each standard) where the concentration is higher than that set down. In order to make useful comparisons between pollutants, for which the standards may be expressed in terms of different averaging times, the number of days on which an exceedence has been recorded is given in the tables.

The standards adopted in the United Kingdom are part of the Air Quality Strategy for England, Scotland, Wales and Northern Ireland adopted by the Government in January 2000. Table 11.4 and 11.5 show exceedences of these standards at monitoring sites in Northern Ireland.

TABLE 11.6

These data refer to non-tidal rivers only.

The classifications have been derived using the chemical General Quality Assessment (GQA), a new method of river classification developed by the Environment Agency for England and Wales and adopted by the Environment and Heritage Service of the Department of the Environment in Northern Ireland in 1995.

The chemical GQA uses three years' data and grades the water into one of six classes based on concentrations of dissolved oxygen, biochemical oxygen demand and ammonia.

The length of rivers monitored has been remeasured, and the totals in Table 11.6 may differ from previously published figures. In 2003, the length of rivers classified was approximately 200km greater than in 2002. A further 600km were classified in 2004.

TABLES 11.7 AND 11.8

Samples of fish, nephrops and winkles landed in Northern Ireland together with seaweeds from three coastal sites are sent on a quarterly basis to the Centre for Environment, Fisheries and Aquaculture Science at Lowestoft for radiochemical analysis.

Fish and seaweeds also contain natural radioactivity, mainly potassium 40 and the decay products of uranium and thorium. The representative values to be expected for natural sources are set out below:

Material	Total beta radioactivity concentrations (wet)	
Fish	40 to 100	Mostly K^{40}
Shell fish	40 to 100	Mostly K^{40}
Seaweed	200 to 600	Mostly K^{40}

The symbols used are as follows:

K	=	Potassium
Cs	=	Caesium

TABLE 11.9

Under the EC Bathing Water Directive 76/160/EEC, Member States are required to identify bathing waters at which bathing is traditionally practised by large numbers of bathers, and to monitor the quality of those waters for a number of prescribed parameters. In 1998 16 sites were identified in Northern Ireland.

The data shown in the table refer to the mandatory standards as set out in the Bathing Water Directive. The mandatory coliform standards require that 95% of samples contain less than or equal to 10,000 colony forming units per 100 millilitres (total coliforms) (expressed as cfu/100mls) and 2000cfu/100mls (faecal coliforms). Two sample failures on the same parameter will cause a bathing water to fail for the whole season.

Faecal coliforms are indicator bacteria, which are so called because they are associated with, and therefore indicate the presence of, human sewage or animal slurry.

During the 2004 season, the bathing waters in Northern Ireland achieved 87.5% compliance with the mandatory coliform bacteria standards of the Bathing Water Directive. T his shows a decline compared with 100% during 2003. This result does not compare well with the results for the rest of the United Kingdom - England (98.3%), Wales (100%) and Scotland (93.1%).

TABLE 11.10

The gamma dose rate in air is monitored at one metre above intertidal sediments, twice a year at selected points around the Northern Ireland coastline.

The average dose rates in air over intertidal sediments in the British Isles due to naturally occurring radioactivity are: sand 0.03 to 0.05 micrograys per hour: mud 0.05 to 0.10 micrograys per hour.

TABLE 11.11

All grants, except for Conservation Area Grants, are paid under Article 106 of the Planning (Northern Ireland) Order 1991. Conservation Area Grants are paid under Article 52 of the Planning (Northern Ireland) Order 1991.

TABLE 11.12

Buildings of special architectural or historic interest are listed by virtue of Article 42 of the Planning (Northern Ireland) Order 1991. Article 42 allows for the delisting of such a building.

TABLE 11.13

Conservation areas are areas of special architectural or historical importance and are designated under Article 50 of the Planning (Northern Ireland) Order 1991. At 31 March 2004, there were a total of 57 designated conservation areas in Northern Ireland. Article 50 allows for the variation or cancellation of a conservation area.

Further Information

Other publications giving statistical information on the social and economic life of Northern Ireland are listed below. All of the publications referenced are published annually except where otherwise stated.

COMPENDIA

UK PUBLICATIONS:
Annual Abstract of Statistics
Monthly Digest of Statistics
Regional Trends
Social Trends
United Kingdom in Figures

POPULATION AND MIGRATION

UK PUBLICATIONS:
Population Trends (quarterly)
Key Population and Vital Statistics

NI PUBLICATIONS:
Annual Report of the Registrar General
Census of Population Reports (periodic)
Analysis of the Northern Ireland Register of Electors
Population Projections for areas within Northern Ireland

HOUSING AND HOUSEHOLDS

UK PUBLICATIONS:
Family Spending
General Household Survey
Housing Statistics

NI PUBLICATIONS:
Annual Report of the Northern Ireland Housing Executive
Northern Ireland House Condition Survey (periodic)
Northern Ireland Housing Bulletin (quarterly)
Housing Statistics
NISRA Expenditure and Food Survey Monitors (periodic)
NISRA Continuous Household Survey Monitors (periodic)
Family Resources Survey Northern Ireland

SOCIAL AND WELFARE

UK PUBLICATION:
Inland Revenue Statistics

NI PUBLICATIONS:
Disability Living Allowance, Retirement Pension, Pension Credit, Attendance Allowance and Carer's Allowance Summary Statistics
Incapacity Benefit and Severe Disablement Allowance Summary Statistics
Jobseekers' Allowance Summary Statistics
Income Support Summary Statistics
Summary of Social Security Statistics
Client Group Analysis

HEALTH AND CARE

NI PUBLICATIONS:
Annual Report of the Chief Medical Officer
Hospital Statistics Bulletin
Community Statistics Bulletin
Quarterly Waiting List Bulletin
Key Indicators of Personal Social Services

EDUCATION AND TRAINING

NI PUBLICATIONS:

Education Statistics (periodic press releases)
Participation in Full Time Education by 16 and 17 Year Olds in Northern Ireland
Qualifications and Destinations of Northern Ireland School Leavers
Pupil:Teacher Ratios in Grant Aided Schools in Northern Ireland
Enrolments at Schools and in Funded Pre-School Education in Northern Ireland
Enrolments on Vocational Courses at Northern Ireland Further Education Colleges
Student enrolments on Higher Education Courses: Northern Ireland
Students gaining Higher Education qualifications: Northern Ireland
Destinations of leavers from Higher Education: Northern Ireland

CRIME AND JUSTICE

NI PUBLICATIONS:
A Commentary on Northern Ireland Crime Statistics
Digest of Information on the Northern Ireland Criminal Justice System (biennial)
Northern Ireland Judicial Statistics
Report of the Chief Constable, Police Service of Northern Ireland
Northern Ireland Prison Service Annual Report

THE ECONOMY

UK PUBLICATIONS:
Annual Business Inquiry (formerly ACOP)
UK Business: Activity, Size & Location (formerly PA1003)
Economic Trends (monthly)
Digest of Energy Statistics

NI PUBLICATIONS:

Facts and figures from the Inter Departmental Business Register (IDBR)
Statistics Bulletin on the Index of Production (quarterly)
Trade at the principal Ports
Statistics Bulletin on the Index of Services (quarterly)

LABOUR MARKET

UK PUBLICATIONS:

Labour Market Trends (monthly)
Average Earnings Index

NI PUBLICATIONS:

Census of Employment (biennially)
Labour Market Statistics (monthly)
Labour Force Survey – Households Data
Labour Force Survey – Self Employment
Labour Force Survey Quarterly Supplement
Labour Force Survey Historical Supplement
Labour Force Survey Religion Report
Labour Force Survey - Local Area Database
Labour Market Bulletin
Skills Monitoring Survey (biennially)
Skills Forecasting Reports (periodic)
Survey of Business Expenditure on Research and Development in Northern Ireland
Production and Construction Summary Results from the Annual Business Inquiry
Annual Survey of Hours and Earnings
Annual Survey of Hours and Earnings Historical Supplement
Annual Survey of Hours and Earnings – Occupational Pensions Data
Annual Survey of Hours and Earnings – Sub Northern Ireland Data
Women in Northern Ireland fact sheet (biennially)
Quarterly Employment Survey supplement

TRANSPORT, TOURISM AND TRAVEL

NI PUBLICATIONS:

Northern Ireland Transport Statistics
Northern Ireland Road and Rail Transport Statistics (quarterly)
Road Traffic Collision Statistics Annual Report
Road Traffic Collision Statistics 1997-2001
Annual Report of the Northern Ireland Tourist Board
Tourism Facts

AGRICULTURE, FORESTRY AND FISHING

UK PUBLICATIONS:

Agriculture in the United Kingdom

NI PUBLICATIONS:

Statistical Review of Northern Ireland Agriculture
Farm Incomes in Northern Ireland
Size and performance of the NI food and drinks processing sector
Farm Business Data
Agricultural Census Data for Northern Ireland
EU structure survey (bi/triennial)
Farm Business Survey Gross Margin Results
Agricultural Market Report (weekly & quarterly)
Animal feedstuff statistics (monthly, quarterly & annual)
Fertiliser statistics (quarterly & annual)
Milk utilisation statistics (monthly, quarterly & annual)
Milk price statistics (monthly)
Pig financial results (monthly)

ENVIRONMENT

UK PUBLICATIONS:

Digest of Environment Statistics
The Environment in your pocket
UK Indicators of Sustainable Development

EUROPEAN COMPARISONS

EUROSTAT PUBLICATIONS:

Basic Statistics of the Community
Portrait of the Regions (periodic)
A Social Portrait of Europe (periodic)
Periodic Report on the Social and Economic Situation and Development of the Regions of the Community

THE FOLLOWING INTERNET SITES CONTAIN UP TO DATE INFORMATION ON THE STATISTICAL PRODUCTS AND SERVICES AVAILABLE.

NORTHERN IRELAND STATISTICS AND RESEARCH AGENCY

www.nisra.gov.uk

THE SOURCE (INCLUDING STATBASE)

www.statistics.gov.uk
(provided by National Statistics)

EUROSTAT

http://europa.eu.int/en/comm/eurostat/eurostat.html
(Statistical Office of the European Communities)

Contact Points

DEPARTMENT OF AGRICULTURE AND RURAL DEVELOPMENT

AGRICULTURE STATISTICS

Economics and Statistics Unit,
Department of Agriculture and Rural Development,
Dundonald House,
Upper Newtownards Road
Belfast BT4 3SB

Telephone: 028 9052 4594
Facsimile: 028 9052 4676

E-mail: amanda.keenan@dardni.gsi.gov.uk
Internet: www.dardni.gov.uk

DEPARTMENT OF ENTERPRISE, TRADE AND INVESTMENT

Statistics Research Branch,
Department of Enterprise, Trade and Investment,
Netherleigh, Massey Avenue,
Belfast BT4 2JP

Facsimile: 028 9052 9459
Textphone:028 9052 9304

Internet: www.statistics.detini.gov.uk

EMPLOYMENT STATISTICS

Telephone: 028 9052 9474
E-mail: avril.jardine@detini.gov.uk

UNEMPLOYMENT STATISTICS (CLAIMANT COUNT)

Telephone: 028 9052 9311
E-mail: cathryn.mcburney@detini.gov.uk

UNEMPLOYMENT STATISTICS (LABOUR FORCE SURVEY)

Telephone: 028 9052 9585
E-mail: paul.mckellen@detini.gov.uk

GENERAL LABOUR FORCE SURVEY STATISTICS

Telephone: 028 9052 9585
E-mail: paul.mckellen@detini.gov.uk

EARNINGS STATISTICS

Telephone:028 9052 9385
E-mail: joanne.henderson@detini.gov.uk

PRODUCTION STATISTICS INDEX OF PRODUCTION

Telephone: 028 9052 9426
E-mail: joyce.mercer@detini.gov.uk

SERVICE SECTOR STATISTICS INDEX OF PRODUCTION

Telephone: 028 9052 9655
E-mail: darren.hetherington@detini.gov.uk

R&D STATISTICS

Telephone: 028 9052 9311
E-mail: cathryn.mcburney@detini.gov.uk

PRODUCTION, CONSTRUCTION AND SERVICE SECTOR STATISTICS ANNUAL BUSINESS INQUIRY

Telephone: 028 9052 9228
E-mail: seana.mcilwaine@detini.gov.uk

ENERGY STATISTICS

Telephone: 028 9052 9385
E-mail: steven.roberts@detini.gov.uk

BUSINESS STATISTICS

Telephone: 028 9052 9505
E-mail: n.mcevoy@detini.gov.uk

DEPARTMENT OF EDUCATION

PRE-SCHOOL, NURSERY, PRIMARY AND POST-PRIMARY STATISTICS

Statistics and Research Branch
Department of Education,
Rathgael House,
Balloo Road,
Bangor, BT19 7PR

Telephone: 028 9127 9401
Facsimile: 028 9127 9594

E-mail: statistics2@deni.gov.uk
Internet: www.deni.gov.uk/facts_figures/index.htm

DEPARTMENT FOR EMPLOYMENT AND LEARNING

HIGHER AND FURTHER EDUCATION STATISTICS

Tertiary Education Analytical Services Branch,
Adelaide House,
39-49 Adelaide Street,
Belfast BT2 8FD

Telephone: 028 9025 7606
Facsimile:028 9025 7747

E-mail: statistics@delni.gov.uk
Internet: www.delni.gov.uk/statistics

TRAINING AND VACANCY STATISTICS

Research and Evaluation Branch,
Adelaide House,
39-49 Adelaide Street,
Belfast BT2 8FD

Telephone: 028 9025 7609
Facsimile: 028 9025 7696

E-Mail: reb@delni.gov.uk
Internet: www.delni.gov.uk

DEPARTMENT FOR REGIONAL DEVELOPMENT

Central Statistics and Research Branch,
Department for Regional Development,
Room 4.02,
Clarence Court,
10-18 Adelaide Street,
Belfast BT2 8GB

Facsimile: 028 9054 0782

E-mail: csrb@drdni.gov.uk
Internet: http://csrb.drdni.gov.uk
http://csrb.doeni.gov.uk

TRANSPORT STATISTICS

Telephone: 028 9054 0801

ENVIRONMENTAL STATISTICS

Telephone: 028 9054 0808

DEPARTMENT FOR SOCIAL DEVELOPMENT

SOCIAL SECURITY AND CHILD SUPPORT STATISTICS

Social Welfare Statistics and Consultancy Branch,
Department for Social Development,
Level 4 James House,
2-4 Cromac Avenue,
Gasworks Business Park,
Ormeau Road,
Belfast BT7 2JA

Telephone: 028 9081 9942
Facsimile: 028 9081 9961

E-mail: scb@dsdni.gov.uk
Internet: www.dsdni.gov.uk/index/stats_and_research.htm

SOCIAL AND HOUSING STATISTICS

Statistics and Research Branch,
Department for Social Development,
Level 4 James House,
2-4 Cromac Avenue,
Gasworks Business Park,
Ormeau Road,
Belfast BT7 2JA

Telephone: 028 9081 9939
Facsimile: 028 9081 9961

E-mail: srb@dsdni.gov.uk
Internet: www.dsdni.gov.uk/index/stats_and_research.htm

DEPARTMENT OF FINANCE AND PERSONNEL NORTHERN IRELAND STATISTICS AND RESEARCH AGENCY (NISRA)

SOCIAL SURVEY STATISTICS

Central Survey Unit,
Northern Ireland Statistics and Research Agency,
McAuley House,
2-14 Castle Street,
Belfast BT1 1SY

Facsimile: 028 9034 8205

E-mail: csu@dfpni.gov.uk
Internet: www.csu.nisra.gov.uk

GENERAL ENQUIRIES

Telephone: 028 9034 8200/1

CONTINUOUS HOUSEHOLD SURVEY

Telephone: 028 9034 8246

EXPENDITURE AND FOOD SURVEY

Telephone: 028 9034 8211

VITAL STATISTICS

Demography and Methodology Branch
Northern Ireland Statistics and Research Agency,
McAuley House,
2-14 Castle Street,
Belfast BT1 1SA

Telephone: 028 9034 8160
Fax: 028 9034 8161

E-mail: census.nisra@dfpni.gov.uk
Internet: www.nisra.gov.uk

CENSUS POPULATION STATISTICS

Census Office for Northern Ireland,
Northern Ireland Statistics and Research Agency,
McAuley House,
2-14 Castle Street,
Belfast BT1 1SA

Telephone: 028 9034 8160
Facsimile: 028 9034 8161

E-mail: census.nisra@dfpni.gov.uk

Internet: www.nisra.gov.uk/census

POPULATION STATISTICS

Demography and Methodology Branch
Northern Ireland Statistics and Research Agency,
McAuley House,
2-14 Castle Street,
Belfast BT1 1SA

Telephone: 028 9034 8160
Fax: 028 9034 8161

E-mail: census.nisra@dfpni.gov.uk
Internet: www.nisra.gov.uk

DEPARTMENT OF HEALTH, SOCIAL SERVICES AND PUBLIC SAFETY

HEALTH AND PERSONAL SOCIAL SERVICES

Community Information Branch,
Department of Health, Social Services and Public Safety,
Annexe 2,
Castle Buildings,
Stormont,
Belfast BT4 3SQ

Telephone: 028 9052 2493
Facsimile: 028 9052 3288

E-mail: kieran.taggart@dhsspsni.gov.uk
Internet: www.dhsspsni.gov.uk/stats&research/index.asp

Hospital Information Branch,
Department of Health, Social Services and Public Safety,
Annexe 2,
Castle Buildings,
Stormont,
Belfast BT4 3SQ

Telephone: 028 9052 2800
Facsimile: 028 9052 3288

E-mail: mary.mcavoy@dhsspsni.gov.uk
Internet: www.dhsspsni.gov.uk/stats&research/index.asp

Information and Research Unit
Central Services Agency
25 Adelaide Street
Belfast
BT2 8FH

Telephone: 028 9053 5684

Email: fitzpatricks@csa.n-i.nhs.uk

NORTHERN IRELAND OFFICE

CRIME, COURT AND PRISON

Statistics and Research Branch,
Northern Ireland Office,
Massey House,
Stoney Road,
Belfast BT4 3SX

Telephone: 028 9052 7534
Facsimile: 028 9052 7532

Email: crime.nio@nics.gov.uk
Internet: www.nio.gov.uk

POLICE SERVICE OF NORTHERN IRELAND

RECORDED CRIME STATISTICS
ROAD TRAFFIC ACCIDENT STATISTICS
SECURITY SITUATION STATISTICS

Central Statistics Unit,
Lisnasharragh,
42 Montgomery Road,
Belfast BT6 9LD

Telephone: 028 9065 0222 ext 24135
Facsimile: 028 9092 2998

E-mail: statistics@psni.police.uk
Internet: www.psni.police.uk

NORTHERN IRELAND COURT SERVICE

NORTHERN IRELAND JUDICIAL STATISTICS

Business Support Group,
Northern Ireland Court Service,
3rd Floor Bedford House,
Bedford Street,
Belfast BT2 7DS

Telephone: 028 9072 8903
Facsimile: 028 9032 1458

NORTHERN IRELAND TOURIST BOARD

TOURISM STATISTICS

Research Department,
Northern Ireland Tourist Board,
St Anne's Court,
59 North Street,
Belfast BT1 1NB

Telephone: 028 9044 1565
Facsimile: 028 9024 0960

E-mail: research@nitb.com
Internet: www.nitb.com/research